STEP UP 攀登 to AP®

Chinese Language, Culture, and Society

TEXTBOOK

AP® is a trademark registered by the College Board, which was not involved in the production of, and does not endorse, this product.

陈少元
Carol Chen-Lin
Head Writer

谭大立　　段辰雨
Dali Tan　　**Clara Duan**

with

毕婧
Jing Bi

Australia • Brazil • Mexico • Singapore • United Kingdom • United States

Step Up to AP®:
Chinese Language, Culture, and Society Textbook

Carol Chen-Lin
Dali Tan
Clara Duan
Jing Bi

Regional Director, Marketing:
Melissa Chan

Senior Marketing Manager:
Lee Hong Tan

Senior Editorial Manager:
Lian Siew Han

Assistant Editorial Manager:
Tanmayee Bhatwadekar

Development Editors:
Titus Teo
Kenneth Chow
Wei Yi Ng
Elaine Chew
Cecile Zhang
Iris Poh

Associate Development Editor:
Dawn Chaim

Senior Regional Manager,
Production and Rights:
Pauline Lim

Production Executive:
Rachael Tan

Cover Designer:
Sok Ling Ong

Compositor:
Puey Yan Goh

Illustrator:
Han Boon Ng

© 2019 Cengage Learning Asia Pte Ltd

ALL RIGHTS RESERVED. No part of this work covered by the copyright herein may be reproduced, transmitted, stored or used in any form or by any means graphic, electronic, or mechanical, including but not limited to photocopying, recording, scanning, digitizing, taping, Web distribution, information networks, or information storage and retrieval systems, without the prior written permission of the publisher.

> For product information and technology assistance, contact us at
> **Cengage Learning Asia Customer Support, 65-6410-1200**
> For permission to use material from this text or product, submit all requests online at
> **www.cengageasia.com/permissions**
> Further permissions questions can be emailed to
> **asia.permissionrequest@cengage.com**

ISBN: 978-981-4780-92-6

Cengage Learning Asia Pte Ltd
151 Lorong Chuan
#02-08 New Tech Park
Singapore 556741

Cengage Learning is a leading provider of customized learning solutions with office locations around the globe, including Singapore, the United Kingdom, Australia, Mexico, Brazil, and Japan. Locate your local office at **www.cengage.com/global**

Cengage Learning products are represented in Canada by Nelson Education, Ltd.

To learn more about Cengage Learning Solutions, visit **www.cengageasia.com**

AP® is a trademark registered by the College Board, which was not involved in the production of, and does not endorse, this product.

Every effort has been made to trace all sources and copyright holders of copyrighted material in this book before publication, but if any have been inadvertently overlooked, the publisher will ensure that full credit is given at the earliest opportunity.

Printed in Singapore
Print Number: 01   Print Year: 2018

PREFACE

Step Up to AP®: Chinese Language, Culture, and Society is an all-new intermediate Chinese program designed for high school students taking the AP® Chinese Language and Culture course. It covers one year of instruction and consists of a Textbook and a Workbook with companion websites.

Using the current developmental trends of contemporary China as its focal point, *Step Up to AP®* situates China in the context of increasing globalization to help students understand the interactions and relations between China and the world. Students will engage in a wide range of topics and gain knowledge of China's role in important areas such as technology, economics, trade and business, climate change and green energy, and the film industry. They will also learn about various aspects of contemporary Chinese society, including travel and transportation, urban and rural development, population and community, geography and ethnic diversity, endangered animals and wildlife conservation, health and wellness, sports and leisure, as well as science and technology.

In the realm of Chinese societal relationships, students will explore how the current family structure and the Internet influence the way individuals interact with family members and peers. The program also frames Chinese culture in literary and historical contexts by introducing students to Chinese literature, arts and philosophy, as well as significant persons and events in Chinese history. Through these topics, students will develop an awareness and appreciation of Chinese culture and society, in addition to gaining and enhancing their Chinese language proficiency.

TEXTBOOK

The Textbook follows the journey of two American high school students as they embark on their study exchange and internship in China. Students examine the Chinese society and the issues it faces through the stories from their journey, thereby deepening their understanding of Chinese cultural products, practices, and perspectives. The Textbook offers nine units which engage students in an exploration of culture in both contemporary and historical contexts.

Each unit opens with clear learning objectives and a fun warm-up activity to generate curiosity and interest. It comprises three main reading passages related to the unit theme. Each passage comes with a vocabulary list, grammar explanations, and exercises to allow students to practice language functions, sentence patterns, and theme-based vocabulary they have learned.

Following the three main passages are four sections that aim to enhance students' language skills and cultural knowledge. The **Culture Enrichment** section relates the unit theme to interesting aspects of the Chinese culture and society. The **Vocabulary Building** section facilitates acquisition of a rich variety of useful words and idiomatic expressions to further improve students' communicative competence. The **Reading Comprehension** section deepens exploration of the unit theme and develops students' skills and strategies in interpretive communication. The **Writing Workshop** section gives guidance on writing for different purposes as well as writing strategies. In particular, e-mail response writing and story narration in the AP® Chinese Language and Culture exam are covered in this section, with specific and practical suggestions on how to effectively comprehend the two types of AP® writing stimuli; students are also provided with strategies to address these AP® writing tasks with thoroughness and rich details in well-organized and coherent paragraphs. Finally, the can-do statements at the end of each unit provides a useful checklist for self-assessment.

Beautiful pictures of China are interspersed throughout the book. These pictures feature many places of cultural or historical interest. Students will gain more knowledge of China through these pictures.

WORKBOOK

The Workbook features a wide variety of exercises to help students develop all four language skills across the three communicative modes (interpersonal, interpretive, and presentational). It serves as a skills-builder that provides opportunities for students to apply the language and cultural knowledge acquired from the Textbook in communicative contexts. Many of the questions are modeled after the AP® Chinese exam format to train students to be exam-ready. Also included in the Workbook are two full-length AP® practice exams. One is placed in the middle of the book as a mid-term review, while the other is placed at the end as a final-term review. The Workbook audio program (for listening and speaking sections) can be accessed from the companion website.

COMPANION WEBSITES

> Textbook: www.cengageasia.com/apchinesetb
> Workbook: www.cengageasia.com/apchinesewb

The companion websites host a range of resources to meet the needs of instructors and students. Instructors may register to download complimentary instructor resources including teaching suggestions, audio files, audio scripts, and full answer key. Students do not need to register and may freely access the audio files for the reading passages in the Textbook and listening and speaking exercises in the Workbook.

* AP® is a trademark registered by the College Board, which was not involved in the production of, and does not endorse, this product.

Acknowledgments

Step Up to AP® Textbook is the outcome of many months of hard work. This project could not have been completed successfully without the support and effort of many individuals. I would like to acknowledge and thank each and every one of them.

First and foremost, I would like to give my grateful thanks to my students. They have given me inspiration and motivation to design a book that meets their intellectual curiosity. I am also greatly indebted to my school, Choate Rosemary Hall, for giving me the opportunity to visit China and keep abreast of all its latest developments. The adventures I mentioned in this book—taking the high-speed rail, riding shared bicycles, visiting the pandas and the golden monkeys, participating in community service in rural Xi'an, discussing social and economic issues with professors, living with a Chinese host family—all of these come from real experiences through the school's study abroad program. These unique opportunities have helped us develop a global perspective that I can share with students in the classroom. As a result of these experiences, I was able to conceptualize this book, come up with the main themes for the units, design the structure of each unit, and supervise the entire project to ensure it meets the needs of both teachers and students.

My heartfelt gratitude goes to Cengage Learning Asia. I thank Roy Lee, Managing Director, and Lian Siew Han, Senior Editorial Manager, for supporting this project. I am also deeply indebted to Titus Teo, Development Editor, whom we worked with on an almost daily basis over the past year. His dedication and professionalism in all stages of development have made a significant difference to the quality of the final product. I thank other members of the team, Cecile Zhang and Dawn Chaim, for their meticulous copy editing and careful proofreading. I also thank Puey Yan Goh for her design and typesetting work that make the pages look stunning.

I am hugely appreciative of the reviewers whose thoughtful comments have enhanced the overall quality of this book. Special thanks to Professor Audrey Li, University of Southern California, for her careful review of the grammar sections in each unit. I also thank Lorna Xing, Board Director of the Chinese School Association in the United States, for reviewing Unit 8 of the book.

I sincerely thank Professor Dali Tan for her contribution in writing Unit 1 Part 2 and Unit 6 Part 3, the can-do statements, and her assistance with various sections in each unit: Culture Enrichment, Vocabulary Building, Reading Comprehension, and Writing Workshop. I am thankful for her great encouragement throughout the entire project. Her experience and dedication have made her a most valuable supporter in the preparation of this book.

Finally, I would like to express my sincere gratitude to Clara Duan and Bi Jing for their invaluable contributions, ideas, and writing assistance. Their enthusiasm for and commitment to this project have enabled us to press on toward the successful publication of this book. I thank Clara for writing Unit 7 Part 2 and these sections in each unit: Language Connection, Culture Enrichment, Vocabulary Building, Reading Comprehension, and Writing Workshop. I am grateful to her for providing updated information about China, valuable feedback on many of my initial drafts, and for all the ideas generated from our discussions in the writing process. I also thank Jing for her contribution in writing the Language Connection section in each unit.

The following list shows each of our contributions in greater detail.

	Unit 1	Unit 2	Unit 3	Unit 4	Unit 5	Unit 6	Unit 7	Unit 8	Unit 9
Learning Objectives	Tan	Tan	Tan	Tan	Tan	Tan	Tan	Tan	Tan
Warm Up	Tan	Chen-Lin	Chen-Lin	Duan	Chen-Lin	Tan	Chen-Lin	Chen-Lin, Duan	Chen-Lin, Duan
Part 1 Text	**Chen-Lin**	**Chen-Lin**	**Chen-Lin**	**Chen-Lin**	**Chen-Lin**	**Chen-Lin**	**Chen-Lin**	**Chen-Lin**	**Chen-Lin**
Part 1 Language Connection	Duan	Duan	Bi	Bi	Bi	Bi	Duan	Bi	Bi
Part 2 Text	**Tan**	**Chen-Lin**	**Chen-Lin**	**Chen-Lin**	**Chen-Lin**	**Duan**	**Chen-Lin**	**Chen-Lin**	**Chen-Lin**
Part 2 Language Connection	Bi	Duan	Bi	Duan	Bi	Duan	Duan	Bi	Duan
Part 3 Text	**Chen-Lin**	**Chen-Lin**	**Chen-Lin**	**Chen-Lin**	**Chen-Lin**	**Chen-Lin, Tan**	**Chen-Lin**	**Chen-Lin**	**Chen-Lin**
Part 3 Language Connection	Duan	Duan	Duan	Bi	Duan	Bi, Chen-Lin	Duan	Bi	Duan
Culture Enrichment	Chen-Lin	Chen-Lin, Tan	Chen-Lin	Chen-Lin, Tan	Chen-Lin	Chen-Lin	Duan	Chen-Lin	Chen-Lin
Vocabulary Building	Chen-Lin	Chen-Lin, Tan	Chen-Lin, Tan	Tan	Chen-Lin	Tan	Chen-Lin	Chen-Lin, Duan	Chen-Lin
Reading Comprehension	Chen-Lin, Bi	Chen-Lin, Tan	Duan	Duan	Duan	Duan	Duan	Chen-Lin, Duan	Duan
Writing Workshop	Tan	Duan, Tan	Chen-Lin	Chen-Lin	Chen-Lin	Tan	Chen-Lin	Chen-Lin	Duan
Can-Do Statements	Tan	Tan	Tan	Tan	Tan	Tan	Tan	Tan	Tan

Carol Chen-Lin
Head Writer

Contents

Unit 1
面向全球
CHINA AND THE WORLD
Page 1

Unit 2
中国人的出行
GETTING AROUND IN CHINA
Page 30

Unit 3
人口、住房与就业
POPULATION, HOUSING, AND EMPLOYMENT
page 59

Unit 4
留学生与中西文化交流
INTERCULTURAL EXCHANGES BETWEEN CHINA AND THE WEST
page 85

Unit 5
城乡发展
URBAN AND RURAL DEVELOPMENT
page 114

Unit 6
中国文学与艺术
CHINESE LITERATURE AND ARTS
page 143

Unit 7
地球与我
THE EARTH AND US
page 171

Unit 8
科技与生活
TECHNOLOGY IN OUR LIVES
page 202

Unit 9
中国的经济发展
CHINA'S ECONOMY
page 231

Appendices

1. 生词索引（汉英） Vocabulary Index (Chinese to English) — page 262
2. 生词索引（英汉） Vocabulary Index (English to Chinese) — page 276
3. 语法点 Language Use — page 292
4. 中国地图 Map of China — page 296

Scope and Sequence

KEY READINGS	COMMUNICATIVE TASKS	CULTURE
第一单元　面向全球 **UNIT 1　CHINA AND THE WORLD**		
• Connecting People and Cultures on the Silk Road 丝绸之路与文化传播 • Famous Chinese Explorer: Zheng He and His Voyages 中国著名航海家：郑和 • The Belt and Road Initiative 一带一路	• **Interpretive:** Read and understand a passage about murals in Dunhuang Caves and a famous Chinese musical based on the murals. • **Interpersonal:** Discuss your research findings about a province of China. • **Presentational:** Write an email recommending places of interest, activities, and food on the Silk Road.	• Chinese Geography and Ethnic Groups
第二单元　中国人的出行 **UNIT 2　GETTING AROUND IN CHINA**		
• Subways and High-Speed Rail 捷运与高铁 • Didi and Uber in Their Ride-Hailing Race 滴滴与优步 • Bicycle Sharing: OFO and Mobike 共享单车	• **Interpretive:** Read and understand blog posts on traffic conditions in Beijing. • **Interpersonal:** Discuss the advantages and disadvantages of different modes of transportation in the past and the present. • **Presentational:** Narrate a story about using shared bicycles to get to a place.	• Modes of Transportation in *Along the River During the Qingming Festival*
第三单元　人口、住房与就业 **UNIT 3　POPULATION, HOUSING, AND EMPLOYMENT**		
• China's Population Policy at a Crossroads 中国人口政策的变迁 • The Challenges of Urban Housing 蜗居：大城床与小城房的矛盾 • Hardships and Dreams of Beijing Drifters 北漂一族的辛酸与梦想	• **Interpretive:** Read and understand a passage about the reflections of an only child. • **Interpersonal:** Discuss how posters or slogans reflect the aims of China's one-child policy. • **Presentational:** Prepare a debate script on the topic "He who is an only child has an edge over he who is not."	• Family Planning Slogans and Shifts in the Structure of the Family

LANGUAGE USE	VOCABULARY AND EXPRESSIONS
	1
• 不仅……也…… • 以……为…… • 通过…… • 从……可以看出…… • 向……传播…… • 扮演……角色 • 为/以……(而)感到自豪 • 为……作出了很大贡献 • ……是指…… • 带来…… • 从……角度来看 • 面临……	• **Continents and Seas:** 美洲, 亚洲, 欧洲, 地中海 … • **Trade and Development:** 促进, 往来, 融合, 全球化, 开创, 贡献, 和平共存 … • **Belt and Road Initiative:** 一带一路, 经济带, 基础建设, 做生意, 互补, 角度, 风险 … • **Words Containing 家:** 音乐家, 文学家, 艺术家, 科学家 …
	30
• 无论……都/也…… • 值得……骄傲/庆祝/纪念/学习 • 恐怕…… • 通过/用……来…… • 既……又…… • 只要……就…… • 一……又一……	• **Public Transportation System:** 捷运, 高铁, 四通八达, 大众化, 线路, 便捷, 打工族 … • **Ride-Hailing Services:** 滴滴, 优步, 应用, 预约, 堵塞, 电动车 … • **Bicycle Sharing:** 共享单车, 高科技, 扫二维码, 解锁 … • **Words Containing 化:** 现代化, 城镇化, 自动化, 智能化… • **Four-Character Expressions Related to Traffic Conditions:** 水泄不通, 通畅无阻, 川流不息 …
	59
• 自从…… • 毕竟…… • 也就是说…… • 加以…… • 简直…… • 这就是所谓的…… • 反正…… • 为……而…… • ……室……厅……卫	• **Population-Related Vocabulary:** 独生子女, 一胎化政策, 生育, 老龄化, 小皇帝 … • **Housing-Related Vocabulary:** 住房, 面积, 房价, 飙升, 平米, 寸土寸金 … • **Working in Beijing:** 北漂一族, 求职, 户口, 租金 … • **Words Containing 族:** 上班族, 月光族, 啃老族 … • **Words Containing 党:** 民主党, 共和党, 加班党 …

KEY READINGS	COMMUNICATIVE TASKS	CULTURE
第四单元　留学生与中西文化交流 **UNIT 4　INTERCULTURAL EXCHANGES BETWEEN CHINA AND THE WEST**			
• Studying Abroad in the Late Qing Dynasty 清末留美幼童 • Returned Students and China's Path to Modernization 留学生对中国现代化的影响 • Contributions of the Chinese to the World 华人的贡献	• **Interpretive:** Read and understand the story of a Chinese American writer, Amy Tan. • **Interpersonal:** Discuss ways to deepen your understanding of contemporary China. • **Presentational:** Write a blog entry on how to adapt to a new environment.	• Young Chinese Studying in the United States in the Late Qing Dynasty
第五单元　城乡发展 **UNIT 5　URBAN AND RURAL DEVELOPMENT**			
• Life in Rural China 走进农村——看城乡差距 • SOHO: Urban Development and Cultural Preservation 从SOHO建筑看城市发展与文化传承 • Mass Migration During Spring Festival 春运与人口迁徙	• **Interpretive:** Read and understand the problems faced by people living in Chinese cities. • **Interpersonal:** Discuss each Chinese city listed and place it in the appropriate city cluster. • **Presentational:** Write a review of a microfilm entitled 三分钟.	• City Clusters in China and Around the World
第六单元　中国文学与艺术 **UNIT 6　CHINESE LITERATURE AND ARTS**			
• Chinese Poetry: Reflecting the Times 中国诗歌——时代的烙印 • East Meets West: Contemporary Chinese Painter Wu Guanzhong 融合中西的中国当代画家——吴冠中 • Chinese Elements in Hollywood Movies 好莱坞电影里的中国元素	• **Interpretive:** Read and understand a passage about pop culture in China. • **Interpersonal:** Discuss famous writers and their representative works. • **Presentational:** Write a poem about someone or something you care deeply about.	• Modern and Contemporary Chinese Writers: Lu Xun, Mo Yan, and Liu Cixin

LANGUAGE USE	VOCABULARY AND EXPRESSIONS
	85
• ……正好…… • 比如…… • 加深……对……的认识/了解 • 尤其…… • 其中…… • 没有……就没有…… • 是……之一 • 至于…… • 结合……，形成……的风格/特色/习惯 • ……占……的……分之……/ 　百分之……/大多数	• **Historical Events:** 鸦片战争, 洋务运动, 甲午战争, 辛亥革命, 白话文运动 … • **Famous Chinese:** 容闳, 詹天佑, 孙中山, 严复, 胡适, 邓小平, 李小龙, 贝聿铭, 谭恩美 … • **Loanwords:** IT 人士, 巧克力, 社交媒体, 互联网, 高尔夫球, 白领, B 超, AA 制 …
	114
• 连……也/都…… • 固然……(但是)……也…… • 在……边缘 • 提供…… • 打造…… • ……跟……有关系 • ……一方面……(另) 一方面…… • 迎来……挑战/高峰/机遇 • ……仅……就(有)…… • 并非……	• **Rural Problems:** 辍学, 农民工, 募捐, 缺乏, 留守儿童, 城乡差距, 挣扎 … • **Urban Development:** 雄心, 追逐梦想, 前卫, 未来感, 胡同, 打造, 城市群, 发达, 带动, 改革开放 … • **Spring Festival Mass Migration:** 春运, 大规模, 运输, 迁徙, 前所未有, 解读, 实时 … • **Words Describing Cities:** 地标, 天际线, 摩天大楼, 大都会, 商业区, 枢纽, 魅力 …
	143
• 与其……(倒)不如…… • 即使……也…… • 经过…… • 不愧是…… • 关系到…… • 以……的形式……	• **Chinese Poetry:** 诗圣, 诗仙, 现实主义, 浪漫主义, 思乡情怀, 时代烙印, 人民心声, 儒家, 道教 … • **Chinese Painting:** 　水墨画, 璀璨, 继承, 物由心生, 文化冲击 … • **Chinese Elements:** 忠, 孝, 武侠, 阴阳, 哲理, 天人合一, 境界, 自我价值, 跨文化, 全球视野 … • **Reduplicated Words and Phrases:** 　小小的, 浅浅的, 轻轻松松, 高高兴兴, 准备准备 …

KEY READINGS	COMMUNICATIVE TASKS	CULTURE
第七单元　地球与我 **UNIT 7　THE EARTH AND US**		
• Endangered Animals and Their Conservation 濒临绝种的动物 • Global Warming: An Unprecedented Threat 全球变暖：人类前所未有的威胁 • Developing Sources of Renewable Energy 可再生能源	• **Interpretive:** Read and understand a passage about the world in 2070 if we do not start to protect the environment. • **Interpersonal:** Discuss the poster you wish to display in school for Earth Day. • **Presentational:** Write a creative text to promote an organic farm.	• Eco-Friendly Practices Around the World
第八单元　科技与生活 **UNIT 8　TECHNOLOGY IN OUR LIVES**		
• Cashless Society in China 无现金社会 • Artificial Intelligence and Its Role in Society 人工智能 • How the Internet Has Changed Our Lives 互联网重塑现代生活	• **Interpretive:** Read and understand a passage about face recognition technology. • **Interpersonal:** Discuss how fast food restaurants in China may benefit from technology. • **Presentational:** Write an essay about a smart life in the next five years.	• The Use of High Technology in the Fast Food Industry in China
第九单元　中国的经济发展 **UNIT 9　CHINA'S ECONOMY**		
• The Chinese Economy: What It Really Is? 全球第二经济体—— 先进还是落后？富裕还是贫穷？ • From E-Commerce to the New Retail Model of O2O 从电子商务到新零售 • From Made-in-China to Created-in-China 从中国制造到中国创造	• **Interpretive:** Read and understand a passage about the corporate culture of Alibaba. • **Interpersonal:** Discuss the slogans of famous sports brands in China and around the world. • **Presentational:** Write a cover letter for a job application.	• Hot New Trends in Health and Diet

LANGUAGE USE	VOCABULARY AND EXPRESSIONS
	171
• 有的……，有的……，还有的…… • 之所以……，是因为…… • 为了…… • 究竟…… • 达成…… • 不然／要不然…… • 其实…… • 不乏……	• **Endangered Animals:** 濒临绝种, 稀有动物, 自然保护区, 物种多样性, 存活率, 熊猫, 华南虎 … • **Global Warming:** 全球变暖, 温室效应, 大气层, 海平面, 灾害, 不堪设想, 遭到破坏 … • **Renewable Energy:** 太阳能, 水力发电, 风力发电, 潮汐能, 跨国合作 … • **Words Associated with Environmental Protection:** 节能减排, 植树造林, 低碳生活, 有机农场, 环境友好型社会, 创造绿色未来 …
	202
• 迎合……需求／需要／口味 • 在……和……／他们之间搭建起桥梁／联系／平台 • ……高达／长达／多达…… • 就算……也…… • 可不是吗 • 一旦……就……	• **Cashless Society:** 无现金, 移动支付, 支付宝, 微信支付, 大数据, 交易, 利弊, 隐私 … • **Artificial Intelligence:** 人工智能, 机器, 模仿, 云计算, 分析, 工业革命, 打破格局 … • **The Internet:** 网络, 革新性, 颠覆, 渗透, 应用程序, 高效, 资讯, 包容性 … • **Words Associated with 网:** 互联网, 网购, 网页, 交通网, 网红, 网友 … • **Words Associated with 智能:** 智能手机, 智能冰箱, 智能家居 …
	231
• 不管……都…… • 到底…… • 如果……就…… • 不再……了 • 基本上…… • 不可不…… • 排比句	• **Chinese Economy:** 社会主义, 资本主义, 计划经济, 市场经济, 富裕, 贫穷 … • **E-Commerce:** 消费者, 强劲, 网购, 零售, 热潮, 双十一光棍节, 线上, 线下 … • **Chinese Brands:** 阿里巴巴, 腾讯, 华为, 小米, 联想, 海尔, 比亚迪 … • **Words Associated with the Economy:** 一日千里, 繁荣, 蓬勃, 低迷, 不景气 …

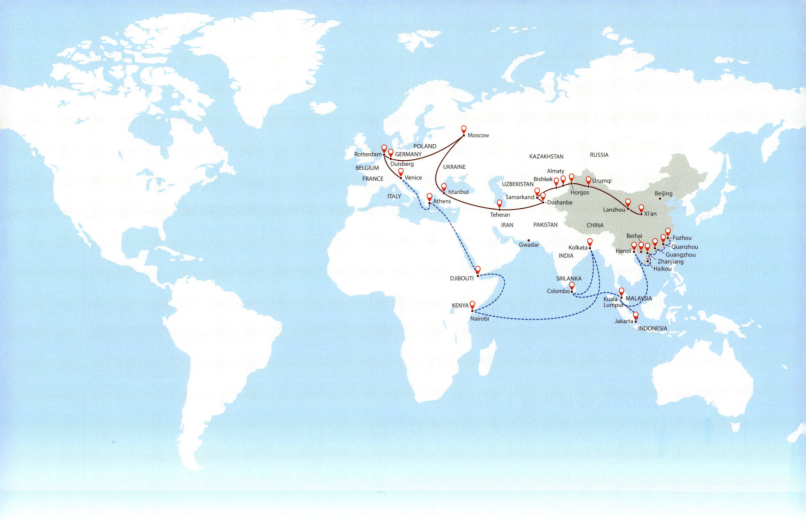

面向全球
CHINA AND THE WORLD

学习目标
LEARNING OBJECTIVES

- Understand the exchanges between China and other countries
- Read about the geography and ethnic groups of China
- Introduce a province of China
- Describe a trip to the Silk Road

单元总览
CONTENTS AT A GLANCE!

导入 WARM UP

- **Part 1: 丝绸之路与文化传播** (Connecting People and Cultures on the Silk Road)
  Language Connection:
  1. 西安<u>不仅</u>是10多个朝代的首都，<u>也</u>是"丝绸之路"的起点。
  2. 那时中国输出到西方的商品<u>以</u>丝绸<u>为主</u>。
  3. 中国的发明也<u>通过</u>丝绸之路传入欧洲。
  4. <u>从</u>一碗牛肉面<u>可以</u>看出文化的交流和融合。

- **Part 2: 中国著名航海家：郑和** (Famous Chinese Explorer: Zheng He and His Voyages)
  Language Connection:
  1. 郑和的船队<u>向</u>各国<u>传播</u>中国的技术。
  2. 郑和的船队一直都在<u>扮演</u>友善大使的<u>角色</u>。
  3. 中国人都<u>为</u>郑和七下西洋与各国人民和平共处的历史事迹<u>而感到自豪</u>。
  4. 郑和开创了海上丝绸之路的极盛时期，<u>为</u>世界航海业<u>作出了很大贡献</u>。

- **Part 3: 一带一路** (The Belt and Road Initiative)
  Language Connection:
  1. "一带一路"<u>是指</u>丝绸之路经济带和21世纪海上丝绸之路。
  2. 这个经济带能为中国和世界<u>带来</u>什么好处？
  3. 我们可以<u>从</u>文化、经济和政治三个不同的<u>角度</u>来看。
  4. 很多国家<u>担心</u>这个计划太大，会<u>面临</u>很大的风险和挑战。

文化剪影：中国的地理和民族
CULTURE ENRICHMENT: Chinese Geography and Ethnic Groups

词汇拓展：……家
VOCABULARY BUILDING: Words Containing 家

阅读理解：敦煌壁画和《丝路花雨》
READING COMPREHENSION: Along the Silk Road

写作工坊：回复电子邮件——去中国旅游
WRITING WORKSHOP: Responding to an Email – Planning a Trip to China

学习总结 I CAN DO!

导入
WARM UP

Do you know who Marco Polo is? Research this person using the Internet and answer the following multiple-choice questions. Make a guess if you could not find the answers.

1. 《马可·波罗游记》是马可·波罗_____。

    Ⓐ 在中国写完的　　　　　　Ⓑ 回国后写完的
    Ⓒ 在中国口述完成的　　　　Ⓓ 回国后口述完成的

2. 马可·波罗是跟谁一起去中国的？

    Ⓐ 自己一个人去的　　　　　Ⓑ 跟他父亲一起去的
    Ⓒ 跟他叔叔一起去的　　　　Ⓓ 跟他父亲和叔叔一起去的

3. 马可·波罗在中国认识的元朝皇帝是哪个民族的人？

    Ⓐ 回族　　Ⓑ 蒙古族　　Ⓒ 汉族　　Ⓓ 藏族

4. 最早的《马可·波罗游记》中文版是哪年完成的？

    Ⓐ 1911年　　Ⓑ 1913年　　Ⓒ 1935年　　Ⓓ 1940年

5. 什么东西是《马可·波罗游记》没有提及的？

    Ⓐ 茶叶　　Ⓑ 玉石　　Ⓒ 丝绸　　Ⓓ 煤

PART 1 第一部分 丝绸之路与文化传播
CONNECTING PEOPLE AND CULTURES ON THE SILK ROAD

宋杰和李静都是美国的高中学生，他们在北京参加了高中留学项目。除了学习中文，他们也住在寄宿家庭体验中国文化。

一个学期很快就过去了，他们都找到了暑期实习工作。宋杰在公益项目"点亮眼睛"工作，李静在一个国际学校的夏令营教英语。

工作之余，他们想到北京以外的地方去旅游。下面是他们跟一位大学历史教授的对话：

宋杰： 王教授，我和李静这个周末打算到西安去玩几天。听说您是从西安来的，可以请您为我们介绍一下西安吗？

王教授： 没问题。西安在古代叫做长安，它不仅是10多个朝代的首都，也是意大利探险家马可·波罗走过的"丝绸之路"的起点。

李静： 我听说丝绸之路连接亚洲、欧洲和非洲，是一条促进中西贸易和文化交流的道路。

项目	n.	xiàngmù	project
体验	v.	tǐyàn	experience
学期	n.	xuéqī	semester
公益	n.	gōngyì	public welfare
夏令营	n.	xiàlìngyíng	summer camp
历史	n.	lìshǐ	history
教授	n.	jiàoshòu	professor
对话	n.	duìhuà	dialog
朝代	n.	cháodài	dynasty
首都	n.	shǒudū	capital city
探险家	n.	tànxiǎnjiā	explorer
丝绸之路	p.n.	Sīchóu zhī Lù	the Silk Road
起点	n.	qǐdiǎn	starting point
连接	v.	liánjiē	link
亚洲	p.n.	Yàzhōu	Asia
欧洲	p.n.	Ōuzhōu	Europe
非洲	p.n.	Fēizhōu	Africa
促进	v.	cùjìn	promote
道路	n.	dàolù	road, route

王教授：没错。汉代的时候，中国的外交家张骞就是从长安出发，经过甘肃、新疆，到中亚、西亚，甚至远到地中海。从那以后，商人开始沿着这条路往来中国和西方。因为那时中国输出到西方的商品以丝绸为主，所以地理学家把这条路称作"丝绸之路"。

宋杰：我了解到中国输出的主要是丝绸、瓷器和茶，而输入的是香料、皮革。葡萄、胡萝卜和菠菜也都是从西方传入的。

王教授：是的。除了商品贸易以外，文化的交流最重要。回教、基督教和佛教都是从丝绸之路传入中国的，而中国的发明——造纸术、印刷术、火药和指南针也通过丝绸之路传入欧洲。

李静：这条路真重要啊！我还听朋友说在西安有很多清真寺，还有一条"回民街"，看来回教对中国的影响很大。

宋杰：我最近看了一个电视节目，里面谈到了回民爱吃的牛肉面，它融合了不同的味道和文化。因为面条是汉族农民的小麦做的，牛肉来自藏族人的牦牛，胡椒和茴香是从蒙古来的，所以从一碗牛肉面可以看出文化的交流和融合。

王教授：说得好！虽然以前没有"全球化"这个词，可是丝绸之路正是古代中西文化交流的通道。你们这个周末去西安，好好地体验一下这个有着千年历史的城市吧。

词语	词性	拼音	英文
汉代	p.n.	Hàndài	Han Dynasty (206 B.C. - 220 A.D.)
外交家	n.	wàijiāojiā	diplomat
张骞	p.n.	Zhāng Qiān	Zhang Qian (an ancient diplomat)
甘肃	p.n.	Gānsù	Gansu (a province in Northwest China)
新疆	p.n.	Xīnjiāng	Xinjiang (a province in Northwest China)
中亚	p.n.	Zhōngyà	Central Asia
西亚	p.n.	Xīyà	West Asia
地中海	p.n.	Dìzhōnghǎi	Mediterranean Sea
往来	v.	wǎnglái	come and go
输出	v.	shūchū	export
地理学家	n.	dìlǐ xuéjiā	geographer
瓷器	n.	cíqì	porcelain
输入	v.	shūrù	import
香料	n.	xiāngliào	spices
皮革	n.	pígé	leather
胡萝卜	n.	húluóbo	carrot
传入	v.	chuánrù	be brought into
回教	p.n.	Huíjiào	Islam
基督教	p.n.	Jīdūjiào	Christianity
佛教	p.n.	Fójiào	Buddhism
清真寺	n.	qīngzhēnsì	mosque
回民	n.	Huímín	Muslim
融合	v.	rónghé	integrate
味道	n.	wèidào	taste
小麦	n.	xiǎomài	wheat
牦牛	n.	máoniú	yak
胡椒	n.	hújiāo	pepper
茴香	n.	huíxiāng	fennel
全球化	n.	quánqiúhuà	globalization
通道	n.	tōngdào	pathway

语言实践
LANGUAGE CONNECTION

1. **Providing additional details: 不仅……也……**

   Structure: 不仅 + feature 1 + 也 + feature 2

   "西安不仅是10多个朝代的首都，也是'丝绸之路'的起点。"

   A number of structures can be used to express "not only ... but also ...." A very common one is 不但……而且……. In this structure, 不但 can be substituted with 不仅, meaning "not only," and must be followed by 而且, 也, or 还. Note that 不仅 is used in formal contexts, while 不但 is used in both formal and informal contexts.

   EXAMPLES:
   1. 马可·波罗不仅是冒险家，也是为中西文化交流作出贡献的外交家。
   2. 李静在北京不仅学习中文，也教英文。

   Make sentences using 不仅……也…… and the phrases provided below.

   EXAMPLE: 宋杰不仅去中国留学，也去中国旅游。

   1. 去中国留学
   2. 坐地铁上学
   3. 每天跑步
   4. 加入球队
   5. 天天看新闻
   6. 经常打游戏
   7. 暑假去实习
   8. 参加社区服务

2. **Describing the function of something: 以……为……**

   Structure: 以 + A + 为 + B

   "那时中国输出到西方的商品以丝绸为主。"

   This pattern means "using/taking ... as ..." in English. We can say 以……为例 (taking ... as an example), 以……为目标 (taking ... as a goal), or 以……为主 (having ... as the priority).

   EXAMPLES:
   1. 她以北京、上海为例谈了大城市的工作机会。
   2. 海外留学课程以培养学生的独立能力为目标。
   3. 我们公司以亚洲市场为主，以欧美市场为辅。

Answer the following questions using 以……为…….

1. 你觉得世界历史课的课程，应该<u>以</u>学习什么<u>为</u>主？
2. 高中生活很丰富，有学习、运动和社交，你觉得你会<u>以</u>什么<u>为</u>主？
3. 你选择大学专业的时候会<u>以</u>什么<u>为</u>标准？
4. 请你<u>以</u>你的学校<u>为</u>例，说一下美国的学校有什么设备？
5. 你这次参加比赛<u>以</u>什么<u>为</u>目标？

3. Indicating a means or method: 通过……

Structure: 通过 + method + outcome

"中国的发明也<u>通过</u>丝绸之路传入欧洲。"

As a preposition, 通过 indicates the use of a method to achieve a desired outcome. It emphasizes the manner or method of doing something, and can be placed before and after the subject.

EXAMPLES:
1. 葡萄和胡萝卜<u>通过</u>丝绸之路传入中国。
2. <u>通过</u>脱口秀，他对时事作出评论。

 Answer the following questions using 通过.

1. 怎样可以多了解中国文化？
2. 你是怎么认识这个新朋友的？
3. 佛教是怎样传入中国的？
4. 听说你不会英语，那你是怎么看得懂美剧(měijù American TV dramas)的？

4. **Introducing an outcome: 从……可以看出……**

> **Structure:** 从 + outcome + 可以看出 + cause/reason

"从一碗牛肉面可以看出文化的交流和融合。"

This pattern is used to explain an outcome. 从 introduces the outcome, and 可以看出 illustrates the cause or reason.

EXAMPLES:
1. 从他的期末考试成绩，我们可以看出他的努力。
2. 从人民生活的水平，我们可以看出一个国家的经济发展水平。

Answer the following questions using 从……可以看出…….

1. 你怎么知道一个学生的中文水平好不好？
2. 你怎么知道一个学校的好坏？
3. 你怎么知道朋友对科学感兴趣？
4. 你怎样可以看出他的身体健康不健康？

China Highlights: Attractions in Beijing

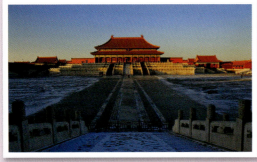
Forbidden City

Tiananmen Square

Summer Palace

Wangfujing (famous shopping street in Beijing)

PART 2 第二部分 中国著名航海家：郑和
FAMOUS CHINESE EXPLORER: ZHENG HE AND HIS VOYAGES

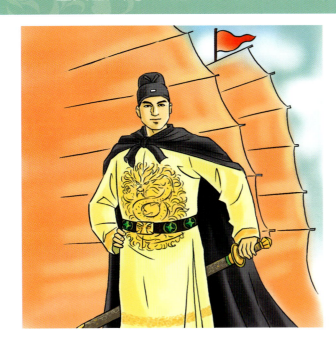

宋杰： 王教授，您好！多谢您建议我们去西安参观名胜古迹，体验那里的风土人情。

李静： 是啊，我们这次西安之行收获很大！我们在西安不但看了有名的清真寺，还逛了"回民街"。我们还听说中国古代有一个很有名的回族人，叫郑和。

王教授： 对，郑和出生在云南的回民家庭，是中国明代伟大的航海家。从1405年到1433年，郑和七次下西洋，经过东南亚、印度洋，最远到达了红海和非洲肯尼亚一带。郑和下西洋的航路，被称为"海上丝绸之路"。

李静： 哦，海上也有一条丝绸之路！

王教授： 你说得对。郑和下西洋，不仅比哥伦布到达美洲大陆早得多，而且船队要大

古代	n. gǔdài	ancient time
郑和	p.n. Zhèng Hé	Zheng He (a famous navigator of China)
云南	p.n. Yúnnán	Yunnan (a province in Southern China)
明代	p.n. Míngdài	Ming Dynasty (1368-1644)
航海家	n. hánghǎijiā	navigator
西洋	p.n. Xīyáng	seas to the west of China
东南亚	p.n. Dōngnányà	Southeast Asia
印度洋	p.n. Yìndùyáng	Indian Ocean
红海	p.n. Hónghǎi	the Red Sea
肯尼亚	p.n. Kěnníyà	Kenya
航路	n. hánglù	sailing route
海上丝绸之路	p.n. Hǎishang Sīchóu zhī Lù	Maritime Silk Road
哥伦布	p.n. Gēlúnbù	Christopher Columbus
美洲	p.n. Měizhōu	the Americas
船队	n. chuánduì	fleet

得多、航海人数多得多。郑和第一次下西洋，有船只62艘，一共有27,800人参加。郑和的船队里都是当时世界上最大的船只，其中最大的一艘有四层楼高。

宋杰： 是啊，哥伦布发现新大陆是在1492年，他的船队只有三艘船、80多个船员，比郑和1405年第一次下西洋晚了87年。

王教授： 郑和七次下西洋，促进了海上丝绸之路的发展。郑和的船队把中国的丝绸、瓷器、茶叶等带到各地，又从各国换回珠宝、香料、药材等特产，还向各国传播中国的技术。

李静： 可以说，郑和下西洋不仅为各国带去了先进的技术，也建立了中国和各国之间的友谊。

王教授： 是的。虽然中国人有着当时最先进的航海技术，但是郑和的船队一直都在扮演友善大使的角色，友好地与各国人民交流技术、交换特产。因此，中国人都为郑和七下西洋与各国人民和平共处的历史事迹而感到自豪。

宋杰： 郑和开创了海上丝绸之路的极盛时期，为世界航海业作出了很大贡献，真是了不起！

语言实践
LANGUAGE CONNECTION

1. **Promoting something on a large scale: 向……传播……**

   Structure: 向 + person/place + 传播 + something

   "郑和的船队向各国传播中国的技术。"

   This pattern is used to express the idea of publicizing or spreading something on a large scale. It can also mean to publicize, popularize, or promote something.

   EXAMPLES:
   1. 学校举办了多次活动，向学生和家长们传播保护环境的重要性。
   2. 学校向学中文的学生传播了很多中国的传统文化。

   Answer the following questions using 向……传播.
   1. 你觉得学校可以通过哪些方式向你们传播中国的传统文化？
   2. 美国可以向世界传播哪些先进的技术和文化？
   3. 你知道中国的造纸术是什么时候、通过什么方式传播到世界各地的吗？

   Complete the following sentences using 向……传播.
   1. 哥伦布发现美洲新大陆时，除了带去了马、牛、猪、小麦及大麦等以外，也……。
   2. 学校的工作不仅是……，也应该是培养学生解决问题的能力。
   3. 孔子一生中教了三千个学生，其中的很多学生后来又……。
   4. 他是美国公共外交大使，他的工作是……。

2. **Describing one's role: 扮演……角色**

   > Structure: 扮演 + modifier + 角色

   "郑和的船队一直都在扮演友善大使的角色。"

   The origin of this expression comes from actors/actresses playing the role of certain characters in a play, musical or movie. This pattern can be used to describe both positive and negative roles in events.

   If we want to express "playing an important role," we can use 扮演了重要的角色.

   EXAMPLES:
   1. 寄宿学校的教师们一直扮演着学生父母的角色。
   2. 自从父母去世以后，姐姐一直扮演着妈妈的角色，照顾弟弟妹妹。
   3. 移动互联网在今年的"双十一"购物节中扮演了重要的角色。

   Answer the following questions using 扮演……的角色.
   1. 如果你和你的朋友玩家庭游戏，你想扮演什么角色？为什么？
   2. 你觉得老师可以扮演哪些角色？（妈妈、朋友、家人、心理医生等）将句子补充完整，例如"老师可以扮演朋友的角色，在我遇到困难的时候帮助我鼓励我。"
   3. 互联网在哪些方面扮演了重要的角色？

3. **Expressing a sense of pride for something or someone: 为/以……（而）感到自豪**

   > Structure: 为/以 + person/entity + (而) 感到自豪

   "中国人都为郑和七下西洋与各国人民和平共处的历史事迹而感到自豪。"

   In this pattern, 为 or 以 means 因为, and is usually followed by a short sentence or a noun phrase.

   EXAMPLES:
   1. 作为一名运动员，我一向为在世界各地代表美国比赛(而)感到自豪。
   2. 很多学校常常为它们的名人校友(而)感到自豪。

Answer the following questions using 为……（而）感到自豪.

1. 你会为什么(而)感到自豪？
2. 你的祖父祖母会为什么事情(而)感到自豪？
3. 你以你们国家的哪些方面(而)感到自豪？

Complete the following sentences using 为……（而）感到自豪.

1. 我们的篮球校队今年在校际联赛中得了第一名，……。
2. 张老师的儿子考上北京大学了，……。
3. 居住在世界各地的海外华人都……。
4. 2008年，北京举办了夏季奥运会，很多中国人都……。
5. 屠呦呦2015年得了诺贝尔医学奖，……。

4. Highlighting one's contributions: 为……作出了很大贡献

   Structure: 为 + person/entity + 作出了很大的贡献/牺牲/努力

   "郑和开创了海上丝绸之路的极盛时期，为世界航海业作出了很大贡献。"

   This structure means "make big contributions for …" in English. Besides 贡献, two other nouns that can be used in this structure are 牺牲 and 努力. They carry different meanings:

   ➢ 为……作出了很大牺牲: make big sacrifices for …
   ➢ 为……作出了很大努力: make big efforts in …

   EXAMPLES:
   1. 中医中药为人类健康作出了很大贡献。
   2. 我妈妈放弃了中国的工作陪我到国外读书，为我作出了很大牺牲。
   3. 这个组织为保护儿童作出了很大努力。

Complete the following sentences using 为……作出了很大贡献／牺牲／努力．

1. 国父孙中山先生为建立中华民国作出了……。
2. 杨利伟是中国航天第一人，为中国航天事业的发展作出了……。
3. 很多人为了事业的成功作出了……。
4. 这个学校的每一位老师都为每一个学生的进步作出了……。
5. 我们要时时告诉自己，每天都要为实现自己的理想作出……。

Answer the following questions.

1. 有哪些人为社会的进步作出了很大的贡献？
2. 你的父母为你作出过哪些牺牲？
3. 你以前为什么事情作出过很大的努力？

China Highlights: Attractions in Beijing

Badaling Great Wall

Temple of Heaven

Old Summer Palace

National Stadium

第三部分 一带一路
PART 3 THE BELT AND ROAD INITIATIVE

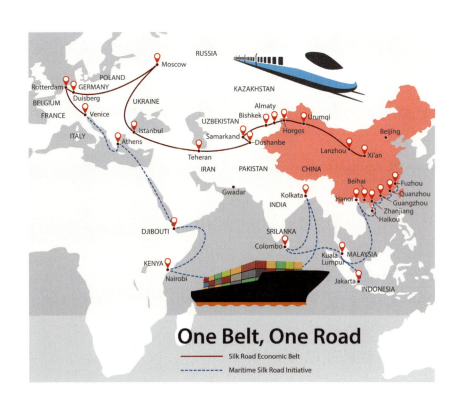

李静： 我在报纸上常看到"一带一路"的报道，英文称为"新的丝绸之路"。王教授，您能为我们解释一下吗？

| 一带一路 | p.n. | Yí Dài Yí Lù | the Belt and Road Initiative |
| 解释 | v. | jiěshì | explain |

王教授："一带一路"是指丝绸之路经济带和21世纪海上丝绸之路，是中国在2013年倡议的。

经济带	phr.	jīngjì dài	economic zone
世纪	n.	shìjì	century
倡议	v.	chàngyì	propose, initiate

宋杰： 这跟古代的"丝绸之路"有什么区别？

| 区别 | n. | qūbié | difference |

王教授：这个新的经济带包括古代的"丝绸之路"，有一条通往欧洲的新陆地通道，还有一条直通东南亚、中东与地中海的海上线路，所以合称为"一带一路"。

| 陆地 | n. | lùdì | land |
| 中东 | p.n. | Zhōngdōng | the Middle East |

宋杰：	"一带一路"的报道中常提到促进周围国家的基础建设。请问什么是基础建设？

基础建设	phr.	jīchǔ jiànshè	infrastructure

王教授：那是指几方面的建设，最重要的是交通网络，比如公路、铁路和桥梁；还有通讯系统，比如网络、邮政；另外还有能源方面的油气管道等等。

桥梁	n.	qiáoliáng	bridge
通讯	n.	tōngxùn	communications
系统	n.	xìtǒng	system
邮政	n.	yóuzhèng	postal
能源	n.	néngyuán	energy
油气管道	phr.	yóuqì guǎndào	oil and gas pipelines

李静：这个经济带能为中国和世界带来什么好处？

王教授：这个问题问得很好。我们可以从文化、经济和政治三个不同的角度来看。"一带一路"倡议首先能促进各国文化交流，其次可为中国带来做生意的好机会，因为各国资源可以互补，大家可以一起合作。从政治上来看，这可以提高中国对世界的影响力。

政治	n.	zhèngzhì	politics
角度	n.	jiǎodù	angle, perspective
做生意	v.o.	zuò shēngyì	do business
互补	v.	hùbǔ	complement one another
合作	v.	hézuò	collaborate

宋杰：我想知道其他国家对"一带一路"倡议有什么不同的看法？

王教授：这个计划是很大的，它包括了全球60多个国家，44亿人口，可以说给世界带来了极大的机会。但是也有很多国家担心这个计划太大，会面临很大的风险和挑战。

风险	n.	fēngxiǎn	risk

语言实践
LANGUAGE CONNECTION

1. Clarifying a term: ……是指……

Structure: subject + 是指 + phrase/clause

"'一带一路'<u>是指</u>丝绸之路经济带和21世纪海上丝绸之路。"

是指 is used to illustrate or clarify the meaning of a term. The part after 是指 is usually a phrase or a clause. Another structure which has the same function is 指的是.

EXAMPLES:
1. 基础建设<u>是指</u>为提供公共服务而建设的基本设施。
2. AP<u>指的是</u>让美国高中生提前学习的大学水平的课程。

Class discussion

1. "少数民族"是指什么?
2. "生活水平"是指什么?
3. "低头族"是指什么样的人群?
4. "早晚高峰"是指什么时候?
5. "晒步数"是指什么?
6. "生活的节奏"是指什么?

2. Useful verb: 带来……

Structure: subject + 带来 + noun/noun phrase

"这个经济带能为中国和世界<u>带来</u>什么好处?"

带来 originally means "to bring." It can be used with nouns or noun phrases, such as 带来了一箱苹果. It can also be used with nouns of abstract concepts, for example:

- 带来好处　　　　bring advantages/benefits
- 带来机遇/机会　bring opportunities
- 带来变化　　　　bring changes
- 带来问题　　　　bring problems
- 带来挑战　　　　bring challenges

EXAMPLES:

1. 共享经济通过节约资源给本地环境<u>带来</u>了好处。
2. 科技创新给世界<u>带来</u>机遇和挑战。
3. 网络信息共享会<u>带来</u>更多的好处还是更多的问题呢?

Class discussion

你看下面的事情为我们带来了什么?

1. 新的学生中心
2. 附近新建的地铁站
3. 社区新开的洗衣店
4. 学校最近取消了期末考试
5. 电视台推出了一个新的访谈节目
6. 药店推出一种新的保健品

3. **Indicating a perspective taken: 从……角度来看**

Structure: 从 + aspect/area + 角度来看/来说

"我们可以<u>从</u>文化、经济和政治三个不同的<u>角度来看</u>。"

To indicate the adoption of a certain perspective, we can use the structure 从……角度来看, which means "from the perspective of ...." A noun or noun phrase follows 从 to indicate the perspective taken.

EXAMPLES:

1. <u>从文化角度来看</u>,这些音乐太商业化了。
2. <u>从政治角度来说</u>,这些措施会引起很大的争议。

Write three sentences based on the question below.

春运是中国新年前后交通堵塞的现象,请从文化、经济和交通这三个不同的角度来写三个句子。

4. Facing a certain situation: 面临……

Structure: subject + 面临 + noun

"很多国家担心这个计划太大,会<u>面临</u>很大的风险和挑战。"

面临 means "facing or confronting with something." It is usually used with nouns which have negative meanings. Here are some commonly used phrases:

- 面临困难　face difficulties
- 面临挑战　face challenges
- 面临危机　face a crisis
- 面临考验　face a test

EXAMPLES:

1. 当你<u>面临</u>困难时,你可以向老师求助。
2. 进入国际舞台后,阿里巴巴集团<u>面临</u>了多种挑战。
3. <u>面临</u>危机时,要保持冷静。

Class discussion

1. 我们面临困难的时候,应该用什么样的态度来解决?
2. 你最近面临了什么样的挑战或问题?最后是用什么方法来解决的?

文化剪影
CULTURE ENRICHMENT

中国的地理和民族
Chinese Geography and Ethnic Groups

1. **中国的地理**

   中国位于亚洲的东部，面积仅次于俄罗斯和加拿大，是世界上第三大的国家。中国有34个省级行政区❶，其中包括：

   23个省：
   名字中有东、南、西、北、江等字的有14个省：
   - 东西：广东、山东、山西、江西、陕西
   - 南北：河南、河北、湖南、湖北、云南、海南
   - 江：浙江、江苏、黑龙江

   其他的9个省份❷是：
   吉林、辽宁、甘肃、青海、四川、贵州、安徽、福建、台湾★

   4个直辖市❸：
   北京、天津、上海、重庆

   5个自治区❹：
   内蒙古自治区、新疆维吾尔自治区、宁夏回族自治区、广西壮族自治区、西藏自治区

   2个特别行政区❺：
   香港、澳门

   ❶ 省级行政区 shěngjí xíngzhèngqū administrative divisions at the provincial level
   ❷ 省份 shěngfèn province
   ❸ 直辖市 zhíxiáshì municipality
   ❹ 自治区 zhìzhìqū autonomous region
   ❺ 特别行政区 tèbié xíngzhèng qū special administrative region

2. 中国的民族

中国有56个民族，汉族约占总人口的92%，主要的少数民族❻有壮族、满族、回族、苗族、维吾尔族、土家族、彝族、藏族和蒙古族。他们主要分布在中国的边境地区，例如内蒙、新疆、宁夏、广西、西藏、云南和贵州。少数民族的文化、宗教、语言和文字都跟汉族很不一样。

汉族　　壮族　　满族　　苗族　　维吾尔族　　藏族　　蒙古族

❻ 少数民族 shǎoshù mínzú ethnic minority

课堂活动 CLASS ACTIVITIES

Interpretive

In groups, choose a province and research it online to answer the following questions.

1) 地理位置在哪儿？邻近有其他哪些省？
2) 人口有多少？
3) 省会在哪儿？有什么重要的城市？
4) 有什么重要的旅游景点与历史名胜？
5) 交通发达吗？有什么高铁线经过？
6) 经济发展怎么样？有什么重要的工业、商业和农业？
7) 有什么特产？
8) 有什么文化特色？
9) 为什么你们选择这个省？

Interpersonal

Discuss the answers to the questions above with your group mates.

Presentational

Prepare a presentation of 10-15 slides introducing the province your group has chosen.

Let's Sing

大中国

词曲：高枫

Wǒmen dōu yǒu yí gè jiā, míngzi jiào Zhōngguó.
我们都有一个家，名字叫中国。
Xiōngdì jiěmèi dōu hěnduō, jǐngsè yě búcuò.
兄弟姐妹都很多，景色也不错。
Jiālǐ pán zhe liǎng tiáo lóng, shì Chángjiāng yǔ Huánghé.
家里盘着两条龙，是长江与黄河。
Háiyǒu Zhūmùlǎngmǎfēngr, shì zuìgāo shānpō.
还有珠穆朗玛峰儿，是最高山坡。

Wǒmen dōu yǒu yí gè jiā, míngzi jiào Zhōngguó.
我们都有一个家，名字叫中国。
Xiōngdì jiěmèi dōu hěnduō, jǐngsè yě búcuò.
兄弟姐妹都很多，景色也不错。
Kàn nà yì tiáo Chángchéng wànlǐ, zài yúnzhōng chuānsuō.
看那一条长城万里，在云中穿梭，
Kàn nà Qīngzàng Gāoyuán, bǐ nà tiānkōng hái liáokuò.
看那青藏高原，比那天空还辽阔。

Wǒmen de dà Zhōngguó ya, hǎo dà de yí gè jiā.
我们的大中国呀，好大的一个家！
Jīngguò nàge duōshǎo, nàge fēng chuī hé yǔ dǎ.
经过那个多少，那个风吹和雨打。
Wǒmen de dà Zhōngguó ya, hǎo dà de yí gè jiā.
我们的大中国呀，好大的一个家！
Yǒngyuǎn nàge yǒngyuǎn, nàge wǒ yào bànsuí tā.
永远那个永远，那个我要伴随她。

Zhōngguó, zhùfú nǐ, nǐ yǒngyuǎn zài wǒ xīn li.
中国，祝福你，你永远在我心里。
Zhōngguó, zhùfú nǐ, búyòng qiān yán hé wàn yǔ.
中国，祝福你，不用千言和万语。

Highlights of China

In groups of three or four, go online and find the answers to the following questions. The group that finds the answers in the shortest time wins.

1) 中国最高的山是？
2) 中国最长的河是？
3) 中国人口最多的城市是？
4) 中国最大的岛是？
5) 中国历史上最长的朝代是？
6) 第一位统一中国的皇帝是？
7) 中国最大的广场是？
8) 中国人口最多的民族是？

词汇拓展
VOCABULARY BUILDING

1. Words Containing "家"

The character 家 means family (家庭) or family members (家人). It also refers to someone who has specialized knowledge or mastery in a skill. A 音乐家 is someone well versed in music, while a 画家 is someone well versed in drawing.

家 (family): 家庭, 家人, 家乡, 回家, 老家

家 (specialized in): 音乐家, 画家

Match each meaning to the correct profession:

1) 对外交事务有专长　　　　　　　　Ⓐ 文学家
2) 对科学研究有贡献　　　　　　　　Ⓑ 作家
3) 不断探险、探索新航线　　　　　　Ⓒ 钢琴家
4) 钢琴表演技术非常好　　　　　　　Ⓓ 科学家
5) 对文学有研究　　　　　　　　　　Ⓔ 艺术家
6) 写作有成就　　　　　　　　　　　Ⓕ 哲学家
7) 从事艺术工作有成就　　　　　　　Ⓖ 外交家
8) 从事哲学的研究　　　　　　　　　Ⓗ 探险家

Give a famous person outside China and a famous person from China for each of the professions below:

EXAMPLE: 音乐家：贝多芬 (outside China)　　郎朗 (from China)

1) 外交家　　　　5) 探险家
2) 科学家　　　　6) 哲学家
3) 文学家　　　　7) 作家
4) 钢琴家　　　　8) 艺术家

2. Fun with Characters

Provide a Chinese character to form a word with the character in the center.

Unit 1 China and the World · 面向全球

阅读理解
READING COMPREHENSION

Read the passage and answer the questions that follow.

敦煌壁画和《丝路花雨》
Along the Silk Road

丝绸之路上一个重要的城市是敦煌，它以石窟和壁画而闻名于世。汉代的时候，敦煌是边境玉门关和阳关的所在地。唐代很多诗词都提到这两个地方，例如王维的诗句"劝君更进一杯酒，西出阳关无故人"，意思是说希望你多喝一杯酒，因为从阳关出去到了塞外❶就很难再遇见你的老朋友了。

另外一首是王之涣的《凉州词》，其中"羌笛❷何须怨杨柳，春风不度玉门关"提到了玉门关。在唐代，当朋友要离开到很远的地方去时，人们习惯把柳树的树枝折下来送给朋友。这首诗里说羌笛不用吹着哀怨❸的杨柳曲，因为春风吹不到玉门关那么远的地方，那里很荒凉❹，根本没有杨柳树可以折枝为朋友送别。

从这两首诗歌可以看到玉门关和阳关是中原❺与塞外、文明与野蛮❻、繁荣与荒凉的分界线，出了这两个地方就是走出了文明的中原，到了荒凉的塞外。

敦煌壁画

敦煌石窟包括莫高窟、西千佛洞、榆林窟和东千佛洞。其中莫高窟最为有名，现存492个洞窟。石窟中的壁画是世界上最大的壁画群，也是佛教艺术的经典。壁画以佛像为主，还有很多画是讲佛教的故事，用简单易懂的艺术形式来表达佛教复杂深奥❼的哲学❽。敦煌石窟可以说是一个宗教和艺术的博物馆。

丝路花雨

《丝路花雨》是甘肃省歌舞剧院在1979年以敦煌莫高窟为背景创作的大型歌舞剧。故事发生在唐代最繁盛的时期,有一个老画匠名字叫神笔张,他有一个漂亮的女儿英娘,非常热爱舞蹈,但小时候不幸走失了。后来神笔张在一个敦煌的市集上遇到英娘,她已经是戏班子里面的歌伎❾。幸亏一个波斯商人同情她,帮助英娘脱离戏班子,让他们父女再团聚。神笔张模仿女儿的舞蹈姿态画出了他的代表作《反弹琵琶伎乐天》。这部大型的歌舞剧曾在世界各地演出,深受观众的欢迎。

❶ 塞外 sàiwài north of the Great Wall
❷ 羌笛 qiāngdí a vertical flute used by the Qiang ethnic group
❸ 哀怨 āiyuàn sad and melancholy
❹ 荒凉 huāngliáng bleak and desolate
❺ 中原 Zhōngyuán Central Plains (comprising the middle and lower reaches of the Yellow River)
❻ 野蛮 yěmán uncivilized, barbaric
❼ 深奥 shēn'ào profound
❽ 哲学 zhéxué philosophy
❾ 歌伎 gējì female singer

1. 敦煌为什么在世界上很有名?
   A 因为中国古代很多诗词都提到了这个地方。
   B 因为这里是玉门关和阳关的所在地。
   C 因为这里是丝绸之路上的重要城市。
   D 因为这里的石窟和壁画很有名。

2. 作者在《凉州词》中想要表达什么样的感情?
   A 不舍得朋友离开
   B 玉门关太远,太荒凉
   C 对杨柳的喜爱
   D 对玉门关的喜爱

3. 关于玉门关和阳关的描述,以下哪一项是<u>错误</u>的?
   A 它们是汉朝的边境。
   B 唐代很多诗词都提到过。
   C 那里在古代有很多人居住。
   D 它们都位于敦煌。

4. 关于敦煌壁画的描述,以下哪一项是<u>错误</u>的?
   A 它包括莫高窟。
   B 它全部都是佛像。
   C 它是世界上最大的壁画群。
   D 它结合了宗教和艺术。

5. 关于《丝路花雨》的描述,以下哪一项是<u>错误</u>的?
   A 它是唐代时期创作的。
   B 故事中的女孩很喜欢跳舞。
   C 爸爸和女儿后来见面了。
   D 这部歌舞剧曾在世界各地演出。

写作工坊
WRITING WORKSHOP

回复电子邮件 Responding to an Email

Read this email from a friend and then type a response.

发件人：小明

邮件主题：去中国旅游

小红，
你好！

　　我们的中文老师明年夏天要带我们去中国游学，打算走"丝绸之路"旅游线。中文班的同学们都高兴极了，因为通过去中国的游学，我们不仅可以参观很多"丝绸之路"上的名胜古迹，也可以体验到沿途各地的风土人情，当然还可以吃到多种多样不同味道的小吃和美食。

　　老师让我们每人提出一个自己最感兴趣的游学主题。我对"丝绸之路"上多种民族文化的交流和融合特别有兴趣，所以想设计一个以了解"丝绸之路"上少数民族风情为主的旅游计划。

　　我知道你今年夏天刚走过"丝绸之路"这条旅游线。请你告诉我，要想更多地了解"丝绸之路"上的少数民族，有哪些名胜古迹一定要去参观？为什么？有哪些活动可以帮我们更好地体验当地的民族风情？对了，别忘了给我建议一些一定要吃的少数民族小吃和美食啊。

　　期待你的回信。

　　祝好！

小明

(380 words)

1. **Interpreting the question**

   The section on responding to an email constitutes 10% of the marks in the AP® Chinese Examination. You should try to read and comprehend the email within 15 minutes. The email is usually one from a peer or penpal.

   The emails in the 2017 and 2016 AP® Chinese Examinations contained about 100 and 120 Chinese characters respectively. The email given in this unit has about 380 Chinese characters, thrice the length of an email in a typical AP® Chinese Examination.

   When you are reading the email, you first need to understand its key purpose. Then you need to check what questions have been asked and respond to them. For example, in the email given above, there are four questions that need to be answered:

   ① 要想更多地了解"丝绸之路"上的少数民族，有哪些名胜古迹一定要去参观？
   ② 为什么？
   ③ 有哪些活动可以帮我们更好地体验当地的民族风情？
   ④ 有哪些一定要吃的少数民族小吃和美食？

   Besides the questions asked, note that in the email, some sentences are actually questions that do not end with a question mark. You have to look out for the questions hidden in such sentences and make sure you answer them accordingly.

2. **Structure of the email**

   A. **Beginning:**

   You may begin with "你好." Then, go straight to the point and show that you have understood the email by answering the questions straightaway. For example:

   你好！很高兴得知你的中文老师明年夏天会带你们走"丝绸之路"。

   B. **Main body:**

   You should try to answer the questions in the sequence as they appear in the email. For example:

   ① 要想更多地了解"丝绸之路"上的少数民族，你们一定要去看西安的清真寺、敦煌的莫高窟壁画及新疆乌鲁木齐的国际大巴扎这些名胜古迹。

   ② 通过参观西安的清真寺，逛那里的回民街，在敦煌看壁画和《丝路花雨》歌舞剧，在乌鲁木齐的国际大巴扎购买有民族特色的小商品这些活动，你们可以更好地体验当地的民族风情。

   ③ 因为这些活动不但可以让你亲身感受到丝绸之路上各族人民的和平共处，而且可以让你体会到不同文化的交流和融合，所以我特别向你推荐。

❹ 从旅游文化的角度来看，饮食文化也是当地风土人情非常重要的一部分。我今年夏天去丝绸之路旅行的时候，特别喜欢吃的美食有西安的羊肉泡馍和麻酱凉皮、兰州的牛肉拉面和手抓饭，还有新疆的大盘鸡和烤包子。这些都是我建议你一定要吃的民族美食和小吃。

C. Conclusion:

Here is a polite way to end the email:

希望我的回答对你会有些帮助。要是你还有别的问题的话，请别客气，随时欢迎你来信。

祝好！

小红

3. Suggested words and sentence patterns

Refer to the new words and sentence patterns at the end of this unit. Try to use them in writing this email.

学习总结
I CAN DO!

Interpretive Communication

- [ ] I can read about the cultural and economic exchanges between ancient China and other countries.
- [ ] I can understand when people talk about Zheng He's voyages to the Western Pacific and the Indian Ocean.
- [ ] I can read and understand some basic information related to the Belt and Road Initiative.
- [ ] I can conduct online search in Chinese and identify some interesting facts related to Marco Polo.

Interpersonal Communication

- [ ] I can discuss the roles of the Silk Road and Maritime Silk Road.
- [ ] I can converse about the cultural and economical exchanges along the Silk Road and Maritime Silk Road.
- [ ] I can share with others some information about the Belt and Road Initiative and its potential benefits to the world.

Presentational Communication

- [ ] I can describe the contributions of Zhang Qian and Zheng He.
- [ ] I can compare and contrast the ancient Silk Road, the Maritime Silk Road, and "the Belt and Road" of today.
- [ ] I can talk about the cultural and economical exchanges between ancient China and other countries.
- [ ] I can describe Marco Polo and his contributions in bringing China to the rest of the world.
- [ ] I can present one of the Chinese provinces and one of the 56 ethnic groups in China.
- [ ] I can compare the historical and cultural significance of Columbus' discovery of the Americas and Zheng He's voyages in the South Seas.

Cultural Knowledge

- [ ] I can talk about the everyday products in China that originally came from trade on the Silk Road.
- [ ] I can describe the ancient Silk Road and Maritime Silk Road.
- [ ] I can talk about the geography of China.
- [ ] I can explain how China opened up to the world in the past and now.

第二单元 UNIT 2
中国人的出行
GETTING AROUND IN CHINA

学习目标
LEARNING OBJECTIVES

- Learn about common modes of transportation in contemporary China
- Read about traffic conditions in different cities
- Compare modes of transportation in different regions
- Explain how the bicycle-sharing system is a useful mode of transportation

单元总览
CONTENTS AT A GLANCE!

导入 WARM UP

- **Part 1: 捷运与高铁** (Subways and High-Speed Rail)
  Language Connection:
  1. 中国的地铁<u>无论</u>从外观、票价、便捷、安全这几个角度来看，<u>都</u>是一流的。
  2. <u>除了</u>地铁<u>以外</u>，高铁<u>更</u>值得我们骄傲。

- **Part 2: 滴滴与优步** (Didi and Uber in Their Ride-Hailing Race)
  Language Connection:
  1. 堵塞<u>恐怕</u>是大城市都要面对的问题。
  2. 用打车软件<u>来</u>打车非常容易。
  3. 拼车<u>既</u>省钱<u>又</u>节能。

- **Part 3: 共享单车** (Bicycle Sharing: OFO and Mobike)
  Language Connection:
  1. <u>只要</u>扫车上的二维码，<u>就</u>能把车解锁。
  2. 这是时代带来的<u>一波又一波</u>的变革。

文化剪影：《清明上河图》中的交通工具
CULTURE ENRICHMENT: Modes of Transportation in *Along the River During the Qingming Festival*

词汇拓展：……化；四字词（短）语
VOCABULARY BUILDING: Words Containing 化; Four-Character Expressions

阅读理解：一个高中生眼中的中国式的出行
READING COMPREHENSION: A High School Student's Blog Posts on Modes of Transportation in China

写作工坊：看图写故事——共享单车；介绍人物——成功创业人士
WRITING WORKSHOP: Narrating a Story – Bicycle Sharing; Introducing a Person – A Successful Entrepreneur

学习总结 I CAN DO!

导入
WARM UP

Look at the modes of transportation of the past, present, and future below. Work in small groups to share ideas and respond to the questions on each mode of transportation.

PAST

1. 坐船

   好处：_____

   坏处：_____

   安全指数 (zhǐshù index)：_____
   （1到5，1是最不安全，5是最安全）

2. 马车

   好处：_____

   坏处：_____

   安全指数：_____

3. 轿子

   好处：_____

   坏处：_____

   安全指数：_____

4. 骑马

   好处：_____

   坏处：_____

   安全指数：_____

PRESENT

5. 地铁
   什么情况下最适合坐地铁？
   _____

6. 飞机
   什么情况下最适合坐飞机？
   _____

7. 高铁
   什么情况下最适合坐高铁？
   _____

8. 共享单车
   什么情况下最适合骑共享单车？
   _____

FUTURE

9. 未来的出行方式有哪些？
   _____

10. 你觉得哪一种最受欢迎？为什么？
    _____

第一部分 捷运与高铁
PART 1 SUBWAYS AND HIGH-SPEED RAIL

宋杰：李静，给你介绍一下，这是我的朋友，陈海文。他昨天刚从台北回来。

| 台北 | p.n. | Táiběi | Taipei |

李静：海文，你好！

海文：李静，你好！很高兴认识你。

李静：听说台北的捷运跟北京的地铁一样方便，四通八达，是个既大众化又环保的交通工具。

捷运	n.	jiéyùn	rapid transit
四通八达	adj.	sì tōng bā dá	(of road networks) extensive and convenient
大众化	adj.	dàzhònghuà	popular
出行	v.	chūxíng	get around
搭乘	v.	dāchéng	take (a mode of transportation)

海文：没错，我在台北的时候，每天出行都是搭乘捷运，非常方便。

宋杰：既然跟地铁一样，为什么叫"捷运"呢？

海文：全名是"大众捷运系统"，我想可能是从英文 Mass Rapid Transit 翻译过来的。其实大部分都在地下，可是也有一部分是在地面上的轻轨。我很喜欢"捷运"这个词，又简单又贴切。

大众捷运系统	p.n.	dàzhòng jiéyùn xìtǒng	mass rapid transit system
翻译	v.	fānyì	translate
轻轨	n.	qīngguǐ	light rail
简单	adj.	jiǎndān	simple
贴切	adj.	tiēqiè	apt
台湾桃园机场	p.n.	Táiwān Táoyuán Jīchǎng	Taiwan Taoyuan Airport

李静：听说台湾桃园机场捷运已开始运营了。

| 运营 | v. | yùnyíng | operate |

海文：是的，我这次就是从桃园机场搭乘捷运到台北车站，只需要半个小时。台湾也有一卡通，跟北京的一样，不但可以乘坐公交车，而且还可以在超市和便利店买东西，甚至可以买电影票和景点的门票，非常方便。

宋杰：听起来真不错，有机会我也要去台北看看，体验那里的地铁文化。

海文：谈到地铁，在我小时候，北京只有一线和环线，非常简单。2001年申奥成功以后拓展了很多线路，现在北京的地铁有20多条线，可谓纵横交错，是联系人们工作和生活的重要交通网络。很多外地人来北京打拼，只能住在近郊，每天搭地铁上班。打工族挤地铁是一件很不容易的事。

李静：我刚来北京的时候很惊讶，因为北京的地铁既干净又安全。我去过世界很多大城市，但我认为中国的地铁无论从外观、票价、便捷、安全这几个角度来看，都是一流的。

海文：除了地铁以外，高铁更值得我们骄傲。2017年的总里程已经高达2.5万公里，覆盖几乎所有的省。

宋杰：听说中国已经掌握了高铁先进技术！

海文：中国幅员辽阔，人口众多而且流动频繁，所以对高铁的需求是非常大的。高铁的建设使中国人的工作和生活发生了重大的变化。

李静：我希望下次有机会外出的时候，能乘搭高铁好好地体验一下。

一卡通	p.n.	Yìkǎtōng	iPASS (a card used for traveling on public transporation in Taiwan)
申奥	v.o.	shēn Ào	bid to host an Olympic Games
拓展	v.	tuòzhǎn	expand
线路	n.	xiànlù	route
可谓	v.	kěwèi	it can be said that ...
纵横交错	phr.	zònghéng jiāocuò	crisscross
打拼	v.	dǎpīn	work hard in one's job
近郊	n.	jìnjiāo	suburbs, outskirts
打工族	n.	dǎgōngzú	the working class
惊讶	adj.	jīngyà	surprised
安全	adj.	ānquán	safe
外观	n.	wàiguān	exterior appearance
便捷	adj.	biànjié	convenient
一流	adj.	yìliú	first class
高铁	n.	gāotiě	high-speed rail
值得	v.	zhídé	be worthy of
总里程	n.	zǒnglǐchéng	total mileage
覆盖	v.	fùgài	cover
省	n.	shěng	province
幅员	n.	fúyuán	the extent of a country
辽阔	adj.	liáokuò	vast
人口	n.	rénkǒu	population
众多	adj.	zhòngduō	numerous
流动	n.	liúdòng	(of people) flow
频繁	adj.	pínfán	frequent
需求	n.	xūqiú	demand
建设	n.	jiànshè	construction
使	v.	shǐ	cause
发生	v.	fāshēng	take place
重大	adj.	zhòngdà	major
变化	n.	biànhuà	change

语言实践
LANGUAGE CONNECTION

1. Emphasizing a state that holds true in all circumstances: 无论……都/也……

   Structure: 无论 + possible condition + 都/也 + state

   "中国的地铁无论从外观、票价、便捷、安全这几个角度来看，都是一流的。"

   无论 means "no matter" or "regardless," and is generally used in the first part of the sentence to introduce possible conditions. 都 or 也 can be used in the second part of the sentence to emphasize that the state will not be changed by the preceding condition. It is more formal than 不管. Note that the clause that follows 无论 includes phrases such as "how hard you try" and "wherever you go," and thus will normally include interrogative pronouns such as 怎么, 多（么）, 什么, and 谁.

   EXAMPLES:
   1. 无论多么成功，他都觉得自己不够好。
   2. 无论在什么地方，我都会给你写信。

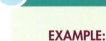 Give out warnings using 无论……都／也…… in response to the pictures below.

EXAMPLE:

无论怎么样，你都不能吸烟！

1.
2.
3.
4.

Use 无论 to express your New Year resolution with reference to the pictures below.

EXAMPLE:

无论怎么样，我今年都要上理想的大学！

❶  ❷  ❸  ❹

2. Expressing something that is worthy of a certain response:
   值得……骄傲/庆祝/纪念/学习

   Structure: 值得 + (pronoun) + 骄傲/庆祝/纪念/学习

   "除了地铁以外，高铁更<u>值得</u>我们<u>骄傲</u>。"

   This phrase expresses that something is worthy of or deserves a certain response. A response follows 值得 to form a phrase such as 值得骄傲 (worth being proud of), 值得庆祝 (worth celebrating), 值得纪念 (worth remembering), and 值得学习 (worth learning). A noun such as 我们 may be placed between 值得 and the response to indicate the doer of the action.

   EXAMPLES:
   ❶ 昨天我们学校拿到了网球比赛的全国冠军，这真的是一个<u>值得骄傲</u>的成绩。
   ❷ 在过去一年有很多事情<u>值得庆祝</u>：我考上了大学，我姐姐结了婚，还有我奶奶的90大寿。
   ❸ 对于任何一名美国人来说，7月4日都是<u>值得记念</u>的日子。
   ❹ 他和别人沟通的技巧非常<u>值得我们学习</u>。

Interview a classmate using the following questions. Your classmate will answer them using 值得……骄傲／庆祝／纪念／学习.

1. 你最近有什么值得庆祝的事？
2. 什么事情值得你骄傲？为什么？
3. 什么日子对你来说是值得纪念的？为什么？
4. 什么东西是值得你学习的？

China Highlights: Beijing Rail Transit Lines

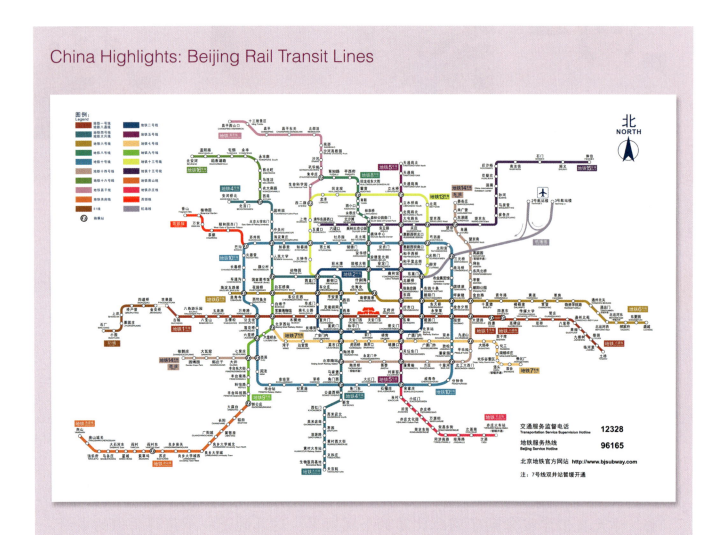

第二部分 滴滴与优步
PART 2 DIDI AND UBER IN THEIR RIDE-HAILING RACE

李静：对不起，让大家久等了，虽然不是早晚高峰，可是路上还是堵得很厉害。

海文：堵塞恐怕是大城市都要面对的问题。工作日堵，周末也堵，北京的堵塞程度应该是世界之最了。

宋杰：那么政府有什么方法来治堵呢？

海文：限行和限购是两种比较直接的治堵方法。尾号限行目前在北京、天津、杭州、成都等多个城市实施。例如北京，在工作日早上七点到晚上八点，每天有两个尾号的汽车不许行驶，否则会罚款。可是限行只针对传统燃油车，电动车仍然能自由行使。另一个措施是限购，就是要通过摇号取得许可才可以买车。

李静：我听同事他们说用打车软件来打车非常容易，一般下单以后五分钟就到了，所以也就暂时不考虑买车了。

堵塞	n.	dǔsè	traffic jam
程度	n.	chéngdù	extent, degree
政府	n.	zhèngfǔ	government
限购	v.	xiàngòu	limit one's purchase
直接	adj.	zhíjiē	direct
天津	p.n.	Tiānjīn	Tianjin (a municipality of China)
杭州	p.n.	Hángzhōu	Hangzhou (the capital city of Zhejiang Province, China)
成都	p.n.	Chéngdū	Chengdu (the capital city of Sichuan Province, China)
实施	v.	shíshī	implement
行驶	v.	xíngshǐ	drive
否则	conj.	fǒuzé	otherwise, else
罚款	v.	fákuǎn	impose a fine on
针对	v.	zhēnduì	direct at
燃油车	n.	rányóu chē	vehicle that runs on gasoline or diesel
电动车	n.	diàndòng chē	electric car
仍然	adv.	réngyóu	still
自由	adj.	zìyóu	free (to do something)
摇号	n.	yáohào	lottery system
许可	n.	xǔkě	permit, license
下单	v.	xiàdān	place an order
暂时	adv.	zànshí	temporarily

海文：你说的这个应用是滴滴，2012年创立，是汽车预约手机应用，希望这样能减少私家车的使用，缓解交通压力。

宋杰：我哥哥的朋友在三藩市的优步公司工作，他们也进入中国的市场了。

海文：对！美国的优步公司在2014年进入中国，和滴滴公司为争夺市场展开了一场激烈的战斗。优步价格特别便宜，而且推出拼车这个新的项目，既省钱又节能，还可以缓解堵塞，可谓一举多得。可是当优步把打进100个城市作为目标的时候，滴滴已经打进了三四百个中国城市，其中包括二三线城市。2014年滴滴打车与对手快的打车合并，改名为"滴滴出行"，口号是"让出行更美好"，2016年8月终于收购中国优步。滴滴出行还拓展了很多的项目，包括代驾、快车和专车等等。

李静：对了，今年滴滴出行的首席运营官柳青登上了《时代周刊》2017年最具影响力人物的百人榜。

词	词性	拼音	英文
应用	n.	yìngyòng	app
滴滴	p.n.	Dīdī	Didi (a Chinese ride-sharing company)
创立	v.	chuànglì	found
预约	v.	yùyuē	make a reservation or booking
三藩市	p.n.	Sānfānshì	San Francisco
优步	p.n.	Yōubù	Uber
争夺	v.	zhēngduó	vie
战斗	n.	zhàndòu	battle, fight
推出	v.	tuīchū	roll out, launch
一举多得	phr.	yì jǔ duō dé	achieve several aims with one action
合并	v.	hébìng	merge
口号	n.	kǒuhào	slogan
终于	adv.	zhōngyú	finally
收购	v.	shōugòu	acquire
代驾	n.	dàijià	designated driver service (a Didi service)
快车	n.	kuàichē	an express ride (a Didi service)
专车	n.	zhuānchē	an exclusive ride (a Didi service)
首席运营官	n.	shǒuxí yùn yíng guān	chief operating officer
时代周刊	p.n.	Shídài Zhōukān	Time Magazine

语言实践
LANGUAGE CONNECTION

1. Making a conjecture: 恐怕……

   Structure: circumstance + 恐怕 + conjecture/prediction

   "堵塞恐怕是大城市都要面对的问题。"

   恐怕 means "I'm afraid that …." It can be used to make a conjecture or prediction based on a given circumstance. The conjecture or prediction is usually negative.

   EXAMPLES:
   1. 作业太多了，恐怕我今天做不完。
   2. 我最近特别忙，明天恐怕不能和你吃饭。

   Respond to the following situations using 恐怕.

   1. 那双运动鞋已经穿了两年了。
   2. 模拟联合国虽然是一个很好的课外活动，但是需要花很多时间。
   3. 物理课太难了。
   4. 我对音乐和美术都很感兴趣。
   5. 这个饭馆离家太远了。
   6. 我昨天晚上熬夜了。

2. Introducing a method: 通过/用……来……

   Structure: 通过/用 + instrument/method + 来 + verb phrase

   "用打车软件来打车非常容易。"

   The word 来 can be used to connect two verb phrases. The first verb phrase contains 通过 or 用 and indicates a method to be used in order to achieve a certain purpose, which is expressed by the second verb phrase. 来 is placed between the two verb phrases to connect them.

EXAMPLES:

① 很多人都是<u>通过</u>这个网站<u>来</u>找工作的。
② 摩拜单车现在<u>通过</u>微信<u>来</u>推广自己的产品。
③ 在过去几年里，这个商店一直<u>用</u>打折<u>来</u>吸引消费者。

> Help your friends solve the following problems using 通过 / 用……来……
> (You may search for solutions online.)

① 朋友A：哎呀，我的信用卡被人盗用了！
我：

② 朋友B：我后天去北京，我不知道上哪儿去找好吃的饭馆。
我：

③ 朋友C：我去中国忘了带人民币，你觉得我可以出门吃饭吗？
我：

④ 朋友D：留守儿童特别需要社会的关爱，我好想帮助他们！
我：

⑤ 朋友F：放暑假后我一直没有运动，都胖了10磅了！
我：

3. Highlighting two characteristics: 既……又……

Structure: 既 + feature 1 + 又 + feature 2

"拼车<u>既</u>省钱<u>又</u>节能。"

既 can be used with 又 to express that something has two features of the same importance. The features can be expressed by adjectives or verb phrases. They usually take the same form—if feature 1 is an adjective, feature 2 will also be an adjective.

EXAMPLES:

① 这个房子<u>既</u>明亮<u>又</u>宽敞。
② 这个产品的设计<u>既</u>时尚<u>又</u>人性化。

Imagine you are a salesperson at a shopping mall. Promote the products below to your customers using 既……又…….

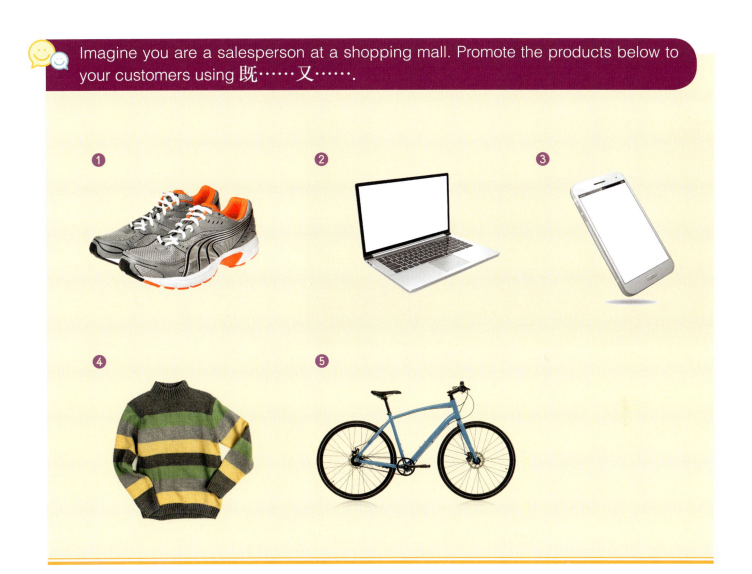

PART 3 第三部分 共享单车
BICYCLE SHARING: OFO AND MOBIKE

宋杰：刚才经过地铁站，看见那里停放着不少黄色和橘色的自行车。

海文：黄色和橘色这两种鲜艳夺目的自行车已成为中国大都市一道亮丽的风景线。黄色的自行车叫"OFO"，橘色的是"摩拜"单车，从2016年冬天开始，这些共享单车就是人们茶余饭后的热议话题，真可谓风靡一时。

李静：共享单车是怎么样操作的？

海文：是利用高科技操作。首先下载手机应用，然后登录输入个人资料和付款方法。用车的时候只要扫车上的二维码，就能把车解锁，收费很便宜，付完押金后，半小时的收费从五毛到一元。用完以后就把车停放在路边。这最适合短途出行。比方说上班的地方在两个地铁站之间，打车太贵，走路又太远，共享单车就是最好的选择了。

宋杰：为什么小黄车取名叫"OFO"？

橘色	adj.	júsè	orange (color)
鲜艳夺目	adj.	xiānyàn duómù	bright and eye-catching
风景线	n.	fēngjǐngxiàn	scenery
共享单车	phr.	gòngxiǎng dānchē	bicycle sharing
茶余饭后	phr.	chá yú fàn hòu	at one's leisure
风靡一时	phr.	fēngmí yì shí	be all the rage
操作	v.	cāozuò	operate
高科技	n.	gāo kējì	high technology
登录	v.	dēnglù	log in
付款	v.o.	fùkuǎn	pay (a sum of money)
扫	v.	sǎo	scan
二维码	n.	èrwéimǎ	QR code
解锁	v.o.	jiěsuǒ	undo a lock, unlock
收费	n.	shōufèi	fee
押金	n.	yājīn	deposit
停放	v.	tíngfàng	park (a vehicle)
短途	n.	duǎntú	short distance
比方	v.	bǐfang	for example
取名	v.o.	qǔmíng	give a name to, be named as

海文：OFO你一看就能联想到单车的两个轮子。当中的"F"是单车的车身，非常形象化。它的创始人戴威，是北京大学毕业的90后。他在创业的道路上遇到很多困难，有一次公司账目上只剩下400多元，连员工的薪酬都不能支付。他不断地改革创新，终于成功地融资，这样公司才继续下来。摩拜单车的创始人胡玮炜，是从杭州来的一个80后。现在摩拜单车不仅在国内使用，甚至已经推广到欧洲的几个大城市了。

李静：我记得在80年代，一般中国人的交通工具都是自行车，外国报道中国的图片都是骑自行车的人潮。到了90年代，汽车逐渐多起来了。到了现在，大城市一到了晚高峰就拥堵不堪。共享单车的确解决了不少短途出行的问题。既经济又环保，可说是从两个轮的自行车到四个轮的汽车，又重新回到两个轮子。这是时代带来的一波又一波的变革。

海文：共享单车这种智能出行的模式不仅为大众提供了便捷的出行，而且在一定程度上缓解了日趋严重的雾霾等环境问题。可是也同时带来值得我们反思的几个问题。第一是胡乱停放，因为使用后可以自由停放，而且数量很多，所以占用了很多道路资源，影响交通和城市美观。第二，共享单车跟爱彼迎和优步的经济模式不一样，后面两个都是利用闲置资源，你不用的公寓租出去，你不用汽车的时候给他人服务。可是共享单车必须购买单车，成本比较高，这样的经济模式能成功吗？

宋杰：看来也只有时间才能给我们答案了。

词	词性	拼音	英文
联想	v.	liánxiǎng	associate with
轮子	n.	lúnzi	tire
形象化	adj.	xíngxiànghuà	visual
创始人	n.	chuàngshǐrén	founder
90后	phr.	jiǔlínghòu	post-90s generation (a Chinese term referring to people born between 1990 and 2000)
创业	v.	chuàngyè	start a business
账目	n.	zhàngmù	accounts
薪酬	n.	xīnchóu	salary
支付	v.	zhīfù	pay
不断	adv.	búduàn	continuously
改革	v.	gǎigé	reform
创新	v.	chuàngxīn	innovate
融资	v.	róngzī	raise funds
推广	v.	tuīguǎng	promote, spread
年代	n.	niándài	decade, era
人潮	n.	réncháo	crowd
不堪	adj.	bùkān	unbearable
重新	adv.	chóngxīn	again
带来	v.	dàilái	bring
波	n.	bō	wave
变革	n.	biàngé	reform, transformation
模式	n.	móshì	mode, model
日趋	adv.	rìqū	increasingly, day by day
反思	v.	fǎnsī	reflect
胡乱	adv.	húluàn	casually, carelessly
爱彼迎	p.n.	Àibǐyíng	Airbnb
闲置	v.	xiánzhì	leave unused
公寓	n.	gōngyù	apartment
租	v.	zū	rent
购买	v.	gòumǎi	purchase
成本	n.	chéngběn	cost

语言实践
LANGUAGE CONNECTION

1. **Describing a condition to be fulfilled for a certain result: 只要……就……**

   Structure: 只要 + condition + 就 + result

   "只要扫车上的二维码，就能把车解锁。"

   In this structure, 只要 is placed at the beginning of a sentence to indicate a condition. 就 begins the second part of the sentence to express the result if the condition is fulfilled. The auxiliary verbs 可以 and 能 can be used interchangeably after 就 to indicate ability or capability.

   EXAMPLES:
   1. 只要不堵车，我们就能准时到。
   2. 只要大家省水省电，就能为环保尽一份力。

   > Imagine that your friend has encountered some difficulties and is feeling stressed. Share with him/her some ways to relieve stress using 只要……就…….

   EXAMPLE:
   只要你努力，就会成功。

   Suggested answers: 休息，运动，跟朋友聊天，出去走走，换个角度看问题

2. **Expressing successive or repeated occurrences: 一……又一……**

   Structure: 一 + measure word + 又一 + measure word

   "这是时代带来的一波又一波的变革。"

   This structure is used to express "one after another" or "again and again." Commonly used phrases include:

   - 一波又一波
   - 一年又一年
   - 一次又一次

   EXAMPLES:
   1. 随着共享单车在国内的发展，摩拜公司收到了一波又一波的资金支持。
   2. 我们都很好奇他是如何一年又一年地坚持理想的。
   3. 他们一次又一次地犯这种小错误。

Complete the following sentences with the appropriate options provided. Then make a new sentence for each option.

一波又一波的好消息　　一年又一年的努力　　一次又一次的失败

① 今年我家迎来了……：我考上了大学，我姐姐结了婚，我哥哥也开了自己的公司。

② 这支球队经过了……，终于在2018年获得了全国比赛的冠军。

③ 马云自从创业以来，经历了……，但是最后他还是获得了巨大的成功。

China Highlights: Shanghai

Shanghai Bund

Pudong

文化剪影
CULTURE ENRICHMENT

《清明上河图》中的交通工具
Modes of Transportation in *Along the River During the Qingming Festival*

张择端（1085-1145）是中国北宋（960-1127）时期最伟大的画家。他出生在今日的山东省，年轻时代在都城汴京(Biànjīng)(现在的河南省开封市)游学，后来学习绘画。他画的《清明上河图》是中国最有名的一幅画，也是一件值得所有中国人骄傲的国宝。画中生动地表现了清明节时汴京和汴河上的热闹景象以及汴京郊外的田园风光。

清明节在每年的阳历四月五日前后，是中国的传统节日。人们常常在清明节那一天扫墓祭祖，有点像墨西哥的"亡灵节"(Day of the Dead)。清明节那天，人们也常常去郊外春游、放风筝。北宋时期100多年没有大战争的和平稳定带来了汴京人口的快速增长和城市建筑的高速发展。

张择端在《清明上河图》中画了很多种交通工具，比如客船、轿子、马、驴、骡、骆驼、马车、牛车等。据统计，《清明上河图》中有20多辆车、8顶轿子、28条大大小小各种各样的客船和货船。当时中国的水陆交通网纵横交错，四通八达。只要你看一看《清明上河图》，就能感觉到中国那时的市场经济非常发达，都市居民的日常生活非常方便，都市的文化娱乐生活也非常丰富。

《清明上河图》中那座最大的桥叫虹桥。值得我们注意的是，虹桥上可以说是拥堵不堪。跟现代大都市一样，900多年前中国都市经济的发展和人口的增长也带来了严重的交通拥堵的问题。

课堂活动
CLASS ACTIVITIES

Interpretive

Answer the question below.

1) 在《清明上河图》中,哪一种交通工具是你以前没有见过的?

Interpersonal

In your group, choose one of the questions below. Research online to find the answers.

1) 宋朝时西方是什么时代?那个时代的欧洲或者世界其他地区都有哪些交通工具?
2) 为什么汴京那么热闹?在你的国家,什么节日时交通会特别拥挤?

Presentational

As a group, share your findings with the class.

How to manage traffic congestion

Read the passage below. In groups, research online to complete the following table.

拥堵是大城市最令人头疼的问题之一。我们先看看中国有哪些解决的方法。

北京市为了缓解交通压力,实行了尾号限行。在周一到周五的工作日,每天有两个尾号(一个是单号,一个是双号)的私人机动车在早上七点到晚上八点在五环内不能行使。比方说周一是1和6,周二是2和7,周三是3和8,周四是4和9,周五是5和0;每三个月更换一次。这样在工作日,在路上行驶的机动车可以减少五分之一。这个政策是从2007年开始的。当时,政府为了准备奥运,确保交通畅通,开始试验单双号限行。这项试验后来就变成了尾号限行的长期措施。

除了尾号限行以外，北京市还严格限制购车，这个方法简称"**摇号限牌**❶"，每年发出的汽车牌照指标有一定的**配额**❷。比如，2017年有15万个指标，2018年有10万个。如果没有北京的**户籍**❸或者没有在北京住满5年，是不可以申请摇号上牌的。如果符合摇号规定还得看运气好不好。所以，要拿到汽车牌照是非常不容易的。

北京也不断地**发展公共交通工具**，地铁现在已经有20多条线路、300多个车站，四通八达，是目前世界上最大的地铁系统之一。除此以外，还有公交车等非常便捷的公共交通工具。公共交通非常便宜，这可以鼓励市民多使用。

当然，**提高停车费**、**控制城市人口增长**、**更好地规划城市**，这些都是解决交通拥堵的方法。不同的城市有不同的方法，让我们来看看世界其他大城市有什么治堵的好方法。

❶ 摇号限牌 yáo hào xiàn pái license plate lottery system　　❷ 配额 pèi'é quota　　❸ 户籍 hùjí household registration

城市	人口	面积	机动车数量	公共交通系统素质（5星为最高）	治堵方法
北京	2170.7万	1.64平方公里	564万	*****	1. 尾号限行 2. 摇号限牌 3. 发展公共交通系统 4. 提高停车费 5. 控制人口增长 6. 城市规划
纽约					
东京					
伦敦					
巴黎					

词汇拓展
VOCABULARY BUILDING

1. **Words Containing 化**

   In Unit 1, we learned the word 全球化 and in this unit, we have just learned the word 大众化. You may have also learned the words 化学 and 变化. 化 may be used to form many words. Equivalent to the suffix "-ize," it is added to nouns or adjectives to form verbs meaning to cause (someone or a situation) to become (something). It takes two main forms:

   ➤ Noun + 化: to cause someone/something to have the characteristics of this noun
   ➤ Adjective + 化: to cause someone/something to become the state described by this adjective

   Both forms can function as both verb and adjective. For example, 现代化 means "to cause something to become modern"; 简化 means "to cause something to become simple."

   1) Guess the meaning of each word below:
      城镇化, 自动化, 标准化, 智能化, 美化, 绿化, 深化, 优化, 强化

   2) In a pair, write as many words comprising 化 as you can within two minutes. In a contest, each pair will take turns to say a word with 化 in it out loud. You may not repeat what other groups have said. The last group that is able to say a word with 化 in it wins.

2. Four-Character Expressions

Read the four-character expressions below and their meanings. They are commonly used to describe traffic conditions and getting around. Fill in the blank in each sentence below with one of the expressions. You may use each expression only once.

> 1) 水泄不通：路上的人特别多，拥挤得不得了，甚至连水都流不过去。
> 2) 畅通无阻：完全没有堵车，很通畅的交通情况。有时候也可以描写政策的实行非常顺利。
> 3) 拥堵不堪：不堪就是受不了，意思就是非常拥挤，让人受不了。
> 4) 人来人往：用来形容路上到处都是人，有的从别的地方来，有的去别的地方，非常热闹。
> 5) 川流不息：人或车在路上像河流一样不停地穿行着。
> 6) 车水马龙：车辆像流水一样不停地穿行，马车一辆接一辆，像一条龙似的；指街上满满都是人群和车辆。

1) 张择端的《清明上河图》反映了北宋都城交通发达的景象，路上可说是_____，非常繁忙。

2) 春节前，赶着办年货准备过新年的人群把超市挤得_____。

3) 在北京开车出行的人都知道，二环路上的车辆一到上下班高峰时间就_____。

4) 昨天晚上，这家旅店旁边高速公路上的车辆_____，吵得我一夜都没睡。

5) 广西桂林的夜市美食一条街与桂林的山水一样有名。在那里，既有外来的游客，又有本地的居民，_____，非常热闹。

6) 春节的时候，大城市的交通反而_____，因为大多数进城打工的农民工都回家过节了。

阅读理解
READING COMPREHENSION

Read the blog posts and answer the questions that follow.

一个高中生眼中的中国式出行
A High School Student's Blog Posts on Modes of Transportation in China

李静来自美国德州休斯顿附近的一个小镇。她在中国呆了几个月，一方面观察，一方面体验新事物。她把这些难忘的经历都写在她的博客上跟朋友分享。下面是她有关在中国出行的几篇博客短文。

博客（一）

我在中国已经有几个月了。这段日子里，我观察到不少新鲜的事物。北京的拥堵是出了名的，所以很多人说北京不是"首都"，而是"首堵"。车多人多本来就是大城市的一个现象。可是北京车实在是太多了。一到了早晚高峰时间，路上满满都是车。我的中文老师以前教我们"水泄不通"这个形容拥挤的词语。当时我不太了解，现在我真的体会到了。

博客（二）

我记得朋友告诉我，中国的第一辆汽车是在清朝末年，袁世凯❶送给慈禧太后❷的。那时候的贵族❸一般都用轿子❹，用马达❺发动的汽车是前所未有❻的。当司机坐在慈禧前面开车时，慈禧非常生气，她觉得司机是仆人❼，应该在她的后面，再说司机不但不能坐着，而且应该跪着开车。这种中西文化的冲突❽，闹出不少的笑话。到了民国，汽车慢慢进入中国上层社会，是一个又新鲜又时髦❾的玩意儿❿。汽车代表一个人在社会上的身份和地位。

博客（三）

　　我到中国的第一个周末，我们的老师就教我怎么乘坐地铁了。她说地铁既方便又便宜，而且是个绿色环保的出行方式。特别是在早晚高峰时间，几条主干道都挤得水泄不通。地铁虽然满满都是人，可是还是畅通无阻的。北京的地铁可以说是四通八达，周末我可以从家坐6号线到南锣鼓巷逛胡同，然后从6号线换乘5号线到天坛公园游玩，从公园出来还可以在红桥市场购买纪念品，然后在附近的老北京炸酱面馆吃顿饭。我还可以坐10号线到三里屯逛商场、看电影。有了方便的地铁系统，<u>我们在北京的生活也就更多姿多彩了</u>。

1. 袁世凯 Yuán Shìkǎi an emperor, general, statesman and warlord famous for his influence during the late Qing Dynasty.
2. 慈禧太后 Cíxǐ Tàihòu Empress Dowager Cixi (the empress who controlled the Chinese government during the late Qing Dynasty)
3. 贵族 guìzú aristocrat
4. 轿子 jiàozi sedan
5. 马达 mǎdá motor
6. 前所未有 qián suǒ wèi yǒu unprecedented
7. 仆人 púrén servant
8. 冲突 chōngtū conflict
9. 时髦 shímáo trendy, fashionable
10. 玩意儿 wányìr plaything

1. 汽车是什么时候进入中国的？

2. 第一辆汽车进入中国的时候，闹出了什么笑话？这个笑话反映了中西文化哪些矛盾？

3. 请用一个四字词语形容北京早晚高峰时间的交通。为什么选用这个词语？

4. 在最后一句"我们在北京的生活也就更多姿多彩了"中，"多姿多彩"的意思是什么？李静的周末可以有哪些活动？

写作工坊
WRITING WORKSHOP

1. 看图写故事 Narrating a Story

1. **Interpreting the question**

   The section on story narration constitutes 15% of the marks in the AP® Chinese Examination. You should try to study the four pictures given and understand the story they convey within 15 minutes.

   You should try to organize your plot in an effective and efficient manner, and use rich and appropriate vocabulary to tell a complete and interesting story that matches closely the story as suggested by the pictures. Vary the sentence structures with both simple and complex sentences. Use four-character phrases or idioms where possible and appropriate.

2. **Structure**

   The story narration test in the AP® Chinese Examination usually uses the format below:
   1) Picture 1 sets the scene/stage so you will need to use rich vocabulary to describe the scene and elaborate on important details of the picture, such as the characters in the story as well as the setting and occasion.
   2) Picture 2 usually shows something unexpected happening or a problem arising.
   3) Picture 3 usually shows the characters in the story thinking quickly and creatively to solve the problem or resolve the issue.
   4) Picture 4 usually shows a happy ending, where the problem/issue is resolved successfully and everyone is pleased with the outcome.

3. **Writing strategies and techniques**

   1) Make sure that your story has a beginning, middle and an end.
   2) Look closely at each picture and describe the characters by giving them names and focusing on their key actions and thought. Provide significant details for your story where appropriate.
   3) Pay special attention to your plot or storyline, ensuring that it is logical.
   4) Check that your narration is cohesive and consistent. You may use conjunctions to connect your sentences and paragraphs, such as 先……, 再……, 然后……, 最后……, and 不但……, 而且……。

4. **Practice**

The four pictures present a story. Imagine you are writing the story to a friend. Narrate a complete story (with a beginning, middle and end) as suggested by the pictures and provide details to demonstrate your proficiency in Chinese language and culture.

2. 介绍人物 Introducing a Person

In your group, choose one of the entrepreneurs below or any other successful entrepreneur. Complete the tasks below.

> 柳青　　雷军　　马云　　戴威　　马化腾

1. Research your chosen entrepreneur online using his/her name as the keyword. You may look at text or videos.

2. Discuss the following questions.
   a. 他/她的教育经历或工作经验给他/她的成功带来了哪些帮助？
   b. 他/她在创业之路上遇到了哪些困难？为什么？
   c. 他/她有什么值得我们学习的地方？
   d. 他/她的公司或项目有什么特别的地方？为什么他/她的公司或项目会成功？

3. Prepare a report of your discussion and present it to the class. You may use the words and sentence structures below.

> 80后/90后/00后　　高科技　　操作　　下载　　资料　　投资　　形象
> 创始人　　不断地　　融资　　继续　　推广　　变革　　日趋　　项目
> 运营　　难度　　体验　　巨大　　针对　　应用　　合并　　对手　　收购

值得学习/值得纪念；无论……都……；通过/用……来……；既……又……；一波又一波/一次又一次；带来……问题/挑战/麻烦/机遇；只要……就……

EXAMPLE:

胡玮炜，浙江人，中国著名的80后成功人士。她在2014年创办了摩拜单车项目，并且在3年期间让摩拜单车成为了中国甚至全球最大的共享单车公司之一。胡玮炜在成立摩拜单车以前有过10年的汽车科技媒体经验，在腾讯、极客公园以及《新京报》等公司工作过。这些经历最终给她带来了成功。

摩拜单车利用自行车来解决人们短途出行的问题，并且用二维码、定位功能等高科技来帮助人们使用自行车。因此，摩拜单车很快就成了大公司。

虽然摩拜单车现在这么成功，但是在刚开始创业的时候，胡玮炜还是因为用户使用习惯等问题，遇到了一波又一波的挫折。但是无论是投资还是市场的问题，胡玮炜都没有被打败。只要努力，没有完成不了的事。最后，她还是带着摩拜单车骑出了一道自己的风景！

学习总结
I CAN DO!

Interpretive Communication

- ☐ I can read about the rapid development and popularity of the vast mass transportation systems in China.
- ☐ I can understand when people talk about some taxi-hailing and bicycle sharing companies and their apps.
- ☐ I can read and understand some basic information on traffic jams and automobile exhaust pollution in some big cities in China and some of the strategies adopted to alleviate them.
- ☐ I can conduct online search in Chinese and identify some interesting information on the founders of a few Chinese start-up companies.

Interpersonal Communication

- ☐ I can discuss common Chinese mass transportation systems.
- ☐ I can converse about the strategies that some big cities in China have adopted to alleviate traffic jams and automobile exhaust pollution.
- ☐ I can talk about some taxi-hailing and bicycle sharing companies and their apps.
- ☐ I can talk about and explain the positive impact these companies have made on traffic conditions and the environment.

Presentational Communication

- ☐ I can describe popular mass transportation systems in China.
- ☐ I can compare briefly the operating models of bicycle sharing companies (such as OFO and Mobike) with that of Airbnb and Uber.
- ☐ I can make a brief presentation on the market competition in China between Didi Chuxing and Uber before Uber sold its China business to Didi.
- ☐ I can compare the founders of a few Chinese start-up companies with those from the United States and other parts of the world.
- ☐ I can write a complete story with details based on a series of pictures.

Cultural Knowledge

- ☐ I can talk about popular everyday mass transportation systems in China.
- ☐ I can describe some taxi-hailing and bicycle sharing companies in China and their apps.
- ☐ I can talk about the founders of a few Chinese start-up companies.
- ☐ I can use several common Chinese idioms appropriately in communicative situations.
- ☐ I can talk about the most famous painting in China—Zhang Zeduan's *Along the River During the Qingming Festival*.

人口、住房与就业
POPULATION, HOUSING, AND EMPLOYMENT

学习目标
LEARNING OBJECTIVES

- Comprehend the population policies as well as housing and employment issues in China
- Understand changes in the structure of the Chinese family
- Discuss posters and slogans related to China's one-child policy
- Debate whether an only child has an edge over another who is not

单元总览
CONTENTS AT A GLANCE!

导入 WARM UP

- **Part 1:** 中国人口政策的变迁 (China's Population Policy at a Crossroads)
  Language Connection:
  1. <u>自从</u>2015年开放二胎，我有些朋友已经开始考虑生二胎了。
  2. 我有些朋友已经开始考虑生二胎了，<u>毕竟</u>有个兄弟姐妹比较好。
  3. <u>也就是说</u>，一般千禧一代、90后都是独生子女。
  4. 人口政策是按照社会情况，随时<u>加以</u>调整的！

- **Part 2:** 蜗居：大城床与小城房的矛盾 (The Challenges of Urban Housing)
  Language Connection:
  1. 100多平米的公寓就要200万美元一套，我<u>简直</u>不能相信。
  2. 这就是<u>所谓的</u>"寸金寸土"。
  3. 这些选择让年轻人觉得很纠结，<u>反正</u>是不同的人有不同选择，可谓"见仁见智"。

- **Part 3:** 北漂一族的辛酸与梦想 (Hardships and Dreams of Beijing Drifters)
  Language Connection:
  1. 毕业生<u>为</u>选择工作的城市<u>而</u>烦恼。
  2. 这是一套<u>三室一厅一卫</u>的房子。

文化剪影：计划生育标语口号和家庭结构的变迁
CULTURE ENRICHMENT: Family Planning Slogans and Shifts in the Structure of the Family

词汇拓展："族"、"党"、词语辨析
VOCABULARY BUILDING: Words Containing 族 and 党;
Differentiating Between Similar Words

阅读理解：独生子女的困扰
READING COMPREHENSION: What an Only Child Is Troubled by

写作工坊：准备辩论稿——独生子女的优势
WRITING WORKSHOP: Preparing the Script for a Debate –
He Who Is an Only Child Has an Edge over He Who Is Not

学习总结 I CAN DO!

导入
WARM UP

1. The population of a country or territory refers to the total number of people living in it. Research online for information on the five most populous countries in the world and fill in the table below in descending order of population.

国家	首都	哪个洲	人口数目	占全球人口百分比
中国	北京	亚洲	大约14亿❶	大约18.50%

❶ 亿 yì hundred million

Which of these five countries has the fastest rate of population growth?

2. Work in small groups to share ideas and respond to the questions below. You may look at the images for clues.

a) What are some factors that contribute to the increase or decrease in a country's population?

b) Which aspects of life will the population size of a country affect? Two of them, education and housing, have been labelled on the image. Think of as many aspects as you can and see which group comes up with the most in five minutes.

Education   Housing

第一部分 中国人口政策的变迁
PART 1 CHINA'S POPULATION POLICY AT A CROSSROADS

海文：自从2015年<u>开放二胎</u>，我有些朋友已经开始考虑生二胎了，<u>毕竟</u>有个兄弟姐妹比较好。

| 开放 | v. | kāifàng | lift a ban or restriction |
| 二胎 | n. | èr tāi | second child |

宋杰：我的中国同事和朋友基本上都是独生子女！

| 独生子女 | phr. | dúshēng zǐnǚ | only child |

海文：当然，你的同事都是90后，朋友一般都是千禧一代的。

| 千禧一代 | phr. | qiānxǐ yí dài | millennials |

李静：这跟90后和千禧一代有什么关系？

海文：因为一胎化政策是在上世纪80年代开始实行的。<u>也就是说</u>，一般千禧一代、90后都是独生子女。

| 一胎化政策 | phr. | yìtāihuà zhèngcè | one-child policy |

宋杰：那为什么上世纪70年代后期有这样的一个政策呢？

海文：在上世纪70年代政府提倡"晚，稀，少"的生育方针，就是说要晚生孩

提倡	v.	tíchàng	advocate
稀	adj.	xī	rare
生育	v.	shēngyù	give birth to
方针	n.	fāngzhēn	policy

子，少生孩子，到了1978年提倡"一对夫妇生育子女数最好一个最多两个，生育间隔3年以上"。到了1982年计划生育就变成了一个基本国策。

宋杰：这跟以前中国的传统观念"多子多孙多福气"背道而驰，实施起来不容易。

海文：那是当然的，特别是在思想保守而且需要劳动力的农村。到了21世纪以后开始出现了低生育水平。所以初步开放二胎，先是"双独二孩"，就是父母双方都是独生子女可以生二胎，后来是"单独二孩"，就是父母只要其中一方是独生子女就可以了。人口政策是按照社会情况，随时加以调整的！

宋杰：我在美国上中文课的时候，老师也提到中国人口结构的变化，以前是大家庭，现在是"一二四"结构，就是说一个孩子以后得照顾父母两人和四名祖父母，这可是很沉重的负担。

海文：是呀！除了人口结构发生了很大变化以外，一胎化也造成了老龄化，男女比例的失衡和独生子女的教育问题。专家估计到了2025年，60岁以上的人就占人口的百分之三十五。在一个正常社会的男女比例是100个女婴有105个男婴，可是现在是100比115，这就意味着很多男孩子长大以后找不到女孩子结婚。

李静：我想独生子女的教育也是一个很大问题。我们都有兄弟姐妹，从小就在家里学习怎么样跟人相处。

海文：对呀，现在父母对孩子特别溺爱。独生子女都是家里的"小皇帝"。父母的期望也很高，所以他们长大以后也承担很大的压力。一胎化政策实施30年，真的存在不少的问题。如果不改变的话，中国的劳动人口会不断地减少，这些问题都是对政府严峻的考验，所以2015年政府决定开放二胎。

宋杰：这真是一个好消息！

老龄化	n.	lǎolínghuà	aging
比例	n.	bǐlì	ratio
失衡	v.	shīhéng	lose balance
估计	v.	gūjì	estimate
占	v.	zhàn	constitute
百分	n.	bǎifēn	percent
正常	adj.	zhèngcháng	normal
婴	n.	yīng	infant
意味	v.	yìwèi	imply, mean

溺爱	v.	nì'ài	spoil (a child)
小皇帝	n.	xiǎohuángdì	(lit.) little emperor (a term used to describe an only child who gains excessive amounts of attention from his/her parents and grandparents)
承担	v.	chéngdān	bear
存在	v.	cúnzài	exist
劳动人口	n.	láodòng rénkǒu	work force
严峻	adj.	yánjùn	severe
考验	n.	kǎoyàn	test

语言实践
LANGUAGE CONNECTION

1. Indicating a time or event in relation to a continuing situation: 自从……

   Structure: 自从 + time/event

   "自从2015年开放二胎，我有些朋友已经开始考虑生二胎了。"

   自从 means "since" and is used to indicate a situation that has continued from then until now. It is normally followed by a time phrase or a noun phrase that implies a certain time or event, such as 自从那时 (since then) and 自从2015年开放二胎 (since the implementation of the policy of allowing a second child). 以后 may be added at the back in the form of 自从……以后, such as 自从那时以后 and 自从2015年开放二胎以后. Note that 自从 can only indicate the starting point of a certain length of time in the past. Use only 自 (without 从) if you want to talk about the starting point of a future time, such as 自今天起 and 自下个星期六起.

   EXAMPLES:
   1. 自从1978年中国改革开放以后，越来越多的外国人决定学习中文。
   2. 自从我跟他分手以后，我们再也没有联系过。

   Answer the following questions using 自从…….
   1. 你读高中以后有哪些变化？
   2. 谁有弟弟妹妹？自从你的弟弟／妹妹出生以后，你家或者你的生活有什么变化呢？
   3. 你学了中文以后，对中国的看法有什么改变？

2. Emphasizing the reason for an outcome: 毕竟……

   "我有些朋友已经开始考虑生二胎了，毕竟有个兄弟姐妹比较好。"

   毕竟 is an adverb used for giving emphasis or for indicating a certain conclusion. It is normally used in the later part of a sentence.

EXAMPLES:

① 您别生他的气了，他<u>毕竟</u>还是个没长大的孩子。

② 虽然北京有很好的工作机会，但是他还是选择回家乡，<u>毕竟</u>他是父母唯一的孩子。

Role play

① In a pair, role-play as two persons who have been learning Mandarin for five years. One of you is determined to continue with your learning while the other is thinking of giving up. Practice using 毕竟 in a dialog giving each other advice.

② In a pair, role-play as a mother and her daughter. The mother wants to have a second child but her daughter is against the idea. Practice using 毕竟 in a dialog dissuading each other.

3. Giving further explanation: 也就是说……

"<u>也就是说</u>，一般千禧一代、90后都是独生子女。"

To further explain the meaning of a word, a set phrase, an idiomatic expression, or a point made earlier, start with 也就是说. It means "that is to say ... " in English. It can be used interchangeably with 换句话说(就是) and 换(而)言之.

EXAMPLES:

① 我姐姐今年念高中三年级，<u>也就是说</u>她马上要上大学了。

② 中国传统的婚恋方式是"包办婚姻"，<u>也就是说／换句话说／换(而)言之</u>，年轻人的婚姻是由双方父母决定，不可以自己选择。

Complete the following sentences.

① 我的暑假马上就要结束了，也就是说，……。

② 中国人常说"多子多福"，也就是说，……。

③ 今年我上高中三年级，也就是说，……。

④ 奶奶周末会来我们家，也就是说，……。

4. **Describing the treatment of someone or something: 加以……**

"人口政策是按照社会情况，随时加以调整的！"

加以 is a verb used to indicate that the action is directed toward something or someone mentioned earlier in the sentence. It is used in formal speech or writing. The verb after 加以 is always a word with two characters and refers to an action that has not yet taken place. Commonly used set phrase expressions with 加以 include: 加以推广, 加以利用, 加以讨论, 加以关注, 加以肯定, and 加以赞赏.

EXAMPLES:

① 推广绿色环保生活的一个好方法就是对所有可以回收的垃圾加以利用。

② 老师应该对学生的进步及时加以肯定，这样学生才能有信心学得更好。

Discuss the following questions.

① 你认为你们学校的学生会应该对什么活动加以推广呢？

② 中国的环境污染问题越来越严重，你觉得中国政府可以做些什么？

China Highlights: Chongqing

A river view

People's Square

第二部分 蜗居：大城床与小城房的矛盾
PART 2 THE CHALLENGES OF URBAN HOUSING

宋杰：我听说几年前有一部电视剧描述大城市的居住问题，非常受欢迎，是吗？

海文：你说的是《蜗居》吧，改编自作家六六的小说，故事是一对年轻夫妻因为没钱在上海买房子，所以暂时租了一套里弄的公寓，孩子出生以后因为住房面积太小，只好把孩子送回乡下让父母照顾。电视剧把当时社会上大家关注的热点问题搬到戏剧的舞台上，反映老百姓在房价飙升的压力下遇到的种种波折。这套电视剧播出后引起大家的共鸣，收视率创了新高。

李静：我来北京几个月了，我对这个大城市的居住问题非常感兴趣。我来自美国德州休斯顿附近的一个小镇。我们一般同学的家都有三四个卧室，还有很大的院子。我们常在朋友家的后院烤肉和打排球。

宋杰：我来了北京以后才知道居住问题那么严重。我的寄宿家庭在海淀区，附近有一个全国有名的高中，这里的房子特别贵。寄宿家庭的妈妈王阿姨告诉我这里

词	词性	拼音	英文
电视剧	n.	diànshìjù	TV series
描述	v.	miáoshù	describe
居住	v.	jūzhù	reside
蜗居	p.n.	Wōjū	Dwelling Narrowness (name of a Chinese TV series)
改编	v.	gǎibiān	adapt from
小说	n.	xiǎoshuō	novel
夫妻	n.	fūqī	husband and wife
套	m.w.	tào	suite (measure word for houses)
里弄	n.	lǐlòng	lanes and alleys in Shanghai
住房	n.	zhùfáng	housing, lodging
面积	n.	miànjī	area
热点	adj.	rèdiǎn	hot (topics)
戏剧	n.	xìjù	drama, play
舞台	n.	wǔtái	stage
反映	v.	fǎnyìng	reflect
老百姓	n.	lǎobǎixìng	ordinary people
房价	n.	fángjià	price of housing
飙升	v.	biāoshēng	soar, surge
波折	n.	bōzhé	twists and turns, setbacks
共鸣	n.	gòngmíng	sympathetic response
新高	n.	xīngāo	new high
德州	p.n.	Dézhōu	Texas
休斯顿	p.n.	Xiūsīdùn	Houston
烤肉	v.o.	kǎoròu	grill meat, barbecue
排球	n.	páiqiú	volleyball
海淀区	p.n.	Hǎidiànqū	Haidian District (a district in Beijing)

是学区房100多平米的公寓就要200万美元一套，我简直不能相信。我们社区30多万已经是很好的房子了。我想谁能买得起200万元的房子呀？

海文：这就是所谓的"寸金寸土"，形容房子非常贵，这种现象在大城市很普遍的。特别是"北上广深"。

宋杰：什么是"北上广深"？

海文：是北京、上海、广州和深圳四个一线城市的简称。就以北京为例吧，五环以内一平米六万元人民币不足为奇，也就是说一个100平米的小公寓差不多是百万美元了。

李静：那么贵，谁买得起呀？

海文：正因为一线城市房价太高，所以很多年轻人想到二线城市去发展。前一阵子有一个脱口秀节目在讨论"大城床还是小城房"。

李静：我因为是暂时来中国实习，所以房价对我没有太大的影响。可是我想如果我是一个中国大学毕业的年轻人，我还是喜欢大城市。虽然房价高，可是工作机会多，发展的空间大。这对年轻人还是很有吸引力的。年轻时就应该努力去拼搏一番。

宋杰：大城市的挑战也很大，虽然大城市有更广阔的视野、更开放的平台、更丰富的资源，可是竞争激烈，生活节奏特别快。我倒是喜欢去小城市，那里比较安稳，日子过得舒心点儿。

海文：这些选择让年轻人觉得很纠结，反正是不同的人有不同选择，可谓"见仁见智"。

平米	m.w.	píngmǐ	square meter
美元	n.	měiyuán	U.S. dollar
简直	adv.	jiǎnzhí	simply, at all
所谓	v.	suǒwèi	what is called
寸金寸土	phr.	cùn jīn cùn tǔ	worth a lot of money
现象	n.	xiànxiàng	phenomenon
普遍	adj.	pǔbiàn	common
广州	p.n.	Guǎngzhōu	Guangzhou (a city in Guangdong Province, China)
深圳	p.n.	Shēnzhèn	Shenzhen (a city in Guangdong Province)
一线	adj.	yī xiàn	first-tier
简称	n.	jiǎnchēng	the abbreviated form of a name
五环	p.n.	Wǔhuán	5th Ring Road (a major expressway in Beijing)
人民币	n.	rénmínbì	Chinese yuan
不足为奇	phr.	bù zú wéi qí	be nothing strange
一阵子	n.	yízhènzi	a period of time
脱口秀节目	phr.	tuōkǒuxiù jiémù	talk show
实习	v.	shíxí	work as an intern
拼搏	v.	pīnbó	go all out in work
番	m.w.	fān	(measure word) turn
广阔	adj.	guǎngkuò	broad
视野	n.	shìyě	vision, horizon
安稳	adj.	ānwěn	stable
舒心	adj.	shūxīn	relaxed
纠结	v.	jiūjié	be tangled, torn between
反正	adv.	fǎnzhèng	all the same, in any case
见仁见智	phr.	jiànrén jiànzhì	a matter of opinion

语言实践
LANGUAGE CONNECTION

1. **Expressing amazement: 简直……**

   "100多平米的公寓就要200万美元一套，我<u>简直</u>不能相信。"

   简直 is an adverb used to add a tone of amazement on the part of the speaker by modifying adjectives or verbs.

   EXAMPLES:
   1. 她长得和她妈妈年轻的时候<u>简直</u>一模一样。
   2. 她化完妆之后<u>简直</u>变成了另一个人。
   3. 他20年后回到家乡时，<u>简直</u>不敢相信自己的眼睛，家乡的变化太大了。

    Describe your school, the city you live in, and your country, talking about the things that surprise you. Use 简直 in your description.

   EXAMPLES:
   1. 小张宿舍房间里的东西<u>简直</u>太多了，连坐的地方都没有。
   2. 纽约的房价<u>简直</u>太高了。

2. **Summarizing an explanation: 这就是所谓的……**

   "<u>这就是所谓的</u>'寸金寸土'。"

   This pattern means "this is what is called ..." and is used to explain a term. It can also be expressed in this form: 所谓 + term + 就是 + explanation. The explanation may also be an example.

   EXAMPLES:
   1. 在大城市，很多年轻人居住的地方只有一张床，只能在里面睡觉，就像蜗牛一样，<u>这就是所谓的</u>"蜗居"。
   2. 现在，很多年轻人从不存钱，每个月都把自己的收入全部花光，<u>他们就是所谓的</u>"月光族"。

Answer the following questions using 这就是所谓的.

① 什么是"尾号限行"？ ② 什么是"见仁见智"？ ③ 什么是"丝绸之路"？

3. **Disregarding earlier considerations: 反正……**

"这些选择让年轻人觉得很纠结，反正是不同的人有不同选择，可谓'见仁见智'。"

反正, meaning "anyway" in English, is used to disregard a previous statement, particularly those involving options or choices.

EXAMPLES:
① 不管你有什么事情，反正你今天要完成这些工作。
② 爸爸妈妈想让我学经济，但是他们怎么想不重要，反正我已经决定学历史了。

Respond to the following scenarios using 不管……，反正…….

① 虽然你知道住在小城市有很多问题，但是你还是喜欢住在小城市。
提示：大城市有更多的工作机会；大城市的学校比较好
② 虽然你知道住在大城市有很多问题，但是你还是喜欢住在大城市。
提示：小城市空气清新；房子比较便宜

 Answer the following question using 简直, 这就是所谓的……, 以……为例, and 反正.

你会选择在大城市生活还是小城市生活？

EXAMPLE:
我想在小城市生活。因为大城市的租金简直太贵了。以北京为例，因为房租太高，很多年轻人会租一个非常小的房间，只可以放得下一张床，这就是所谓的"蜗居"。所以不管大城市的经济有多发达，工作机会再多，反正我会选择在小城市生活。

PART 3 第三部分 北漂一族的辛酸与梦想
HARDSHIPS AND DREAMS OF BEIJING DRIFTERS

海文：跟你们介绍一下，这是我公司的同事林峰。

宋杰：林大哥，您好。

林峰：宋杰，你好。

海文：我趁着五一长假的时候回老家合肥跟家人聚聚，看到了在深圳工作10多年的表哥，他说没办法承受不断"涨涨涨"的房价，终于离开了深圳，在我们老家三线城市的热门地段买了一套商品房。

林峰：最近我听到不少人逃离"北上广深"。在北京生活的确不容易。每年一到了毕业求职的季节，就看见毕业生为选择工作的城市而烦恼。

海文：在我身边有不少朋友，他们自称为"北漂一族"。

合肥	p.n.	Héféi	Hefei (capital city of Anhui Province)
涨	v.	zhǎng	rise
热门地段	phr.	rèmén dìduàn	popular sites
商品房	n.	shāngpǐn fáng	commercial housing
逃离	v.	táolí	get away from
求职	v.o.	qiúzhí	apply for a job
烦恼	adj.	fánnǎo	worried, vexed
北漂一族	phr.	běi piāo yì zú	(a term describing people working in Beijing who are not registered residents there)

宋杰：什么是"北漂一族"？

海文：就是在北京工作，可是还没有"扎根"、拿到北京户口人。

| 扎根 | v. | zhāgēn | take root, settle down in a place |
| 户口 | n. | hùkǒu | registered residence |

林峰：我哥哥为了存钱买房子，现在跟两个北漂合租了公寓。今天是周末，咱们要不要下午去他公寓看一看，了解一下北漂一族的生活？

宋杰：好极了，百闻不如一见，我很希望跟北漂一族聊聊。

| 百闻不如一见 | phr. | bǎi wén bù rú yí jiàn | seeing is believing |

（林峰带海文和宋杰到他哥哥林浩的公寓。）

林峰：我来介绍，这是林浩，我的哥哥。这是他的两个室友：王伟和张晓丽。

（大家打招呼。）

林浩：你们随便参观！这是一套三室一厅一卫的房子。

海文：挺宽敞明亮的，主厅不但大而且采光好。

| 宽敞 | adj. | kuānchang | spacious |
| 采光 | n. | cǎiguāng | natural lighting (for an indoor space) |

宋杰：你们这个公寓让我想起了美剧《老友记》，剧里的一群年轻男女也是住在一起。我想知道你们是怎么样决定留在北京的呢？

王伟：我是东北人，现在在三环一家公司担任市场推广。

晓丽：我来自昆明，在电脑公司编写代码。在北京留下不是一个容易的决定，我有过彷徨，有过失落，也有过困惑，可是每次都在失望的边缘重新找到希望。

王伟：我来北京的第一年最难过，堵车、雾霾和不断上涨的物价都是让人头疼的事。跟晓丽一样，常有失落的感觉，我也曾多次想离开北京，可是每次在地铁站等车看到其他在北京奋斗的年轻人，他们眼神中的期待和憧憬，给了我勇气继续坚持下去。

宋杰：我觉得你们的情况跟我姐的很相似。她大学毕业以后有两个工作机会。一个在美国中部的小城市，一个在三藩市。她一再考虑，最后决定去三藩市。因为三藩市的租金特别贵，她现在跟两个在网上认识的朋友合租一个公寓。他们一个在优步工作，一个在谷歌工作，除了周末下午偶尔会看见他们，其他时间他们都在加班，很难才见上一面。看来美国硅谷的生活步调跟北京一样紧张。

林浩：是的，无论在美国还是在中国，年轻人在大城市拼搏都不容易。

担任	v.	dānrèn	hold a post
市场推广	n.	shìchǎng tuīguǎng	marketing
昆明	p.n.	Kūnmíng	Kunming (capital city of Yunnan Province)
编写	v.	biānxiě	write
代码	n.	dàimǎ	code
彷徨	adj.	pánghuáng	hesitant, not knowing where to go in life
失落	adj.	shīluò	lost
困惑	adj.	kùnhuò	bewildered
边缘	n.	biānyuán	verge, brink, edge
奋斗	v.	fèndòu	strive
眼神	n.	yǎnshén	the expression in one's eyes
期待	n.	qīdài	expectation
憧憬	n.	chōngjǐng	yearning
勇气	n.	yǒngqì	courage
相似	adj.	xiāngsì	similar
租金	n.	zūjīn	rental
谷歌	p.n.	Gǔgē	Google
加班	v.	jiābān	work overtime
硅谷	p.n.	Guīgǔ	Silicon Valley

语言实践
LANGUAGE CONNECTION

1. Describing cause and effect or purpose and action: 为……而……

Structure: subject + 为 + cause/purpose + 而 + effect/action (烦恼/努力/忧伤/伤心)

"毕业生为选择工作的城市而烦恼。"

因/为……而…… is a structure that expresses cause and effect or purpose and action. The cause/purpose appears after 因/为 and the effect/action appears after 而.

EXAMPLES:

1. 很多年轻人都为了买房而努力，但是也因为高房价而烦恼。
2. 我的姐姐今年没有申请上理想的实习，她正因此而伤心难过呢。
3. 我们队去年拿了全国联赛的冠军，现在正在为今年再得冠军而努力。

In a pair, complete the following activities.

1. "为中华之崛起而读书！" This statement was spoken by Zhou Enlai, the first Premier of the People's Republic of China, in his youth. Research the story online and share it in class.
2. Interpret the meaning of 崛起 based on the story and your knowledge of Chinese history.
3. The youth of China aspired to fight for the rise of China 100 years ago. What do you think the youth of America should strive for today?

2. **Describing the layout of a house:** ……室……厅……卫

> Structure: numeral + 室 + numeral + 厅 + numeral + 卫

"这是一套<u>三室一厅一卫</u>的房子。"

This structure can be used to describe the layout of a house or an apartment. In English we can describe a home as having "three bedrooms, two bathrooms." Similarly, in Chinese, we can describe a home with 室 (bedroom), 厅 (living room or dining room), and 卫 (bathroom). A numeral is placed before each room type to indicate the number. Typically, 一室一厅一卫 (one bedroom, one living room, one bathroom) describes an apartment for one person; 两室一厅一卫 (two bedrooms, one living room, one bathroom) describes an apartment for a small family under China's one-child policy; 三室两厅两卫 (three bedrooms, one living room and one dining room, two bathrooms) describes an apartment for a bigger family.

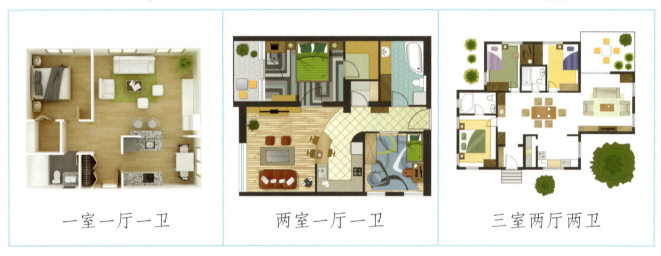

一室一厅一卫　　　　两室一厅一卫　　　　三室两厅两卫

In a pair, complete the following activities.

❶ Search on 58.com for houses using 一室一厅一卫, 两室一厅一卫, and 三室两厅两卫. Record their locations and prices in the table below.

房型	位置	价格
一室一厅一卫		
两室一厅一卫		
三室两厅两卫		

❷ Discuss with your classmates how much you should be earning every month, working in Beijing, in order to afford the rental for the house you wish to live in, based on those you have found above.

文化剪影
CULTURE ENRICHMENT

计划生育标语口号和家庭结构的变迁
Family Planning Slogans and Shifts in the Structure of the Family

1. 计划生育海报和标语口号

中国人喜欢用简单的词语来表情达意。在推行一胎化政策时,为了让老百姓了解推行这项政策的原因,政府使用了许多标语口号。它们容易读,容易记。上世纪80年代在城市和农村都可以看见。

海报标语一:
利国利民利家,优生优育优教

海报标语三:
少生优生,振兴中华

海报标语二:
搞好计划生育,促进经济发展

2. 家庭结构的变迁

自从实行了一胎化政策，中国人的家庭结构发生了很大的变化。现在，大多数的中国家庭都只有一个孩子，这样的情况其实为中国社会带来了一些问题，比如一个孩子在成年后，除了必须照顾自己的父母，还得照顾四名祖父母，这对他们来说是非常沉重的负担。

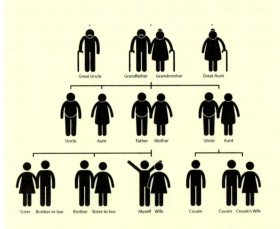

图一：
传统的家庭结构

图二：
一胎化以后的家庭结构

图三：
一胎化以后的家庭结构

Interpretive/Interpersonal

1. In a pair, search online for other posters or slogans related to the implementation of the one-child policy. You may use "一胎化海报和标语" as the key words. Choose one poster or slogan and discuss how it reflects the aims of the policy.

2. In groups, discuss and research online to answer the following questions.

   1) 以上每一张图代表什么？
   2) 第二和第三张图显示的都是独生子女家庭，它们有什么不同？
   3) 在第二和第三张图片里都有四个老年人。社会上老年人多会带来什么影响？
   4) 在美国，什么时代是"婴儿潮"(yīng'ércháo baby boomers)？为什么？
   5) 在你知道的名人中有在"婴儿潮"年代出生的吗？请说出两位名人的名字。
   6) 你的祖父母或者你认识的人有在"婴儿潮"年代出生的吗？他们还在工作吗？他们的生活怎么样？

词汇拓展
VOCABULARY BUILDING

1. **Words Containing 族**

   In this unit, we have learned about the term 北漂一族. The character 族, the rough equivalent in English being "tribe," originally refers to an ethnic group. There are 56 ethnic groups in China: the Han people make up 94% of the total population of China, while the other 55 groups are ethnic minorities. On the Internet, many people use "……族" to refer to a specific group of people.

   Can you guess the meaning of each term below?

   1) 上班族

   2) 单身贵族
      (Hint: What do 单身 and 贵族 mean as individual words? What do they refer to when combined?)

   3) 月光族

   4) 啃老族

   5) 丁克族

If you could form a 族 with a group of friends, what would this new 族 be?

Write the name of your 族 on the whiteboard. In your group, write down six sentences to describe it. Share these sentences with your classmates for them to guess the type of 族 you have created.

Hints:
1. Which modes of transportation do you take to go to school?
2. Do you support recycling?
3. Do you stay up late at night?

2. **Words Containing 党**

The character 党 is usually used to refer to political parties. For example, 民主党 (Mínzhǔdǎng, Democrats), 共和党 (Gònghédǎng, Republicans), and 共产党 (Gòngchǎndǎng, Communists). 党 is also used to refer to a group of people who share the same characteristic.

In a group, answer the following questions.

1) 常常熬夜的是什么"党"?
2) 常常加班的是什么"党"?
3) 要准备考SAT的是什么"党"?
4) 学生属于什么"党"?
5) 你一个星期去三次健身房,你属于什么"党"?
6) 如果你爸爸妈妈常常出差,他们属于什么"党"?
7) 你在"饿了么"*工作,请你写一段广告 (guǎnggào advertisement) 给"加班党",告诉他们晚上八点以后推出便宜的外卖服务。

*"饿了么"是一个像 Uber Eats 一样的外卖订餐平台。

3. **Differentiating Between Similar Words**

严峻 and 严重

	Used with	Examples
严峻	表情 形势 考验	1. 他知道父亲去世的消息以后表情严峻,说不出一句话来。 2. 目前就业的形势很严峻,大学生毕业以后不容易找到理想的工作。 3. 全球变暖对我们来说是一个严峻的考验。
严重	问题	这个问题很严重,我们得马上解决。

沉重 and 繁重

	Used with	Examples
沉重	心情 代价 负担	1. 他没有考进大学,心情非常沉重。 2. 如果我们只重视经济的加速发展,而不关心环境保护的话,以后会付出很沉重的代价。 3. "一胎化政策"实施以后,一个孩子长大得照顾父母和四名祖父母,这可是很沉重的负担。
繁重	作业 工作	1. 高中二年级的学生为了准备高考,作业非常繁重。 2. 他的工作很繁重,经常要加班和出差。

阅读理解
READING COMPREHENSION

Read the passage and answer the questions that follow.

独生子女的困扰
What an Only Child Is Troubled by

刘文是一个在加州上高中的北京女孩。在加州的学校里她很快认识了一些朋友，包括同年级的海伦。刘文常常听海伦抱怨她的姐姐，比如说抢她的衣服、嘲笑❶她的发型❷等。刘文也能感受到在美国的家庭里，孩子们为了争夺❸"谁是爸爸妈妈最喜欢的孩子"会有很多矛盾。开始刘文很开心，因为她是独生子女，没有<u>那种压力</u>。但是刘文也渐渐发现有兄弟姐妹其实并不坏：哥哥姐姐会在你需要帮助的时候给你建议；弟弟妹妹能让你更快长大、更早成熟；过生日、过节的时候，一个大家庭能给你更多的礼物和温暖。每年的4月10号是美国的国家兄弟姐妹日（National Siblings Day），刘文看到社交媒体上都是同学们和他们的兄弟姐妹的照片，下面还加上了几句温暖的话。看到这些，刘文真的开始羡慕美式大家庭的生活了！

❶ 嘲笑 cháoxiào　laugh at, mock　　❷ 发型 fàxíng　hairstyle, hairdo　　❸ 争夺 zhēngduó　fight, contend

1. 在刘文看来，有兄弟姐妹的家庭有哪些问题？
2. "那种压力"指的是什么压力？
3. 为什么刘文开始羡慕有兄弟姐妹的家庭？
4. 其实中国也有"中式大家庭"，那就是爸爸妈妈、爷爷奶奶和孩子们住在一起，你觉得这样的家庭好不好？这样的家庭会有什么问题？
5. 你的兄弟姐妹或者好朋友有没有让你羡慕的地方？请分享一下。

写作工坊
WRITING WORKSHOP

准备辩论稿 Preparing the Script for a Debate

Since the implementation of the one-child policy in China in the 1980s, families with only one child have become the norm. Children in China who have no siblings are often showered with a great amount of love and grow up to be confident people. This is the edge they have. Being an only child, however, also means that their parents may have greater expectations of them, which may affect them adversely. So does an only child have an edge over another who is not? Have a debate on this.

1. **Taking a side**

    Divide yourselves into two groups. The proposition team (正方, affirmative) will take this stand: 独生子女占有优势 He who is an only child has an edge over he who is not. The opposition team (反方, negative) will argue against this.

2. **Preparing your script**

    You should first look at what a child needs in his growing-up years. Then decide which child has an edge, the only child or one with a sibling or siblings, in each aspect. Use the table below to help you.

	独生子女	有兄弟姐妹的家庭
父母的关爱		
家庭经济		
自信		
独立		
懂得与人相处		
教育		

    In your group, discuss and prepare a speech for the main debater (主辩). The speech should be between 300 and 350 words, and last three minutes.

3. **The sequence of debate**

   Your debate will take the sequence below.

   ❶ 发言（立论）：每人3分钟
   由正方主辩先发言，再由反方主辩发言。

   ❷ 攻辩一：提问10秒，回答20秒
   首先，由正方二辩向反方二辩提问，反方二辩回答提问。接着，由反方二辩向正方二辩提问，正方二辩回答提问。

   ❸ 攻辩二：提问10秒，回答20秒
   首先，由正方三辩向反方三辩提问，反方三辩回答提问。接着，由反方三辩向正方三辩提问，正方三辩回答提问。

   ❹ 总结：每人2分钟
   先由反方主辩作结论，再由正方主辩作结论。

学习总结
I CAN DO!

Interpretive Communication

- [ ] I can read about the evolution of family planning policies in China from the one-child policy, which was implemented in the late 1970s amidst conflicts with traditional Chinese values, to the current two-child policy.
- [ ] I can understand when people talk about the extremely high prices of housing in big metropolitan cities in China.
- [ ] I can read and understand basic information on the life and work of "Beipiao" youths and what made them decide to stay in Beijing.
- [ ] I can conduct online search in Chinese and identify some interesting information on the changes in the slogans used in China's family planning policies over different periods.

Interpersonal Communication

- [ ] I can discuss the pros and cons of China's one-child policy and two-child policy.
- [ ] I can converse about the high prices for housing in big cities in China and the dilemma between "a bed in a big city and a house in a small city."
- [ ] I can talk about the life and work of some "Beitpiao" youths.
- [ ] I can talk about and explain the positive impact of China's one-child policy and some problems it has led to.

Presentational Communication

- [ ] I can describe the basic evolution of family planning policies in China over the past few decades.
- [ ] I can make a brief presentation on the housing situations in China's first-tier, second-tier and third-tier cities.
- [ ] I can present briefly on who "Beipiao" youths are and their hopes and struggles.
- [ ] I can compare the life and work of "Beipiao" youths with that of American youths who are working very hard to make it in the Silicon Valley in San Francisco.

Cultural Knowledge

- [ ] I can talk about the traditional Chinese value of "the more descendants one has, the more happiness one gets" and the impact of China's one-child policy.
- [ ] I can describe who "Beipiao" youths are.
- [ ] I can name some third-tier cities in China and talk about basic housing market situations in different types of cities in China.
- [ ] I can use several common Chinese four-character set phrases appropriately in communicative situations.

留学生与中西文化交流
INTERCULTURAL EXCHANGES BETWEEN CHINA AND THE WEST

学习目标
LEARNING OBJECTIVES

- Read about famous Chinese who studied abroad
- Appreciate the contributions of the Chinese
- Talk about historical events and persons
- Explain how to adapt to a new environment

单元总览
CONTENTS AT A GLANCE!

导入 WARM UP

- **Part 1: 清末留美幼童** (Studying Abroad in the Late Qing Dynasty)
  Language Connection:
  1. 他们到耶鲁参观的时候，接待的同学正好是中国人。
  2. 也有在外交和在教育界发展的，比如：中华民国的第一任总理唐绍仪和担任清华大学第一任校长的唐国安。
  3. 他们的后人有很多珍贵的照片和回忆，能加深我们对早期留美学生的认识。

- **Part 2: 留学生对中国现代化的影响** (Returned Students and China's Path to Modernization)
  Language Connection:
  1. 他促进了中国人尤其是年轻知识分子对外国先进科技思想的认识。
  2. 那是因为庚子赔款选拔了很多优秀的学生来美国学习，其中就有胡适。
  3. 可以说没有留学生，就没有今天的现代化的中国。

- **Part 3: 华人的贡献** (Contributions of the Chinese to the World)
  Language Connection:
  1. 他也是《时代周刊》选出的20世纪最具影响力的百位名人之一。
  2. 至于贝聿铭，我好像在哪里听过他的名字。
  3. 贝聿铭18岁以前在中国受教育，后来在美国上大学，所以他能结合东西方艺术，形成他个人的独特风格。
  4. 差不多有400多万华裔，大约占美国人口的百分之一。

文化剪影：留学美国的中国幼童
CULTURE ENRICHMENT: Young Chinese Studying in the United States in the Late Qing Dynasty

词汇拓展：外来词语；探索词语的由来
VOCABULARY BUILDING: Loanwords; Exploring the Origin of Words

阅读理解：著名美籍华裔：谭恩美
READING COMPREHENSION: Famous Chinese American: Amy Tan

写作工坊：写一篇博客短文——怎样适应新环境
WRITING WORKSHOP: Writing a Blog Entry – Adapting to a New Environment

学习总结　I CAN DO!

导入
WARM UP

Imagine that your friends and you have completed an immersion and community service program overseas. Some of you have also traveled overseas for leisure. You are preparing a basic travel guide for your schoolmates who have not traveled to the cities below. Your guide will help them understand the culture and customs of the countries these cities are in, and adapt to life there more easily.

Work in small groups to collect information and fill in the blanks below.

城市：曼谷（泰国）

主要语言	：	泰文
主要宗教	：	_____
气候	：	全年都很热，温度在摄氏_____度和35度之间
特色美食	：	_____
主要习俗	：	进屋要脱鞋；不要随便摸别人的_____

城市：伊斯坦布尔（土耳其）

主要语言	：	_____
主要宗教	：	伊斯兰教
气候	：	夏季时间长，气温_____
特色美食	：	融合了_____的美食
主要习俗	：	不能带_____进入

城市：卡萨布兰卡（摩洛哥）

主要语言	:	_____、法语
主要宗教	:	_____
气候	:	气候_____
特色美食	:	羊肉炖土豆、橄榄炖鸡
主要习俗	:	不能带猪肉进入，不能_____

城市：马德里（西班牙）

主要语言	:	西班牙语
主要宗教	:	_____
气候	:	气候比较温和
特色美食	:	西班牙_____、火腿
主要习俗	:	_____以后休息；晚饭在十点左右，比较_____

城市：圣保罗（巴西）

主要语言	:	葡萄牙语
主要宗教	:	_____
气候	:	_____、多雨
特色美食	:	以肉多、菜_____出名
主要习俗	:	每个人都喜欢_____；与熟人和亲人见面一般会互相拥抱

第一部分 清末留美幼童
PART 1 STUDYING ABROAD IN THE LATE QING DYNASTY

李静和宋杰两人一边喝咖啡，一边聊天。

李静：上个月我寄宿家庭的姐姐去美国波士顿参加了一个夏令营。周末的时候，老师带他们去康州的耶鲁大学参观，也去了麻州的春田市。她回来后很兴奋地告诉我，原来早在19世纪，也就是清朝的时候，已经有中国人到美国去留学了。

宋杰：我也听说第一个留学美国的学生是容闳。他是1850年进入耶鲁大学，1854年毕业的。

李静：我姐姐说，他们到耶鲁参观的时候，接待的同学正好是中国人，于是就为他们介绍这一段历史。他说容闳是广东人，从小在教会学校读书，所以英语有一定的基础。他在耶鲁参加过很多社团活动，还在英语比赛中两次获奖。

宋杰：中国人获得这种奖项，真是不可思议！

李静：是呀！而且我还真没有想到，中国人在美国留学有那么悠久的历史。

波士顿	p.n.	Bōshìdùn	Boston
康州	p.n.	Kāng Zhōu	Connecticut
耶鲁大学	p.n.	Yēlǔ Dàxué	Yale University
麻州	p.n.	Má Zhōu	Massachusetts
春田市	p.n.	Chūntián Shì	Springfield (a city in Massachusetts)
清朝	p.n.	Qīng Cháo	Qing Dynasty (1644-1912)
留学	v.	liúxué	study abroad
容闳	p.n.	Róng Hóng	Yung Wing (1828-1912) (the first Chinese to graduate from an American college)
接待	v.	jiēdài	receive (visitors, guests, etc.)
正好	adv.	zhènghǎo	happen to
广东人	n.	Guǎngdōng rén	Cantonese
教会学校	phr.	jiàohuì xuéxiào	mission school
社团	n.	shètuán	club, association
奖项	n.	jiǎngxiàng	award
不可思议	adj.	bù kě sī yì	unimaginable, inconceivable
悠久	adj.	yōujiǔ	long, age-old

宋杰：我学中国历史的时候，知道鸦片战争以后，中西文化开始有更频繁的接触。中国人迫切希望国家强大，不受外国人的欺负，所以有了学习西方科技的洋务运动。

李静：容闳后来得到清朝政府的支持，把120个幼童带到美国学习。这些幼童不但克服了语言的障碍，而且很快就适应了美国的生活，在学校取得了优异的成绩。他们回国后为中国的现代化作出了很大的贡献。

宋杰：我念书的高中就在耶鲁附近，我知道耶鲁跟中国有着很深厚的情谊。除了容闳以外，幼童中有二三十人都是耶鲁毕业的，

其中的一位是詹天佑。他修筑了第一条中国自主设计并建造的铁路。

李静：除了修筑铁路以外，还有不少回国的幼童成为了电报、矿冶、机械制造、水师等新的产业的领军人物。也有在外交和在教育界发展的，比如：中华民国的第一任总理唐绍仪和担任清华大学第一任校长的唐国安。

宋杰：中央电视台有一套纪录片《留美幼童》，里面访问了几个当年在春田市接待中国学生的家庭，他们的后人有很多珍贵的照片和回忆，能加深我们对早期留美学生的认识。

李静：谢谢你的介绍，我以后有机会一定会看这部纪录片。

词语	词性	拼音	英文
鸦片战争	p.n.	Yāpiàn Zhànzhēng	Opium Wars (1840-1842; 1856-1860)
欺负	v.	qīfu	bully
洋务运动	p.n.	Yángwù Yùndòng	Self-Strengthening Movement (1861-1895) (a drive to learn Western concepts of modernization)
幼童	n.	yòutóng	young child
克服	v.	kèfú	overcome
障碍	n.	zhàng'ài	obstacle, barrier
适应	v.	shìyìng	adapt to
优异	adj.	yōuyì	excellent, outstanding
深厚	adj.	shēnhòu	deep, solid
情谊	n.	qíngyì	friendship
詹天佑	p.n.	Zhān Tiānyòu	Jeme Tien Yow (1861-1919) (a pioneering Chinese railroad engineer)
修筑	v.	xiūzhù	build, construct
自主	v.	zìzhǔ	act on one's own
铁路	n.	tiělù	railway
电报	n.	diànbào	telegram
矿冶	n.	kuàngyě	mining and metallurgy
机械制造	phr.	jīxiè zhìzào	manufacture of machinery
水师	n.	shuǐshī	navy (a term used in ancient times)
产业	n.	chǎnyè	industry
领军	adv.	lǐngjūn	leading
中华民国	p.n.	Zhōnghuá Mínguó	the Republic of China
总理	n.	zǒnglǐ	premier
唐绍仪	p.n.	Táng Shàoyí	Tang Shaoyi (1862-1938) (the first premier of the Republic of China who took office in 1912)
清华大学	p.n.	Qīnghuá Dàxué	Tsinghua University
唐国安	p.n.	Táng Guó'ān	Tong Kwo On (1858-1913) (the founding president of Tsinghua University)
中央电视台	p.n.	Zhōngyāng Diànshìtái	China Central Television
访问	v.	fǎngwèn	interview
后人	n.	hòurén	later generations
回忆	n.	huíyì	memory
加深	v.	jiāshēn	deepen

语言实践
LANGUAGE CONNECTION

1. Expressing coincidence: ……正好……

Structure: subject + 正好 + predicate

"他们到耶鲁参观的时候，接待的同学正好是中国人。"

正好 can be used as an adverb to express a coincidence. It means "happen to be."

EXAMPLES:

1. 今年的情人节正好是春节，因此很多西餐厅的生意都没有往常情人节那么好。
2. 我正好要出门，垃圾我来倒吧。
3. 我到达车站的时候，客车正好来了。

Answer the following questions using 正好.

1. 明天你能送我去机场吗？
（建议答案：周六，要去机场接朋友，放假……）
2. 这个暑假你要去中国学中文，有哪些事情是你一直想去中国做的呢？
例如：这个暑假我要去中国学中文，正好去看看我的中国朋友。

In a pair, role-play as two persons studying at the same boarding school in China or the United States. Practice using 正好 to invite each other to visit your hometown for Thanksgiving or the Spring Festival.

EXAMPLES:

1. 我家住在成都，你跟我坐高铁回去正好可以亲眼看看中国人怎么过春节。
2. 我爸妈住在纽约，你跟我回去正好可以感受一下美国人怎么过感恩节。

2. Giving examples: 比如……

"也有在外交和在教育界发展的，比如：中华民国的第一任总理唐绍仪和担任清华大学第一任校长的唐国安。"

比如 means "for example," "for instance" or "such as." It can be used interchangeably with 例如 or 比如说.

EXAMPLES:
1. 一年来，同学们做了许多好事，比如有的同学积极参加植树活动，有的同学去老人中心打扫卫生，还有的同学为灾区的孩子捐赠自己的玩具和学习用品。
2. 锻炼身体有很多方法，比如散步、跑步、游泳、打太极拳等。
3. 很多有名的大人物出身贫困家庭，比如林肯、爱迪生。

Complete the following sentences below.

1. 我的兴趣很广泛，比如……。
2. 当我心情不好的时候，我会试着调整自己的心情，比如……。
3. 中国是一个历史悠久的国家，有很多名胜古迹，比如……。
4. 中国年轻人的爱好跟美国年轻人在很多方面都很相似，比如……。
5. 自从有了丝绸之路以后，很多中国的先进技术都通过丝绸之路传到了欧洲各地，比如……。

3. Deepening one's understanding of something: 加深……对……的认识/了解

Structure: 加深 + noun + 对 + noun phrase + 认识/了解

"他们的后人有很多珍贵的照片和回忆，能加深我们对早期留美学生的认识。"

This structure is usually used in a positive situation. A noun is usually placed after 加深 to indicate for whom the action is meant.

EXAMPLES:

1. 了解文学作品的作者与写作背景，能够加深我们对这些作品的认识。
2. 国家与国家之间只有互相尊重彼此的文化，才能够加深对彼此的了解。
3. 选修环保科学加深了我对全球变暖的认识。

 Discuss the following questions.

1. 做哪些事情可以加深你们对当代中国的认识？
2. 做什么事情可以加深对朋友的了解？
3. 父母应该做什么样的事情才能加深对孩子的了解？

China Highlights: North China

Beijing: CCTV HQ

Tianjin: Urban skyline

Hebei: The Imperial Summer Resort, Chengde

Shanxi: The ancient town of Ping Yao

Inner Mongolia: Yurts on the grassland

PART 2 留学生对中国现代化的影响
RETURNED STUDENTS AND CHINA'S PATH TO MODERNIZATION

李静、宋杰与历史系的王教授正在讨论留学生对中国现代化的影响。

李静： 我的朋友告诉我现在到美国留学的中国学生越来越多了。

王教授： 其实早在19世纪中国人就开始在美国留学了。自鸦片战争以后，中国的知识分子就了解到，如果要国家富强，必须向西方学习。

宋杰： 这就是您在历史课上谈到的"洋务运动"吗？

王教授： 是的，洋务运动又称为"自强运动"，希望通过学习西方先进的科技和军事设备来救国。可是中国在1895年的甲午战争中被日本打败，于是一部分知识分子觉得日本之所以强大主要是明治维新，所以不单在军事上要改良，在政治上也需要改革。

知识分子	n.	zhīshi fènzǐ	intellectuals
富强	adj.	fùqiáng	prosperous and strong
设备	n.	shèbèi	equipment
甲午战争	p.n.	Jiǎwǔ Zhànzhēng	First Sino-Japanese War (1894-1895) (launched by Japanese imperialism to annex Korea and invade China)
打败	v.	dǎbài	defeat
于是	conj.	yúshì	hence
明治维新	p.n.	Míngzhì Wéixīn	Meiji Reformation
改良	v.	gǎiliáng	improve

李静： 这个政治上的改革是不是"辛亥革命"？最后推翻了2000多年的君主制度。

王教授： 你说得对！孙中山就是跟当时在日本留学的学生成立"同盟会"，最后才革命成功，建立中华民国。

宋杰： 所以中国近代很多的变革都跟留学生有关系。除了留学日本以外，还有去别的国家留学的吗？

王教授： 有留学英国、美国和欧洲各国的。留学英国最有名的是严复。他把重要的西方著作翻译成中文，其中包括亚当·斯密的《原富》和赫胥黎的《天演论》，把权威经济理论和进化论介绍给中国人，促进了中国人尤其是年轻知识分子对外国先进科技思想的认识。

李静： 那留学美国的人是不是更多？

王教授： 是的，那是因为庚子赔款选拔了很多优秀的学生来美国学习，其中就有胡适。他认为民国虽然已经成立了，可是国民的思想还是很封建保守的，

辛亥革命	p.n.	Xīnhài Gémìng	the Revolution of 1911 (the Chinese bourgeois democratic revolution led by Dr. Sun Yat-sen which overthrew the Qing Dynasty)
推翻	v.	tuīfān	overthrow
君主制度	n.	jūnzhǔ zhìdù	monarchy
孙中山	p.n.	Sūn Zhōngshān	Sun Yat-sen (1866-1925) (the first president and founding father of the Republic of China)
同盟会	p.n.	Tóngménghuì	Tung Meng Hui, Chinese Revolutionary League (founded in 1905)
严复	p.n.	Yán Fù	Yan Fu (1854-1921) (Chinese scholar and translator, President of Fudan University)
著作	n.	zhùzuò	book
亚当·斯密	p.n.	Yàdāng Sīmì	Adam Smith (1723-1790) (Scottish economist, philosopher and author)
原富	p.n.	Yuán Fù	The Wealth of Nations (Chinese translated work of Yan Fu, originally written by Adam Smith)
赫胥黎	p.n.	Hè Xūlí	Thomas Henry Huxley (1825-1895) (English biologist)
天演论	p.n.	Tiānyǎn lùn	Evolution and Ethics (Chinese translated work of Yan Fu, originally written by Thomas Henry Huxley)
权威	adj.	quánwēi	authoritative
理论	n.	lǐlùn	theory
进化论	n.	jìnhuàlùn	theory of evolution
庚子赔款	p.n.	Gēngzǐ Péikuǎn	Boxer Rebellion Indemnity (1900)
优秀	adj.	yōuxiù	outstanding, excellent
胡适	p.n.	Hú Shì	Hu Shi (1891-1962) (a scholar widely credited with language reform by advocating the use of written vernacular Chinese)
成立	v.	chénglì	establish
封建	adj.	fēngjiàn	feudalistic

所以他回国以后推动了白话文运动，用白话文来取代文言文，这样用浅易的语言来表达思想，一般老百姓都看得懂，知识更容易普及。

宋杰：这就是我们历史课本上提到的"五四运动"了。还有"新文化运动"，对吗？

王教授：新文化运动主要把"赛先生"(science)和"德先生"(democracy)介绍给中国人，"科学"与"民主"在那个时代是一个新的理念。

李静：那么欧洲的留学生呢？

王教授：很多中国的领导人都在欧洲留过学，比方说周恩来和邓小平都在法国留过学。

宋杰：原来留学潮从清代末年就开始，一直到民国。可以说没有留学生，就没有今天的现代化的中国。

王教授：留学生在中国现代化的道路上起了划时代的作用。不同的文化交流最后都能促进人类的文明。

李静：很感谢王教授给我们上了一堂精彩的中国历史课。我和宋杰都是留学生，我们得好好想一想，怎么样和美国的同学分享我们在中国留学的经验。

宋杰：我想我们可以做文化大使，让我们在美国的同学多了解中国，这就是我们最好的贡献。

词语	词性	拼音	英文
白话文运动	n.	Báihuà wén Yùndòng	Vernacular Language Movement
取代	v.	qǔdài	replace
文言文	n.	wényánwén	classical Chinese
浅易	adj.	qiǎnyì	simple and easy
语言	n.	yǔyán	language
普及	v.	pǔjí	popularize
五四运动	p.n.	Wǔ-Sì Yùndòng	the May 4th Movement (1919) (an anti-imperialist, anti-feudal, political and cultural movement influenced by the October Revolution and led by intellectuals having the rudiments of Communist ideology)
新文化运动	p.n.	Xīn Wénhuà Yùndòng	the New Culture Movement (around the time of the May 4th Movement in 1919)
民主	n.	mínzhǔ	democracy
理念	n.	lǐniàn	idea
领导人	n.	lǐngdǎorén	leader
周恩来	p.n.	Zhōu Ēnlái	Zhou Enlai (1898-1976) (the first premier of the People's Republic of China who took office in 1949)
邓小平	p.n.	Dèng Xiǎopíng	Deng Xiaoping (1904-1997) (leader of the People's Republic of China who is widely credited with the economic reforms of the 1980s which propelled China to the economic powerhouse it is today)
留学潮	n.	liúxué cháo	(a term used to describe the period beginning in late Qing Qynasty, when many young people went abroad to study)
末年	n.	mònián	last years of a dynasty or reign
划时代	adj.	huàshídài	epoch-making
作用	n.	zuòyòng	effect
人类	n.	rénlèi	mankind
文明	n.	wénmíng	civilization

Did you know?

洋务运动 (Yángwù Yùndòng, Self-Strengthening Movement), 1861–1895, refers to the institutional reforms of the late Qing dynasty following a series of military defeats and concessions to foreign powers.

Also known as the Chinese Revolution, 辛亥革命 (Xīnhài Gémìng, the Revolution of 1911) was a revolution that overthrew China's last imperial dynasty (the Qing dynasty) and established the Republic of China (ROC).

新文化运动 (Xīnwénhuà Yùndòng, the New Culture Movement) started in the mid 1910s and continued till early 1920s. It sprang from the disillusionment with traditional Chinese culture following the failure of the Chinese Republic, founded in 1912, to address China's problems. Scholars like Chen Duxiu (陈独秀), Cai Yuanpei (蔡元培), Li Dazhao (李大钊), Lu Xun (鲁迅), and Hu Shi (胡适) led a revolt against Confucianism and called for the creation of a new Chinese culture based on global and western standards, especially in democracy and science.

语言实践
LANGUAGE CONNECTION

1. Emphasizing someone or something: 尤其……

"他促进了中国人<u>尤其</u>是年轻知识分子对外国先进科技思想的认识。"

尤其 is used to indicate that what is being said before it applies especially to a particular thing or a person, the term for which comes after 尤其. It is an adverb and appears before a predicate that generally contains the verb 是. Equivalent to "especially," it is most commonly placed at the start of the second clause in a compound sentence.

EXAMPLES:

① 我喜欢这个村子,<u>尤其</u>是在春天。
② 这个网上广告很多,<u>尤其</u>是电脑的广告。

In a pair, complete the following table. Next, take turns to make sentences using 尤其 by combining the information provided in both columns.

EXAMPLE: 我的妈妈喜欢吃蔬菜,尤其是黄瓜。

Category	Specific item
蔬菜	黄瓜
	牛肉
中国有名的运动员	
	上海
北京的景点	
	棒球
颜色	
	春天

Take turns to ask and answer questions on personal preferences using 尤其.

EXAMPLE:
Student A: 你暑假喜欢做什么？
Student B: 我喜欢打球，<u>尤其</u>是篮球。

1. 你的家人喜欢吃什么菜？
2. 你明年想选修什么课？
3. 你的朋友喜欢看中国电影还是美国电影？
4. 如果你有机会去中国，你会去哪些城市旅游？
5. 周末的时候你喜欢坐什么交通工具去看电影？

2. Introducing someone or something in a group: 其中……

Structure: (category/group/context) + 其中

"那是因为庚子赔款选拔了很多优秀的学生来美国学习，<u>其中</u>就有胡适。"

In classical Chinese, 其 means 那个, 那, or 那些, and refers to people or things mentioned before it in a sentence. 其中 thus means "among the aforementioned," or 那里面, and denotes that something is part of a bigger group. This is similar to "of which." For example, we may say, 我有三条领带，其中两条是丝绸的. (I have three ties, of which two are silk.)

EXAMPLES:
1. 人类目前面临许多问题，<u>其中</u>最严重的是环境问题。
2. 我用过三个手机，<u>其中</u>两个都是苹果的。
3. 篮球训练虽然有时候很累，但是<u>其中</u>有很多乐趣。

Complete the following sentences.

① 现在我们高中生面临很多压力，其中最沉重的是……。因为…… (reason 1)，以及…… (reason 2)。

② 我们觉得现在美国社会有很多问题，其中最难解决的问题是……。因为…… (reason 1)，以及…… (reason 2)。

3. **Giving credit to someone or something:** 没有……就没有……

   Structure: 没有 A，就没有 B

   "可以说没有留学生，就没有今天的现代化的中国。"

   We make conditional clauses with this structure. A is usually the clause that expresses a condition or reason that results in B. Therefore, without A, there would be no B. A and B are usually nouns or noun phrases.

   EXAMPLES:
   ① 没有我们的教练，就没有我们今年的胜利。
   ② 没有大家的努力，就没有今天的成就。

Write a thank-you note to someone using 没有……，就没有……

EXAMPLE:
妈妈，谢谢你！没有你的照顾，就没有我今天的成绩！

第三部分 华人的贡献
PART 3 CONTRIBUTIONS OF THE CHINESE TO THE WORLD

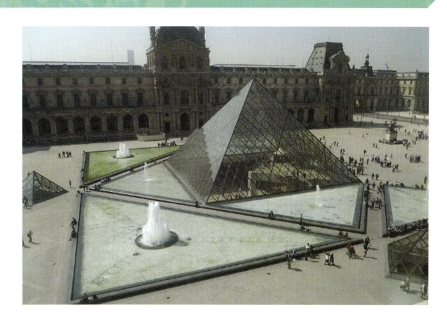

宋杰和李静正在谈论美国有名的华人和重要的华人社区。

宋杰：我发现美国许多城市都有很多中国人居住。

李静：对，像是纽约、洛杉矶、三藩市、芝加哥和波士顿，都有很多华人社区。那里不但有中国城，而且还有中文学校。我家休斯顿附近就有不少中文学校。为了让我有机会学中文，我父母从我一年级开始，就每个周末把我送到中文学校学习。

洛杉矶	p.n.	Luòshānjī	Los Angeles
芝加哥	p.n.	Zhījiāgē	Chicago
中国城	n.	Zhōngguó Chéng	Chinatown

宋杰：难怪你的中文说得那么好。

李静：我是从那时候开始对中文感兴趣的，我父亲又喜欢武术，所以小时候跟他看过不少功夫电影，例如李小龙的《精武门》和《唐山大兄》。虽然我看不太懂

李小龙	p.n.	Lǐ Xiǎolóng	Bruce Lee (1940-1973) (a martial arts actor and martial artist)
精武门	p.n.	Jīngwǔmén	Fist of Fury (Hong Kong martial arts film starring Bruce Lee)
唐山大兄	p.n.	Tángshān Dàxiōng	The Big Boss (Hong Kong martial arts film starring Bruce Lee)

故事的情节，但光是他精彩的武术和优秀的演技，就足以给我留下深刻的印象。

宋杰：一说到"功夫"，我也会马上联想到李小龙。他是1970年代打进好莱坞的中国演员，带领了中国电影走出亚洲，走向世界。那时的功夫电影可以说是风靡一时啊！他也是《时代周刊》选出的20世纪最具影响力的百位名人之一。

李静：除了他以外，还有很多杰出的美籍华人，比方说神探李昌钰和建筑师贝聿铭。

宋杰：我知道李昌钰！他去年来过我们学校演讲，是一个刑事鉴识学的专家，调查过不少重大的案件。他的演讲不但幽默，而且能用轻松简单的语言来解说严肃又复杂的课题，深入浅出。他最后还分享他破案的秘诀，就是尝试从不同的角度去看一个问题。至于贝聿铭，我好像在哪里听过他的名字。

李静：你一定听过！他跟我们学校可是有很密切的关系。

宋杰：我想起来了！我们校园里的艺术中心和科学馆就是他设计的。虽然是70年代的建筑，可是看起来还是那么有现代感。

李静：对啊！他真的是一位出色的建筑师，在世界各地都有他的作品，像是香港的

词	词性	拼音	英文
情节	n.	qíngjié	plot, story
演技	n.	yǎnjì	acting skills
带领	v.	dàilǐng	lead
美籍	n.	Měijí	American
神探	n.	shéntàn	a great detective
李昌钰	p.n.	Lǐ Chāngyù	Henry Chang-Yu Lee (a Chinese American forensic scientist)
贝聿铭	p.n.	Bèi Yùmíng	Ieoh Ming Pei (a Chinese American architect)
刑事鉴识学	phr.	xíngshì jiànshíxué	criminal forensics
调查	v.	diàochá	investigate
案件	n.	ànjiàn	case
解说	v.	jiěshuō	explain
严肃	adj.	yánsù	serious, solemn
深入浅出	phr.	shēnrù qiǎnchū	explain complex matters in simple terms
破案	v.	pò'àn	crack a criminal case
秘诀	n.	mìjué	secret (of success)
尝试	v.	chángshì	try
至于	prep.	zhìyú	as for
现代感	n.	xiàndàigǎn	modern sense
出色	adj.	chūsè	outstanding

中国银行大厦、苏州博物馆和卡塔尔的多哈伊斯兰艺术博物馆。他的代表作是法国卢浮宫前的玻璃金字塔。

宋杰：我记得有一部电影叫《达·芬奇的密码》，最后一幕密码的谜底就藏在这个晶莹剔透的玻璃金字塔下面。

李静：贝聿铭18岁以前在中国受教育，后来在美国上大学，所以他能结合东西方艺术，形成他个人的独特风格。

宋杰：真是了不起啊！我还知道有两位来自中国的科学家，杨振宁和李政道，曾获得1957年诺贝尔物理奖。

李静：美国真的是一个多族群的国家，从外地来这里留学和定居的人可不少呢！谈了那么多优秀的中国人，那华裔究竟占美国人口的多少比例呢？

宋杰：我在网上查了一下。差不多有400多万华裔，大约占美国人口的百分之一。人数虽然不多，可是是一个非常重要的族群啊！

李静：这种开放的精神让我觉得非常骄傲。

语言实践
LANGUAGE CONNECTION

1. **Describing someone or something in a group: 是……之一**

   > Structure: subject + 是 + noun phrase + 之一 or noun phrase + 之一 + 是……

   "他也是《时代周刊》选出的20世纪最具影响力的百位名人之一。"

   之一 is equivalent to "one of the …." It can only follow a noun.

   EXAMPLES:
   1. 纽约是世界国际大都市之一。
   2. 中秋节是中国的重要传统节日之一。
   3. 21世纪最大的特点之一是全球化。
   4. 他有时感到疲劳的原因之一是他常常要加班。

   In a group of five, complete the following activities.
   1. 轮流说说你最喜欢的电影之一。
   2. 轮流说说美国的传统节日之一。
   3. 轮流说说你学中文的原因之一。
   4. 轮流说说有名的美籍华人之一。
   5. 轮流用"之一"说出污染问题越来越严重的原因和解决方法。

2. **Pointing out another issue relating to the previous topic: 至于……**

   "至于贝聿铭，我好像在哪里听过他的名字。"

   至于 means "as for." It is used when the speaker wants to comment on a topic related to the one previously discussed. As a preposition, it points to another topic and emphasizes the change in the subject of conversation.

EXAMPLES:

1. 她跟我说她明天回来，至于具体的时间，我就不知道了。
2. 我已经做了最大的努力了，至于结果会怎么样，只能看运气了。
3. 至于这个问题，我们还需要进一步讨论。

> **Complete the following activities using 至于.**
>
> 1. 分别介绍一下两位有名的美籍华人：李小龙和李昌钰。
> 2. 你告诉今天没来上课的同学明天我们要考试，用"至于"说说更多的考试细节。

3. Describing the result of combining two elements:
   结合……，形成……的风格／特色／习惯

   Structure: 结合A 和 B，形成 + noun phrase + 的风格/特色/习惯

   "贝聿铭18岁以前在中国受教育，后来在美国上大学，所以他能结合东西方艺术，形成他个人的独特风格。"

   This structure is used to indicate that something is a result of combining two elements, A and B. It is usually used in a compound sentence to describe the characteristics of the resulting situation taking the essence of each element. The second clause usually starts with 形成, a word which means "to form."

   EXAMPLES:

   1. 左宗棠鸡结合了中国的烹调技术和美国人的饮食口味，形成了人人喜爱的美式中餐特色。
   2. 由美籍华人建筑师林璎设计的越战纪念碑，结合东西方文化，形成了与自然和谐共处的建筑风格。
   3. 肯德鸡快餐店进入中国餐饮市场以后，结合中国人的口味，形成了中国快餐的特色，比如，椒盐鸡翅、冬菇滑鸡粥等。

Rewrite the following sentences using 结合A和B / 结合……，形成了……的风格/特色.

1. 这个面包店的甜点不仅有法国特色，还有美国的特色，很特别。
2. 这个舞蹈很独特，有芭蕾舞的技巧，也有传统中国舞蹈的技巧。
3. 这个画家与众不同，既有油画的技巧，又有中国传统山水画的技巧。

4. Expressing a proportion: ……占……的……分之……/ 百分之……/ 大多数

   Structure:
   subject A + 占 + subject B + 的…… 分之……/百分之……/大多数/大部分

   "差不多有400多万华裔，大约占美国人口的百分之一。"

   This structure is often used when we need to describe something as a percentage of another. It is similar to "A accounts for … of B", where B usually refers to a total quantity of which A is a part.

   EXAMPLES:
   1. 在美国，全职妈妈差不多占所有妈妈的五分之二。
   2. 这门课期中考试的成绩占总成绩的百分之三十。
   3. 习惯用右手的人占大多数。
   4. 地球海洋面积占地球总面积的71.8%，因此海洋占地球面积的大部分。

Complete the following activities using ……占……的……分之……/百分之…….
Express the area of each continent as a percentage of the total land area of the earth (地球陆地面积, 14900万平方千米).

EXAMPLE: 亚洲，4400万平方千米：亚洲占地球陆地面积的百分之三十。

1. 非洲，3000万平方千米
2. 北美洲，2400万平方千米
3. 南美洲，1800万平方千米
4. 南极洲，1400万平方千米
5. 欧洲，1000万平方千米
6. 大洋洲，900万平方千米

文化剪影
CULTURE ENRICHMENT

留学美国的中国幼童
Young Chinese Studying in the United States in the Late Qing Dynasty

中国幼童在19世纪的末期到美国留学时，面对了重重困难。他们远离了家人，到了一个陌生的环境。当时中国和美国无论在政治、宗教、语言、服装或饮食上，都有很大的差异。他们不但要克服语言上的障碍，还得马上适应不同的生活方式。

这些幼童在留美期间经历了很多既有趣又难忘的事情。他们住在康州的哈特福德市❶（哈市）。当时，中国留学生事务局就设立在哈市。哈市非常有意思，住着很多知名的美国作家，包括大文豪马克·吐温❷和女作家斯托夫人❸。它还有一所历史悠久的公立中学，当时幼童就在那里上学。清朝的传统是男孩都留着辫子❹，所以很多美国人嘲笑他们是女孩，让他们觉得很不好意思。他们打球的时候会把辫子放在衣服里或盘❺在头上。他们对打球很感兴趣，很快就组织了一支全是中国孩子的棒球队。他们当中有些还尝试打冰球或参加其他的运动。

幼童们毕业以后都进入了有名的美国大学，在大学期间也参加各种运动。其中有一个男孩叫钟文耀，他个子特别瘦小，被选中为学校划船队的舵手❻。他们队连续两年跟哈佛大学的比赛都赢了。当然，舵手有很大的功劳，他的队友因此感到非常自豪。

1876年，幼童们被邀请参加了在费城❼格式举办的世界博览会❽，那是中国第一次参加博览会。他们不但跟总统格兰特❾见面，还亲眼看到最先进的科技，比方说柯立斯蒸汽机❿、贝尔⓫发明的世界上第一台电话及爱迪生⓬发明的自动电报系统⓭。博览会让他们留下了难忘的回忆。

❶ 哈特福德市 Hātèfúdé Shì the city of Hartford
❷ 马克·吐温 Mǎkè Tǔwēn Mark Twain
❸ 斯托夫人 Sītuō Fūrén Harriett Beecher Stowe
❹ 辫子 biànzi pigtail
❺ 盘 pán to pin
❻ 舵手 duòshǒu bow coxswain
❼ 费城 Fèichéng Philadelphia
❽ 世界博览会 Shìjiè Bólǎnhuì World Expo
❾ 格兰特 Gélántè President Ulysses Grant
❿ 柯立斯蒸汽机 kēlìsī zhēngqìjī corliss steam engine
⓫ 贝尔 Bèi'ěr Alexander Graham Bell
⓬ 爱迪生 Àidíshēng Thomas Edison
⓭ 自动电报系统 zìdòng diànbào xìtǒng automatic telegraph system

Interpersonal/Interpretive

In groups, research online the key dates related to the events and people below. Then put each of them in the appropriate position on the respective timeline.

南北战争 (Nánběi Zhànzhēng, Civil War)
鸦片战争
英法联军 (Yīng Fǎ Liánjūn, Second Opium War)
甲午战争
洋务运动
林肯总统 (Línkěn Zǒngtǒng, President Abraham Lincoln)
咸丰皇帝 (Xiánfēng Huángdì, Emperor Xianfeng)
慈禧太后
卡尔·本茨 (Kǎ'ěr Běncí, Karl Benz) 发明汽车
贝尔发明电话
爱迪生发明电灯

美国

| 1840 | 1850 | 1860 | 1870 | 1880 | 1890 | 1900 |

中国

| 1840 | 1850 | 1860 | 1870 | 1880 | 1890 | 1900 |

词汇拓展
VOCABULARY BUILDING

1. **Loanwords** (外来词语)

   Over the past 200 years, many western concepts, ideologies, and inventions made their way into the Chinese society. As they did not exist in China prior to this, the Chinese had to create new words to describe and refer to them by translating from the languages of the countries they originated from. This was done through four key methods:

Method	How	Examples
音译 (Transliteration)	Imitating the sound of the foreign word	沙发 (shāfā, sofa) 咖啡 (kāfēi, coffee) 沙拉 (shālā, salad) 巧克力 (qiǎokèlì, chocolate)
意译 (Translation)	Using existing Chinese words to express the meaning of the foreign word	热狗 (règǒu, hot dog) 互联网 (hùliánwǎng, Internet) 社交媒体 (shèjiāo méitǐ, social media)
音译 + 意译 (Transliteration + translation)	Combining transliteration and translation to express the meaning of the foreign word	高尔夫球 (gāo'ěrfū qiú, golf) 汉堡包 (hànbǎobāo, hamburger) 苹果派 (píngguǒpài, apple pie)
字母 + 汉字法 (Letters + Chinese characters)	Using letters and Chinese characters to express the meaning of the foreign word	IT人士 (IT rénshì, IT professionals) B超 (B chāo, B-scan) ATM机 (ATM jī, ATM)

Guess the meaning of each loanword and place it in the correct column in the table below according to the method by which it was created.

超市	绿色食物	黑色星期五	普拉提	瑜伽	柠檬
拷贝	马拉松	智能手机	华氏度	白领	机器人
多媒体	英特网	空中巴士	摄氏度	下载	冰淇淋
香槟	碳足迹	芭蕾舞	AA制	e时代	IP地址

音译外来词	意译外来词	音译法 + 意译法	字母 + 汉字法
	例：黑色星期五		

2. **Exploring the Origin of Words**

In this unit, we have learned about the Self-Strengthening and May 4th Movements. In the term 洋务运动, 洋 refers to the western world, as one had to, setting off from China, sail across the Pacific Ocean (太平洋), Indian Ocean (印度洋), and Atlantic Ocean (大西洋) to reach the western world. Many Chinese words that refer to western people or things thus start with the character 洋, such as 洋人 and 洋房.

When the concepts of science and democracy were introduced to China, the English terms for them were translated into 赛因斯 or 赛先生 (literally Mr Science), and 德摩克拉西 or 德先生 (literally Mr Democracy), respectively through transliteration.

In Unit 1, we learned about Zhang Qian and the journeys he made on the Silk Road. He introduced many types of Central Asian food, animals, and musical instruments to China. With this, many new words were created, such as 葡萄, 菠菜, 狮子, 骆驼, 猩猩, and 琵琶. On the other hand, the ancient Chinese called people who lived in Central Asia 胡人. For this reason, many things that originated from Central Asia have the character 胡 in their Chinese names. Examples are 胡萝卜 and 胡椒.

In a group of four, research online the origins and meanings of a few words (consisting of two or four characters) or phrases that contain the characters 胡 or 洋 respectively. Make a brief presentation in class.

阅读理解
READING COMPREHENSION

Read the passage and answer the questions that follow.

著名美籍华裔：谭恩美
Famous American Chinese: Amy Tan

安琪是一个住在纽约的华裔女孩。她虽然从小在美国长大，说着流利的英语，但她的生活与华裔精英❶息息相关。安琪从五岁开始，几乎每天都会看《傻瓜猫》❷的动画，这部动画是根据华裔作家谭恩美（Amy Tan）的作品拍的。上中学的时候，安琪也会和她的妈妈一起阅读，然后讨论谭恩美的小说，比如《喜福会》❸。因为从她的小说中能读到移民到美国的华人在生活中遇到的酸甜苦辣。好像每一代的华裔都有不同的压力和动力，就像安琪和妈妈之间就有很多不同。不过安琪和她的妈妈都认为：虽然她们是美国人，但是她们的生活与中国和中国文化有很深的关系。华裔不仅代表了西方的文化，也能反映东方的美和传统，华裔应该为这种特别的身份而感到骄傲！

上大四的时候，安琪开始去华裔服装设计师王大仁（Alexander Wang）的公司实习。现在安琪和她的男朋友准备结婚了，她正在准备存钱买另一位华裔设计师王薇薇（Vera Wang）做的婚纱❹。美国社会有很多像他们一样优秀的华裔，他们不仅在文学、时尚、体育等行业为美国作出贡献，也是促进中美文化交流的代表。安琪目前也在为成为一名出色的美籍华裔而努力！

❶ 精英 jīngyīng elite
❷ 傻瓜猫 Shǎguā Māo Sagwa, the Chinese Siamese Cat
❸ 喜福会 Xǐ Fú Huì The Joy Luck Club
❹ 婚纱 hūnshā wedding dress

1. 在文章中，哪一位华裔精英在文学方面取得了很大的成就？你了解她的作品吗？
2. 猜一猜什么是移民的"酸甜苦辣"？你可以从你的生活里举出一个例子吗？
3. 你还知道其他在美国很有名的华裔吗？他们取得了什么成就？
4. 请上网查一查，还有哪些人促进中西文化的交流？

写作工坊
WRITING WORKSHOP

写一篇博客短文 Writing a Blog Entry

1. **Deciding on a topic**

   The topic chosen for discussion is "怎样适应新环境." In the world that we live in, very often, we have to adapt to our environment in order to survive. If we fail to adapt, we may face elimination.

2. **Choosing an event to write about**

   You may have had one or more of the experiences below, which you can write about.

   1) 到一所新的学校上学
   2) 搬到了一个新的社区
   3) 因为父母的工作搬到另一个城市或国家
   4) 去参加一个夏令营
   5) 暑假到亲戚或朋友家里住

3. **Structuring your blog entry**

   Your blog entry should be between 300 and 400 characters, and should focus on your experience of adapting to a new environment. Use the following questions below as a guide.

   1) 你的新环境怎么样？跟以前有什么不同？
   2) 你遇上什么样的挑战？
   3) 你怎么样克服困难？
   4) 如果你有朋友要适应一个新的环境，你会给他什么样的建议？

   Use also the following words and phrases, which are related to 适应, in your writing.

   > 入乡随俗❶   水土不服❷   调整   改变   受得了/受不了   习惯   冲击
   > 跨文化   体验   成长   成熟   变得   成为   凭着……信心/勇气
   > 面对/遇上……挑战/困难   克服……困难   承受/面对……压力

   ❶ 入乡随俗：到了一个新的环境，得适应那里的风俗习惯。
   ❷ 水土不服：在一个新的环境，在气候和饮食上都不习惯。

学习总结
I CAN DO!

Interpretive Communication

☐ I can read about western influences on China in the late 19th century and the early 20th century.

☐ I can read and understand some major events in the modern history of China, from 1840 to 1949, and the contributions of some important figures, such as Sun Yat-sen and Hu Shi, to her modernization.

☐ I can read and understand basic information on some Chinese Americans and their contributions to cross-cultural understanding.

Interpersonal Communication

☐ I can discuss Rong Hong's effort in bringing the first group of students sponsored by the government to the United States and how this contributed to the modernization of China.

☐ I can converse about some famous people who studied abroad and their contributions to the modernization of China.

☐ I can talk about the lives and work of some well-known Chinese Americans.

☐ I can talk about and explain the origins of some loanwords in Chinese.

Presentational Communication

☐ I can describe some amusing incidents that happened because of cultural differences to the first group of Chinese students who studied abroad.

☐ I can make a brief presentation on the contributions of this group of students to the modernization of China.

☐ I can present briefly on the lives and work of some well-known Chinese Americans and their significance.

☐ I can compare briefly the lives of Chinese students studying abroad in the past and at present.

Cultural Knowledge

☐ I can describe briefly the Self-Strengthening Movement and the Xinhai Revolution.

☐ I can name some famous Chinese from the first group of students who studied abroad and their contributions to the modernization of China.

☐ I can name some famous Chinese Americans and their contributions to the world in general and to the American society in particular.

☐ I can explain words in Chinese that came from foreign cultures and how different cultures influenced the creation of some Chinese words.

第五单元 UNIT 5
城乡发展
URBAN AND RURAL DEVELOPMENT

学习目标
LEARNING OBJECTIVES

- Understand the disparity between cities and the rural areas of China
- Learn about city clusters in China and around the world
- State the reasons for the traffic conditions during the Spring Festival travel season
- Discuss the factors to consider when choosing a base in a city

单元总览
CONTENTS AT A GLANCE!

导入 WARM UP

Part 1: 走进农村——看城乡差距 (Life in Rural China)

Language Connection:
1. 打工子弟学校就连农村的学校也不如。
2. 我们的主任常跟我们说在乡下的"留守儿童"固然不容易，跟父母进城的打工子弟也遇上不少挑战。
3. 很多打工者和他们的孩子都在社会的边缘挣扎生存。

Part 2: 从SOHO建筑看城市发展与文化传承
(SOHO: Urban Development and Cultural Preservation)

Language Connection:
1. 听说SOHO还经常邀请一些成功企业家提供讲座和论坛。
2. 中国现在正在打造五大城市群。
3. 你看世界的文明发展跟城市有多密切的关系！
4. 当然一方面发展城市，一方面也得保留传统的文化。

Part 3: 春运与人口迁徙 (Mass Migration During Spring Festival)

Language Connection:
1. 每年都迎来一个前所未有的新高峰！
2. 中国有那么多人，仅北京地区就有800万外地人。
3. 春运并非只有文化的原因，还有经济发展不平衡的原因。

文化剪影：中国和世界的城市群
CULTURE ENRICHMENT: City Clusters in China and Around the World

词汇拓展："天际线"和"地标"；刻画城市的词语
VOCABULARY BUILDING: Skylines and Landmarks; Words Describing Cities

阅读理解：城市病
READING COMPREHENSION: Urban Problems

写作工坊：写一篇影评
WRITING WORKSHOP: Writing a Movie Review

学习总结　I CAN DO!

导入
WARM UP

1. China has many large cities with large populations. Research online the population of each Chinese city below and rank the cities in descending order of population. Can you guess which of these cities are among the 10 most populous in the world?

排名	城市	人口（万人）
第一		
第二	上海	
第三		
第四		
第五		

排名	城市	人口（万人）
第六	广州	
第七		
第八		
第九		
第十	保定	

Chinese cities that are among the 10 most populous in the world: _____

2. China is similar in size to the United States but, unlike the contiguous United States which has four time zones, has only one time zone, the Beijing Standard Time. Why is that so? Research online and look at the demographic distribution of China for a clue to the answer.

第一部分 走进农村——看城乡差距
PART 1 LIFE IN RURAL CHINA

李静：你从农村回来了！

宋杰：是的，我、海文和几个公益项目的朋友在西安附近的永寿县参观了一个农村的小学。虽然我在中国已经好几个月了，可是我一般都在大城市，这次到农村有不少新的体验。

| 永寿县 | p.n. | Yǒngshòu Xiàn | Yongshou County (a county in Shaanxi Province, China) |

李静：快给我介绍一下。

宋杰：我们这个公益项目是斯坦福大学农村教育行动计划（Rural Education Action Program, REAP）的一部分，主要是希望改善落后地区孩子的教育问题。根据斯坦福大学的研究，农村孩子辍学率特别高，有的地区甚至高达百分之六十。

斯坦福大学	p.n.	Sītǎnfú Dàxué	Stanford University
农村教育行动计划	phr.	Nóngcūn Jiàoyù Xíngdòng Jìhuà	Rural Education Action Program (REAP)
地区	n.	dìqū	area, district
辍学	v.	chuòxué	drop out of school
率	n.	lǜ	rate, ratio
高达	phr.	gāo dá	reach up to

李静：什么是辍学？

宋杰：辍学就是停学，中国政府有9年免费的义务教育，可是农村很多孩子因为种种原因，不到初三就不再上学了。

| 义务教育 | phr. | yìwù jiàoyù | compulsory education |

李静：那你们的公益项目怎样帮助这些孩子呢？

宋杰：主要从两方面入手解决，第一是提供营养食品，比方说鸡蛋和维生素。第二就是配戴眼镜，农村孩子一般没有视力检查，所以有近视问题也都不知道，这样视力差当然影响学业成绩。我们的项目叫"点亮眼睛"，主要是卖一些时尚的太阳镜，用募捐得到的钱用来支持农村孩子配戴免费的眼镜。除了我们的项目以外，还有不同的基金会，给孩子定期进行视力检查，如果发现视力有问题，会派发一张"眼镜券"，孩子的家长可以到乡镇医院换取一副免费的眼镜。

李静：这样对孩子的学业一定很有帮助。

宋杰：那帮助可大了，根据研究数据，孩子配戴眼镜半年以后在语文和数学的成绩都赶上同龄的孩子。我这次到永寿县有机会访问学生和家长，学生说他们的世界一下子变得清晰明亮起来了，家长也表示孩子不但学业有了很大的进步，而且也越来越自信了。

配戴	v.	pèi dài	wear
视力	n.	shìlì	vision, eyesight
检查	n.	jiǎnchá	inspection
近视	n.	jìnshì	myopia, short-sightedness
点亮眼睛	p.n.	Diǎnliàng Yǎnjing	Education in Sight (an NGO in China that seeks to improve the eyesight of children in rural areas)
募捐	v.	mùjuān	raise donations
基金会	n.	jījīn huì	foundation
定期	adv.	dìngqī	at regular intervals
派发	v.	pàifā	distribute
券	n.	quàn	voucher
乡镇	n.	xiāngzhèn	villages and towns
换取	v.	huànqǔ	exchange something for
数据	n.	shùjù	data
清晰	adj.	qīngxī	distinct, clear
明亮	adj.	míngliàng	bright
表示	v.	biǎoshì	express, say
自信	v.	zìxìn	have confidence in oneself

李静：我听说部分农民工带着孩子到城里工作，因为户籍的问题孩子不能上公立学校，只能上打工子弟学校。

宋杰：一般打工子弟学校，收费不便宜，可是无论在师资、设备和教学质量方面，都比不上公立学校，就连农村的学校也不如。

李静：随着农民工的增加，他们孩子的教育问题也受到关注。

宋杰：我们的主任常跟我们说在乡下的"留守儿童"固然不容易，跟父母进城的打工子弟也遇上不少挑战。

李静：这些问题都是城乡差距的一个缩影。城市是真的发展起来了，可是因为教育资源的缺乏，很多打工者和他们的孩子都在社会的边缘挣扎生存。

宋杰：你看过《一个都不能少》这部电影吗？

李静：我听说过，可是还没有看过。

宋杰：虽然那是1999年的电影，可是其中反映了农村的教育和城乡差距的问题。已经10多年了，很多问题还未能完全解决。

词	词性	拼音	英文
农民工	n.	nóngmín gōng	migrant worker
户籍	n.	hùjí	household registration
公立	adj.	gōnglì	public
打工子弟	phr.	dǎgōng zǐdì	children of migrant workers
师资	n.	shīzī	teachers
教学	n.	jiàoxué	teaching
质量	n.	zhìliàng	quality
主任	n.	zhǔrèn	director, head
留守儿童	phr.	liúshǒu értóng	left-behind children (children in foster care of grandparents or other relatives while their parents work in other cities)
固然	adv.	gùrán	admittedly, it is true that
城乡差距	phr.	chéngxiāng chājù	urban-rural gap
缩影	n.	suōyǐng	epitome, microcosm
缺乏	v.	quēfá	lack
挣扎	v.	zhēngzhá	struggle
生存	v.	shēngcún	survive

语言实践
LANGUAGE CONNECTION

1. **Emphasizing a situation: 连……也/都……**

   Structure: 连 + X + 也/都 + action

   "打工子学校就连农村的学校也不如。"

   The structure 连 X 也/都…… means "even to the extent that ...." It is used for emphasizing a particular situation by describing a contrasting condition.

   EXAMPLES:
   1. 我不了解他，我连他叫什么名字也不知道。
   2. 他今天很不舒服，连平时最喜欢喝的可乐都喝不下去。
   3. 这个问题太简单了，连三岁的孩子都知道。
   4. 这个汉字太难了，连我的中文老师也不认识。

   Complete the following sentences with 连……也/都…….
   1. 这儿很安静，……。
   2. 奶奶住的地方很不方便，……。
   3. 今天很热，……。
   4. 我们家人人都用微信 (WeChat)，……。
   5. 自从可以网上购物，……。

2. **Emphasizing the equal importance of two aspects: 固然……（但是）……也……**

   Structure: condition 1 + 固然 + adjective + (但是) + condition 2 + 也 + adjective

   "我们的主任常跟我们说在乡下的"留守儿童"固然不容易，跟父母进城的打工子弟也遇上不少挑战。"

   The structure means "It is true that …, but …." It expresses a comparison between two aspects or conditions and emphasizes the equal importance or possibility between the two.

EXAMPLES:

1. 这个办法<u>固然</u>很好，那个办法<u>也</u>不错。
2. 这个建筑的设计<u>固然</u>很漂亮，<u>但是</u>造价<u>也</u>会很高。
3. 对于学生来说，学习成绩<u>固然</u>很重要，<u>但是</u>生活能力<u>也</u>很重要。

> Rewrite the following sentences using 固然……，（但是）……也…….

1. A：我最近太忙了。
   B：你最近确实很忙，但是你还是可以找时间给父母打个电话的。
2. 数量确实很重要，质量也很重要。
3. 骄傲不好，缺少自信也不好。

3. Describing a dismal situation: 在……边缘

"很多打工者和他们的孩子都<u>在</u>社会的<u>边缘</u>挣扎生存。"

This structure means "at the edge of" and is used to describe a dismal situation a person or animal is facing. Usually preceded by the cause of this situation, it is often used in the negative state.

EXAMPLES:

1. 经济的不平等造成很多低收入家庭生活<u>在</u>饥饿的<u>边缘</u>。
2. 现代医学的发展帮助医生治好了成千上万<u>在</u>死亡<u>边缘</u>挣扎的病人。
3. 全球变暖让北极熊身处<u>在</u>灭绝的<u>边缘</u>。

> Imagine that you are in a training session of your school's peer counseling team. Answer the following questions about the pressures that your peers are facing in your school community. Use 在……边缘 in your answers.

1. 你知道为什么有一些同学会感到绝望（完全没有希望了）吗？
2. 你最近面对什么压力？为什么你觉得快要崩溃了？
3. 我们学校有一些同学来自战争的地区，你想如果面临战争，人们会觉得怎么样？

第二部分 从SOHO建筑看城市发展与文化传承
PART 2　SOHO: URBAN DEVELOPMENT AND CULTURAL PRESERVATION

宋杰：李静，我给你介绍一下，这是我的同学李明威。他前天刚和父母一起来北京看望我。

李静：明威，你好！欢迎你来北京。这是你第一次来中国吗？

明威：是的！我以前从没有来过中国，这是第一次，所以我和爸爸妈妈都觉得特别兴奋！

李静：你们去了些什么地方？

明威：我们已经去过上海、成都和西安。北京是我们回国前的最后一站。

宋杰：你来中国已经有10多天了，给你印象最深的是什么？

明威：现代化的城市、摩天大楼和创新科技处处都给我们留下难忘的印象。我们住在纽约曼哈顿，我父母老觉得那里的第五大道和时代广场是美国甚至是世界的中心。可是我们一到了北京，爸爸的朋友就带他们去银河SOHO和望京SOHO❶参观，他们感觉十分惊讶。中国竟有那么现代化的建筑。

李静：是的，我刚到北京的时候，也感到非常震惊，这个城市不但有2000多年的长城，还有那么前卫的未来性建筑物，可说是在一个城市完美地结合了传统与现代。

宋杰：我姐姐一个月前给我转发了一篇《纽约时报》的文章，标题为"摩天大楼，天际线上的亚洲雄心"。内容是说摩天大楼是中国人的自信和雄心的一种表达方式。我觉得是挺有道理的。

明威：我们参观望京SOHO3Q才发现中国有这样先进的想法，整栋楼都是创业的公司，有的小公司真是仅租几张办公桌就可以开始运作了。一进去都是二三十岁的年轻人。在公共区域里可以一起喝喝咖啡，交流一下经验。听说SOHO还经常邀请一些成功企业家提供讲座和论坛，可真是一个创业成长的好地方。

李静：我们项目的中文老师告诉我们，中国现在正在打造五大城市群：京津冀城市

摩天	v.	mótiān	skyscraping
纽约	p.n.	Niǔyuē	New York
曼哈顿	p.n.	Mànhādùn	Manhattan
第五大道	p.n.	Dì Wǔ Dàdào	Fifth Avenue
时代广场	p.n.	Shídài Guǎngchǎng	Times Square
银河SOHO	p.n.	Yínhé SOHO	Galaxy SOHO (a landmark in Beijing, China)
望京SOHO	p.n.	Wàngjīng SOHO	Wangjing SOHO (a landmark in Beijing, China)
参观	v.	cānguān	visit, look around
竟	adv.	jìng	unexpectedly
震惊	adj.	zhènjīng	amazed, shocked
前卫	adj.	qiánwèi	fashionable, modern
未来性	adj.	wèilái xìng	futuristic
转发	v.	zhuǎnfā	forward
纽约时报	p.n.	Niǔyuē Shíbào	New York Times
标题	n.	biāotí	headline
天际线	n.	tiānjìxiàn	skyline
雄心	n.	xióngxīn	great ambitions

运作	v.	yùnzuò	operate
公共	adj.	gōnggòng	public
区域	n.	qūyù	area
经验	n.	jīngyàn	experience
讲座	n.	jiǎngzuò	lecture
论坛	n.	lùntán	forum
打造	v.	dǎzào	make, create
城市群	n.	chéngshì qún	city cluster
京津冀	p.n.	Jīngjīnjì	Jingjinji (a metropolitan region)

---

❶ 银河SOHO和望京SOHO是由世界知名建筑师扎哈·哈迪德（ZahaHadid）设计的。她曾获普利兹克奖（Pritzker Architecture Prize），是前卫流线设计的领军建筑师。

群，就是北京、天津和河北一带的几个城市；长江三角洲城市群是以上海为中心的；珠江三角洲城市群有广州、香港等地；成渝城市群包括西南部的成都和重庆；最后还有以武汉为首的长江中游城市群。

宋杰：这些城市群里有已经很发达的一线城市，也有二三线城市，这样一线城市可以带动周边的二三线城市的发展。

明威：真是很有意思，我在学校不但学习中文，而且也学习拉丁文。我知道"city""城市"、"citizen""公民"，跟"civilization""文明"，这几个词的词根来自拉丁文的"civis""市民"和"civitas""城邦"。你看世界的文明发展跟城市有多密切的关系！

李静：我们中国寄宿家庭的爸爸说改革开放以后，中国的城镇化已经让不少的农民脱离贫困，现在中国一半以上的人口是住在城市的。

宋杰：城市既开放又多样化，还充满了活力，是年轻人追逐梦想的地方！

李静：当然一方面发展城市，一方面也得保留传统的文化。明天我们带你去游胡同！胡同是个特别有北京风味的地方，能代表北京传统的一面。

明威：好的，一言为定！明天见。

词	词性	拼音	英文
河北	p.n.	Héběi	Hebei (a province in Northern China)
长江三角洲	p.n.	Chángjiāng Sānjiǎo Zhōu	Yangtze River Delta (a metropolitan region)
珠江三角洲	p.n.	Zhūjiāng Sānjiǎo Zhōu	Pearl River Delta (a metropolitan region)
成渝	p.n.	Chéngyú	Cheng Yu (a metropolitan region)
长江中游	p.n.	Chángjiāng Zhōngyóu	Yangtze River Valley (a metropolitan region)
发达	adj.	fādá	developed
带动	v.	dàidòng	spur on
拉丁文	n.	Lādīngwén	Latin
词根	n.	cígēn	root word
市民	n.	shìmín	city residents
城邦	n.	chéngbāng	city-state
密切	adj.	mìqiè	close
改革开放	phr.	gǎigé kāifàng	Chinese economic reform
城镇化	n.	chéngzhènhuà	urbanization
脱离	v.	tuōlí	separate oneself from
追逐	v.	zhuīzhú	pursue
胡同	n.	hútòng	hutong (a type of narrow street or alley in northern Chinese cities)
风味	n.	fēngwèi	local flavor
一言为定	phr.	yì yán wéi dìng	that is settled then

语言实践
LANGUAGE CONNECTION

1. **Useful verb: 提供……**

    "听说SOHO还经常邀请一些成功企业家提供讲座和论坛。"

    This verb means "provide" or "offer." Being a transitive verb, it is used with an object, which can be an actual item such as a snack and fruit, or an abstract idea such as a service and opportunity.

    EXAMPLES:
    1. 幼儿园提供午餐，每天下午还提供点心和水果。
    2. 你们医疗中心提供的服务是很不错，但是收费对我来说太贵了。
    3. 学校附近的社区中心给同学提供了很多做义工的机会。

    Answer the following questions using 提供.
    1. 你的父母为你提供了什么？
    2. 学校为你提供了什么？

2. **Useful verb: 打造……**

    "中国现在正在打造五大城市群。"

    This verb means "develop" or "create" and is used with an object. The object can be something concrete, such as metals, jewelry and weapons, or something abstract, such as spirit, culture, and brand. It is always used in a positive situation.

    EXAMPLES:
    1. 中国的体操王子李宁打造了这个体育服装品牌。
    2. 一名成功的教练能帮助运动员打造团队精神。
    3. 很多大学正在努力打造更开放更有包容性的校园文化。

In pairs, discuss and answer the following questions with 我们认为要打造……

1. 你觉得健康饮料应该怎样打造独特品牌？他们是不是应该给运动员提供免费试喝，或者请明星为他们打广告？
2. 你认为怎样可以打造一个开放的校园文化？能不能举办"世界文化节"，展示不同文化的特色？

3. **Making connections:** ……跟……有关系

   Structure: A 跟 B 有关系

   "你看世界的文明发展跟城市有多密切的关系！"

   In this structure, A and B have a connection. It is used to indicate that something (A) is related to something else (B). A, which is placed in the first clause, is usually a result that is determined by B, which is placed in the second clause. It can also show that two things, A and B, share something in common. It can have both positive and negative connotations.

   EXAMPLES:
   1. 我昨晚没睡好，这跟我睡前喝了一杯咖啡有关系。
   2. 一个人的身体状况跟他的生活习惯有很大的关系。
   3. 大部分学生在大学选择的专业跟自己的爱好有关系。

   Complete the following sentences that use ……跟……有关系.
   1. 一个人汉语说得好不好，跟……有关系。
   2. 一个人快乐不快乐，跟……有关系。
   3. 一个学校好不好，跟……有关系。

4. **Stating two aspects of an action:** ……一方面……（另）一方面……

"当然一方面发展城市，一方面也得保留传统的文化。"

The two aspects stated after 一方面 in the two clauses can be similar in tone, or they can be the direct opposite of each other.

EXAMPLES:
1. 自己做饭一方面更健康，另一方面还可以省钱。
2. 抽烟一方面对自己有害，另一方面对别人也有害。
3. 学好一门外语，一方面可以更好地了解外国文化，另一方面也可以有机会去国外工作。
4. 利用太阳能一方面能减少污染，另一方面也可以节省能源。

Complete the following sentences using ……一方面……，（另）一方面…….

1. 我喜欢骑自行车……。
2. 在网上跟朋友聊天……，但另一方……。
3. 科技的发展一方面……，另一方面……。

China Highlights: Northeast China

Heilongjiang:
Large illuminated building made of ice, Harbin

Jilin: Heaven Lake, Mount Changbai

Seaview of Dalian

第三部分 春运与人口迁徙
PART 3 MASS MIGRATION DURING SPRING FESTIVAL

宋杰：海文，你春节回老家的票买好了吗？

海文：还没有呢！要**提前**30天才能**预购**。**春运期间**特别紧张，真是一票难求啊！

李静：什么是"春运"？

海文：春运指的是春节前15天及后25天左右的**大规模**交通**运输**现象。这段期间因为中国人都回家过年，所以交通运输压力特别大，这种现象就叫"春运"。**央视**（中央电视台的简称）**形容**春运是一个全球**罕见**的人口流动现象，也是一个人口大**迁徙**。

宋杰：我记得在美国媒体上看见过**密密麻麻**的迁徙**轨迹图**，真是不可思议呀！

海文：那是**百度**从2014年推出的一个新项目，是利用手机**用户**的**定位**信息，把不同区

提前	v.	tíqián	move to an earlier date
预购	v.	yùgòu	purchase in advance
春运	n.	chūnyùn	passenger transportation during or around the Spring Festival
期间	n.	qījiān	period
大规模	n.	dà guīmó	big scale
运输	v.	yùnshū	transport
央视	p.n.	Yāngshì	China Central Television (abbreviation of 中央电视)
形容	v.	xíngróng	describe
罕见	adj.	hǎnjiàn	rare
迁徙	v.	qiānxǐ	move, migrate
密密麻麻	adj.	mìmimámá	numerous and close together
轨迹图	n.	guǐjì tú	route map
百度	p.n.	Bǎidù	Baidu (a Chinese multinational technology company)
用户	n.	yònghù	user
定位	n.	dìngwèi	location

域的迁徙路线提供给市民，来查询实时信息，也可以查询过去的资料。政府为了解决春运的问题，每年都提前计划。可是每年都迎来一个前所未有的新高峰！真是计划都赶不上变化了！

路线	n.	lùxiàn	route
实时	n.	shíshí	real-time
计划	v.	jìhuà	plan
前所未有	adj.	qián suǒ wèi yǒu	unprecedented

李静：我就不明白，每个国家都要过节，节日期间交通拥挤是很正常的，可是春运可不是一般的拥挤。

宋杰：我觉得这跟中国人的传统思想有关。对中国人来说，春节是最重要的节日，无论离家多远，都会回家过年。而且中国有那么多人，仅北京地区就有800万外地人，如果这些人都要回家过年，火车站和机场肯定会非常拥挤！

| 肯定 | adv. | kěndìng | definitely |

海文：你说得对！但是春运并非只有文化的原因，还有经济发展不平衡的原因。因为中国的经济发展不平衡，工作、教育和文化资源还是集中在一线城市，所以很多人从农村到城里打工，放假的时候再回到老家过春节。春运就是经济发展不平衡的体现。

| 并非 | adv. | bìngfēi | is not |
| 集中 | v. | jízhōng | concentrate |

李静：没想到从一个春运可以解读中国社会那么多情况。最近还有些什么新的变化吗？

| 解读 | v. | jiědú | analyze, interpret |

海文：春运一般是从一线城市到二三线城市。可是最近两年有"逆向迁徙"的现象，北京和上海这些大城市不但是迁出的人口多，迁入的人口也多。可能进城工作的人已经稳定下来，经济状况也不错，所以他们可以请父母去城市过春节。

逆向	v.	nìxiàng	reverse
迁出	v.	qiānchū	move out
迁入	v.	qiānrù	move in
稳定	v.	wěndìng	stabilize

宋杰：这些迁出和迁入的城市都是东部沿海的城市吗？

海文：以前是，可是现在已经慢慢发展到中西部地区，比方说成都、重庆、郑州、合肥这几个中西部的城市的迁出和迁入量都很高。

| 沿海 | n. | yánhǎi | along the coast |

重庆	p.n.	Chóngqìng	Chongqing (a city in Southwest China)
郑州	p.n.	Zhèngzhōu	Zhengzhou (the city capital of Henan Province, China)
量	n.	liàng	capacity

李静：除了坐火车、飞机以外，还有什么便捷的长途旅行方式呢？

海文：有顺风车，也有互联网包车。

长途	adj.	chángtú	long-distance
顺风车	n.	shùn fēngchē	hitch ride
互联网包车	phr.	hùliánwǎng bāochē	online car charter

李静：我在网上也看见了"拼车回家"、"包车回家"的广告。这也是一些好方法。

海文：春运真的太有意思了。我觉得春运比"贴春联"、"放鞭炮"更能代表春节的含义！

语言实践
LANGUAGE CONNECTION

1. Welcoming something: 迎来……挑战／高峰／机遇

   "每年都<u>迎来</u>一个前所未有的新<u>高峰</u>！"

   迎来 originally means "to meet those arriving." It is given a metaphorical meaning when used with words such as 挑战, 高峰, and 机遇, which mean challenges, peaks, and opportunities, respectively. It is equivalent to the term "welcome." These words that follow 迎来 always hold a positive connotation.

   EXAMPLES:
   1. 春节之前每家都会挂起"福"字，希望<u>迎来</u>非常美好的<u>未来</u>。
   2. 我们学校刚赢了加州的机器人大赛，下个月将参加全国大赛，<u>迎来</u>新一轮的<u>挑战</u>！

   > Imagine you are going to study in China in the summer and really look forward to the new opportunities and challenges ahead of you. Write a short text message or email to your Chinese friend and share your excitement with him/her using 迎来……挑战／高峰／机遇.

   Useful structures:
   - 我今年暑假要到中国去学习中文……
   - 我非常兴奋……
   - 虽然这是我第一次离开美国，可是……

2. Emphasizing one part to reflect the whole situation: ……仅……就（有）……

   Structure: 仅 + A + 就 (有) B

   "中国有那么多人，<u>仅</u>北京地区<u>就有</u>800万外地人。"

   This structure means "just ... alone ..." and is usually used to emphasize something impressive or surprising: Just A alone there is B (a surprising amount or figure related to A).

   Unit 5 Urban and Rural Development · 城乡发展

EXAMPLES:

1. 我们学校的运动队一直很强大，<u>仅</u>2017年<u>就</u>拿了三个全国冠军和一个州冠军。
2. 这家公司发展十分快，<u>仅</u>一年<u>就</u>有了5400万用户。

> In pairs, complete the following activity.
>
> Imagine you are the founders of a club. Decide what kind of club it is and create an advertisement for it with the structure 仅……就（有）……. Include the contributions your club has made to your community, as well as its accomplishments.

3. **Refuting an argument: 并非……**

"春运<u>并非</u>只有文化的原因，还有经济发展不平衡的原因。"

Emphasizing negation, 并非 is often used to refute an argument or to clarify a misunderstanding. The second clause that follows the first clause containing 并非 states the true state of affairs.

EXAMPLES:

1. 大城市的压力<u>并非</u>都是因为收入，还和空气、感情等有关。
2. 美国报纸上的中国<u>并非</u>真的中国，你要是想了解这个国家，你得自己去看看。

> Imagine you have studied in China and have gained a better understanding of both Chinese and American cultures. However, some of your friends have some misunderstandings about China/America. Clarify some of their misperceptions below and share your cross-cultural perspective with them using 并非.

1. 美国朋友：中文非常难学！
2. 中国朋友：美国孩子学习很轻松，下课以后都喜欢打球。
3. 美国朋友：中国人除了乒乓球以外，不喜欢别的运动。
4. 中国朋友：美国人天天都吃牛排和汉堡包。

文化剪影
CULTURE ENRICHMENT

中国和世界的城市群
City Clusters in China and Around the World

1957年，法国地理学家让·戈特曼❶提出了大都市带❷的想法。他认为一个城市在发展过程中会带动许多周边的城市一起发展起来。这些城市有很多相像的地方，比方说地理环境与气候❸，也有很多不一样的地方，比方说资源。几个大城市一起发展，能更有效❹地发展这个大区域的经济。后来，这个想法便成了城市群的概念❺。

中国有五个城市群，它们是京津冀城市群、成渝城市群、长江中游城市群、长江三角洲城市群以及珠江三角洲城市群。世界上则有六大城市群，除了中国的长江三角洲城市群，还有日本太平洋沿岸城市群❻、欧洲西北部城市群❼、英伦城市群❽、美国东北部大西洋沿岸城市群❾以及北美五大湖城市群❿。

一个区域要成为城市群，应该具备⓫什么条件呢？首先，它必须是这个国家或地区重要的经济中心，总人口至少2500万。第二，这个城市群里的城市密集⓬，其中有一个或几个是国际性的大城市。第三，这些城市之间必须有分工⓭和密切的经济关系。

❶ 让·戈特曼 Ràng Gētèmàn Jean Gottmann
❷ 大都市带 dà dūshì dài megalopolis
❸ 气候 qìhòu climate
❹ 有效 yǒuxiào effective
❺ 概念 gàiniàn concept
❻ 日本太平洋沿岸城市群 Rìběn Tàipíngyáng yán'àn chéngshì qún Japan Pacific coastal's city cluster
❼ 欧洲西北部城市群 Ōuzhōu xīběi bù chéngshì qún Northwestern Europe's city cluster
❽ 英伦城市群 Yīnglún chéngshì qún England's city cluster
❾ 美国东北部大西洋沿岸城市群 Měiguó dōngběi bù dàxīyáng yán'àn chéngshì qún Northeast megapolis (U.S.)
❿ 北美五大湖城市群 Běiměi Wǔdàhú chéngshì qún Great Lakes megalopolis (U.S.)
⓫ 具备 jùbèi possess
⓬ 密集 mìjí highly concentrated
⓭ 分工 fēn gōng division of work

Interpersonal/Interpretive

In groups, research online to complete the following activities.

1) Place each Chinese city below in the appropriate city cluster.

上海	深圳	北京	长沙	杭州	合肥	成都
重庆	武汉	南昌	广州	天津	苏州	张家口

京津冀城市群　　　　　成渝城市群　　　　　长江中游城市群

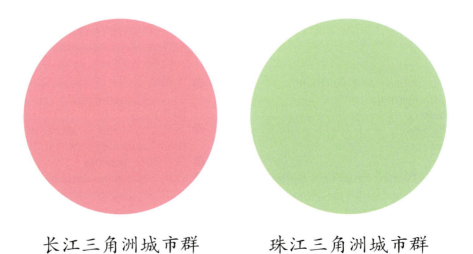

长江三角洲城市群　　　珠江三角洲城市群

2) Read the short introduction below and answer the questions that follow. Research online if you do not know the answers.

北美五大湖城市群以芝加哥为中心，其他城市有底特律 (Dǐtèlǜ, Detroit)、克利夫兰 (Kèlìfūlán, Cleveland)、辛辛拿提 (Xīnxīnnátí, Cincinnati) 以及加拿大的多伦多 (Duōlúnduō, Toronto)。

1. 芝加哥有什么工业？它是美国的金融中心吗？
2. 这几个城市有多少家"财富500强"企业 (Fortune 500 Companies)？
3. 它们有什么有名的大学和摩天大楼？
4. "壮丽 (zhuànglì) 一英里"(Magnificant Mile) 指的是什么？

Presentational

Prepare a presentation based on the following question.

最近，亚马逊 (Yàmǎxùn, Amazon) 正在寻找一个城市作为他们的第二个总部 (zǒngbù, headquarters)。一共有二十个城市入选，包括洛杉矶、费城 (Fèichéng, Philadelphia)、芝加哥、波士顿、奥斯丁 (Àosīdīng, Austin) 以及华盛顿 (Huáshèngdùn, Washington, D. C.)。你认为亚马逊在选择城市时会考虑哪些因素 (yīnsù, factor) 呢？

词汇拓展
VOCABULARY BUILDING

1. **Skylines and Landmarks**

   When we discuss cities, we usually use two words:

   - 天际线 (tiānjìxiàn, skyline)：一个城市的高楼大厦和天空构成的线条。
   - 地标 (dìbiāo, landmark)：一个城市特别的景观，是这个城市的代表。

   1) Guess the cities based on the skylines and landmarks depicted in the pictures below.

   Skylines

   a)    b)

   Landmarks

   c)    d)

   2) Find an image of the skyline or landmark of each city below:

   a) 巴西圣保罗
   b) 阿联酋迪拜
   c) 美国芝加哥
   d) 英国伦敦

2. **Words Describing Cities**

There are many words used to describe a city, from its skyline to its landmarks, and the transportation network and way of life associated with it. Look at the words below and check how many you have already learned and know how to use.

摩天大楼	大都会	天际线	地标	商业中心	商业区	枢纽
近郊	霓虹灯	博物馆	音乐厅	购物中心	火车站	成千上万
川流不息	四通八达	地铁	咖啡馆	电影院	热闹	繁荣
发达	现代化	魅力	充满活力	五光十色	高楼林立	

1) Use an online dictionary to find out the *pinyin* and meaning of those words you find unfamiliar.

2) Place the words into the categories below. Each word may be placed in more than one category.

跟生活有关	跟交通有关	跟建筑有关

3) Imagine the famous writers below are alive today. How would they now describe the cities they had lived in? Write a few sentences on their behalf using the words from the previous page.

1) 雨果 (Yǔguǒ Victor Hugo) 与巴黎
2) 狄更斯 (Dígēngsī Charles Dickens) 与伦敦
3) 马克·吐温与新奥尔良 (Xīn Ào'ěrliáng New Orleans)
4) 余光中与台北

阅读理解
READING COMPREHENSION

Read the passage and answer the questions that follow.

城市病
Urban Problems

小王刚刚从大学毕业,这个秋天他进入一家深圳的金融公司工作。小王很喜欢深圳的开放和现代化。他喜欢公司楼下的日式餐馆,也喜欢周末去看话剧❶和爬山。小王也很快在公司有了一些朋友。但是有一些同事在吃午饭的时候常常抱怨生活在深圳的苦恼❷,比如说房价太高、堵车、空气污染等等。工作了几个月以后,小王也觉得大城市的生活并非那么简单。他开始理解什么是"城市病"。

随着城市的快速发展,越来越多的人涌入❸城市。很多人都想在大城市获得成功和幸福。但是大量的人口也带来了房价问题、污染问题以及生活问题。很多年轻人在一线城市买不起房、开不起车,甚至没时间吃饭。其中一些年轻人因为受不了在一线城市的压力,搬去了二三线城市过"慢生活",因此很多城市也损失❹了不少人才,发展得越来越慢。

政府为了"治好"城市病,想了很多办法,比如说发展城市群,让一线城市带动附近的二三线城市发展;修建更多的城市公园等。小王的老家在惠州❺,一个离深圳一小时车程的小城市,那里的环境很好,房价不太高;同时随着深圳的发展,越来越多的公司去惠州投资❻。小王的父母希望小王可以回老家找工作。但是小王不知道他应该听父母的建议,还是继续留在深圳。

❶ 话剧 huàjù modern drama, stage play
❷ 苦恼 kǔnǎo worry, frustration
❸ 涌入 yǒng rù come pouring in
❹ 损失 sǔnshī lose
❺ 惠州 Huìzhōu Huizhou (a city in Guangdong Province, China)
❻ 投资 tóuzī invest

1. 小王生活的城市是在哪个城市群？
   - Ⓐ 京津冀城市群
   - Ⓑ 长江三角洲城市群
   - Ⓒ 珠江三角洲城市群
   - Ⓓ 成渝城市群

2. "城市病"指的是什么？
   - Ⓐ 大城市的人买不起房子和车子。
   - Ⓑ 大城市的空气特别不好。
   - Ⓒ 因为人口太多、环境不好，大城市的发展受到了影响。
   - Ⓓ 以上都是。

3. 你觉得小王回老家找工作有什么好处？有什么坏处？

4. 你觉得中国的城市病和美国的城市病有什么不同？

5. 你认为还有什么更好的办法可以解决城市病？

写作工坊
WRITING WORKSHOP

写一篇影评 Writing a Movie Review

In this section, you will learn about the basic method of analyzing a movie in order to write a review of it. You will need to watch a video on YouTube and follow these five suggested steps in writing a 400-word review. You will then share it with your classmates.

1. **Gathering information**

    Divide yourself into groups. Each member of the group will be assigned one of these aspects to focus on:

    1) 故事有哪些人物？他们是什么关系？
    2) 故事发生在哪里？是怎样的背景？
    3) 故事发生在什么时候？有什么特别的地方？

    Then search for and watch the microfilm 三分钟 on YouTube. Each group member will look out for details relating to the aspect he/she has been assigned.

2. **Recording the chain of events and exchanging information**

    In your group, pay attention to the chain of events in the movie, recording them on a flowchart. The first three are listed here for you: 乘务员在火车上工作 > 孩子在车站等妈妈的火车进站 > 妈妈让乘客先下车. Then, exchange information gathered relating to the aspects mentioned above.

3. **Making inferences**

    In your group, discuss the following questions.

    1) 为什么车站那么拥挤？
    2) 为什么妈妈不能跟孩子在一起？
    3) 为什么孩子要背乘法表？
    4) 从这个微电影可以看到什么社会问题？

4. **Creating new ideas**

    Now that you have analyzed the plot of the movie as a group, think about how you will answer individually the following question.

    如果你跟家人已经很久没有见面，这次见面只有三分钟，你会怎么样利用这三分钟呢？

5. **Putting it together**

    To put the information you have collected and the ideas you have generated into writing, organize your account into three sections, or paragraphs, following the pointers below:

    1) 故事里有哪些人物，在哪里，发生了哪些事情。
    2) 妈妈和孩子之间的故事反映了什么社会问题。
    3) 你会如何利用和家人见面的三分钟。

学习总结
I CAN DO!

Interpretive Communication

- [ ] I can read about some public service projects that help children in the rural areas of China protect and improve their eyesight and, consequently, their academic performance.
- [ ] I can understand when people talk about the huge disparity between cities and the rural areas of China in aspects such as education, healthcare and employment opportunities.
- [ ] I can read and understand basic information on modern and avant-garde buildings in Beijing and the role they perform in nurturing start-up companies.
- [ ] I can conduct online research in Chinese on recent developments and future plans for the five city clusters of China.

Interpersonal Communication

- [ ] I can discuss the pros and cons of migrant workers bringing their children to the cities with them or leaving their children in the rural areas in the care of their grandparents.
- [ ] I can converse about some public service projects for children in the rural areas of China.
- [ ] I can talk about the unique 春运 phenomenon and the challenges it presents for transportation.
- [ ] I can talk about how SOHO3Q nurtures young entrepreneurs and start-up companies.

Presentational Communication

- [ ] I can describe the fundamental disparity between cities and the rural areas of China in aspects such as education, health care and employment opportunities.
- [ ] I can present briefly on public service projects such as the Rural Education Action Program, and their goals and operations.
- [ ] I can make a brief presentation on SOHO3Q and its business model.
- [ ] I can present briefly on the 春运 phenomenon and its cultural significance.
- [ ] I can compare the five city clusters of China with those in the United States and the world.

Cultural Knowledge

- [ ] I can describe the importance of the compulsory education system of China in improving social mobility.
- [ ] I can name some city clusters of China and talk about the economic advantages they possess.
- [ ] I can describe and explain the annual 春运.
- [ ] I can use several common Chinese four-character set phrases appropriately in describing life in big metropolitan cities.

第六单元 UNIT 6
中国文学与艺术
CHINESE LITERATURE AND ARTS

学习目标
LEARNING OBJECTIVES

- Read about famous Chinese poets and painters
- Understand the significance of Chinese elements in Western popular culture
- Discuss the works of famous writers around the world
- Compose a poem about someone or something you care deeply about

143

单元总览
CONTENTS AT A GLANCE!

导入 WARM UP

- **Part 1:** 中国诗歌——时代的烙印 (Chinese Poetry: Reflecting the Times)
  Language Connection:
  1. <u>与其</u>在饭馆门前排长队、在商场的人群里挤，<u>倒不如</u>跟朋友一起出行，到成都和三峡旅游。
  2. <u>即使</u>对我这样的外国学生来说，这个名字<u>也</u>绝对不陌生。

- **Part 2:** 融合中西的中国当代画家——吴冠中
  (East Meets West: Contemporary Chinese Painter Wu Guanzhong)
  Language Connection:
  1. <u>经过</u>数十年的努力<u>后</u>，他画出了很多影响深远的作品。
  2. 吴冠中真<u>不愧</u>是中西融合的大师！

- **Part 3:** 好莱坞电影里的中国元素 (Chinese Elements in Hollywood Movies)
  Language Connection:
  1. 因为你的一举一动都<u>关系到</u>你家族的光荣和耻辱。
  2. 影片<u>以</u>喜闻乐见<u>的</u>艺术形式给全世界的电影观众带来了惊喜。

文化剪影：中国现当代文学家：鲁迅、莫言、刘慈欣
CULTURE ENRICHMENT: Modern and Contemporary Chinese Writers: Lu Xun, Mo Yan, and Liu Cixin

词汇拓展：重叠词
VOCABULARY BUILDING: Reduplicated Words and Phrases

阅读理解：偶像的诞生——看中国的流行文化
READING COMPREHENSION: The Birth of an Idol: Chinese Pop Culture

写作工坊：写诗——描述人或物
WRITING WORKSHOP: Writing a Poem: Describing a Person or a Situation

学习总结　I CAN DO!

导入
WARM UP

Choose one of the artists or writers below and write down on an index card as much information as you know about him/her and his/her representative works. Include at least two key facts about him/her. If you do not know the person, research online to gather information on him/her.

- Artists: 张择端，齐白石，徐悲鸿，刘小东，艾未未
- Writers: 李清照，徐志摩，巴金，老舍，王安忆，舒婷

Spend no more than five minutes on preparing the index card. You will be the "expert" on this artist or writer.

EXAMPLE:

张择端：北宋时期有名的画家，《清明上河图》是他的代表作。

Your teacher will give a signal for you to mill around the classroom to find a partner to have a conversation with. You will talk to each other about the artist or writer you have chosen to write about. You will have a conversation with at least five partners.

张择端《清明上河图》

徐悲鸿《奔马图》

徐志摩《再别康桥》

第一部分 中国诗歌——时代的烙印
PART 1 CHINESE POETRY: REFLECTING THE TIMES

宋杰五一长假的时候到成都和三峡游玩，途中与朋友讨论中国诗歌。以下是他所写的博客。

| 三峡 | p.n. Sānxiá | Three Gorges |

生活在大都市里，我非常向往大自然的秀丽风景！五一小长假到了，与其在饭馆门前排长队、在商场的人群里挤，倒不如跟朋友一起出行，到成都和三峡旅游。我的朋友天芸是研究中国文学的研究生，每到一个地方就为我们介绍有关这个景点的中国诗歌。这次旅游的收获不但是欣赏名山大川，而且最重要的是了解中国文化。

| 与其 | conj. yǔqí | rather than |

| 名山大川 | phr. míng shān dà chuān | famous mountains and rivers |

成都的杜甫草堂和三峡的白帝城是我这次旅游最难忘的地方。唐代伟大诗人杜甫和李白在这里留下了他们的足迹。我记得在中文课上老师介绍唐代的诗歌，也提到"诗圣"杜甫和"诗仙"李白，他们是中国诗歌最具有代表性的诗人。杜甫草堂

杜甫	p.n. Dù Fǔ	Du Fu (712-770) (a prominent Chinese poet of the Tang Dynasty)
草堂	n. cǎotáng	thatched cottage
白帝城	p.n. Báidìchéng	Baidi City (an ancient temple complex in Chongqing, China)
李白	p.n. Lǐ Bái	Li Bai (701-762) (a prominent Chinese poet of the Tang Dynasty)
足迹	n. zújì	footprint
诗圣	p.n. Shīshèng	Poet-Sage
诗仙	p.n. Shīxiān	Poet Immortal

面积虽然不大，可是园林格局典雅而优美。天芸跟我们解释，杜甫之所以被称为"诗圣"，是因为他是一个忧国忧民的现实主义诗人，他的作品常常描写民生疾苦，表现出儒家的仁爱精神。他最有名的一首诗是《春望》，背景是京城战争后的破落景象，他一方面关怀国事，一方面想念家人。里面有两句"烽火连三月，家书抵万金"，意思是说战火已经持续三个多月，这时候如果收到家人报平安的书信，比万两的黄金都要珍贵。这首诗充分反映了诗人对祖国的热爱和对亲人的挂念。

我们离开成都到达重庆，坐船游览长江三峡，非常壮观。我们到了白帝城的时候，天芸又给我介绍了一首流传千古的佳作——李白的《早发白帝城》："朝辞白帝彩云间，千里江陵一日还，两岸猿声啼不住，轻舟已过万重山。"这首诗描写李白愉快的心情，早上从白帝城出发，长江水流急速，两岸都是高山，传来猴子不停的叫声，他坐的小船已经经过很远的路程。诗人用壮丽的江山和轻快的行舟来衬托他的喜悦心情。后人称李白为"诗仙"。他

格局	n.	géjú	structure, format
典雅	adj.	diǎnyǎ	elegant
忧国忧民	phr.	yōu guó yōu mín	concerned about one's country and people
现实主义	n.	xiànshí zhǔyì	realism
描写	v.	miáoxiě	depict, portray
民生疾苦	phr.	mínshēng jíkǔ	sufferings of the people
儒家	p.n.	Rújiā	Confucianism
仁爱	n.	rén'ài	benevolence
背景	n.	bèijǐng	background
京城	n.	jīngchéng	capital
景象	n.	jǐngxiàng	scene, sight
关怀	v.	guānhuái	care for
两	m.w.	liǎng	tael (a unit of weight)
黄金	n.	huángjīn	gold
充分	adv.	chōngfèn	as fully as possible
祖国	n.	zǔguó	home country
挂念	n.	guàniàn	miss
流传千古	phr.	liúchuán qiāngǔ	pass down through the ages

| 衬托 | v. | chèntuō | be a foil to |
| 喜悦 | adj. | xǐyuè | happy |

对唐代政治不满，可是也没有办法改变，只好寄情于祖国美丽的自然风光来表达他道教出世的思想，诗歌好像行云流水一样潇洒自如，想象力特别丰富，表现出浪漫主义的精神。

中国古典文学除了唐诗以外，还有宋词和元曲，它们都代表着一个时代的文学特色。天芸说现代诗中也有很多伟大的作品。她给我介绍了享有盛名的台湾诗人余光中。即使对我这样的外国学生来说，这个名字也绝对不陌生。学校中文朗诵节就有他的作品《乡愁》。我还记得"小小的邮票"、"窄窄的船票"、"矮矮的坟墓"和"浅浅的海峡"。这几个形象的事物把"乡愁"这样抽象的感情变得具体化了。这首诗表达了人生不同阶段的分离——小时候母子分离，青年时与妻子分离，中年时与母亲生死相隔，晚年时游子与家乡分离。短短的几个句子，把强烈的思乡情怀表达出来。

我觉得诗歌最有意义的地方就是通过精练的语言来表达人们的心声，带着时代的烙印。这是中国文化遗产中最珍贵的一部分，希望我以后有更多机会进一步学习中国的诗歌。

寄情	v.	jìqíng	give expression to one's feelings
自然风光	phr.	zìrán fēngguāng	natural scenery
道教	p.n.	Dàojiào	Daoism
出世	n.	chūshì	renounce the world, keep aloof from worldly affairs
行云流水	phr.	xíngyún liúshuǐ	natural and spontaneous
潇洒自如	phr.	xiāosǎ zìrú	natural and unrestrained
想象力	n.	xiǎngxiànglì	imagination
浪漫主义	n.	làngmàn zhǔyì	romanticism
宋词	p.n.	Sòng Cí	classical Chinese poetry of the Song Dynasty
元曲	p.n.	Yuán Qǔ	*Qu*, a form of poetry from the Yuan Dynasty
盛名	n.	shèngmíng	great reputation
余光中	p.n.	Yú Guāngzhōng	Yu Kwang-Chung (1928-2017) *(a famous Taiwanese writer, poet, educator, and critic)*
绝对	adv.	juéduì	absolutely
陌生	adj.	mòshēng	unfamiliar
朗诵	n.	lǎngsòng	recitation
窄	adj.	zhǎi	narrow
坟墓	n.	fénmù	tomb
浅	adj.	qiǎn	shallow
海峡	n.	hǎixiá	straits
形象	adj.	xíngxiàng	vivid
乡愁	n.	xiāngchóu	yearning for home
抽象	adj.	chōuxiàng	abstract
分离	n.	fēnlí	separation
游子	n.	yóuzǐ	a person traveling or residing in a place far away from home
家乡	n.	jiāxiāng	home
思乡	v.	sīxiāng	miss one's hometown
情怀	n.	qínghuái	emotion, sentiment
精练	adj.	jīngliàn	succinct
烙印	n.	làoyìn	mark, imprint
文化遗产	phr.	wénhuà yíchǎn	cultural heritage

语言实践
LANGUAGE CONNECTION

1. **Expressing preference: 与其……（倒）不如……**

   > Structure: 与其 + option A + （倒）不如 + option B

   "<u>与其</u>在饭馆门前排长队、在商场的人群里挤，<u>倒不如</u>跟朋友一起出行，到成都和三峡旅游。"

   This structure is used to express preference by indicating two contrasting options. The speaker prefers option B to option A, seeing option B being much better than option A. The speaker uses this structure to place a strong emphasis on his/her attitude or opinion.

   EXAMPLES:
   1. <u>与其</u>浪费时间，<u>倒不如</u>做一些有意义的事情。
   2. 天气这么好，<u>与其</u>在家里呆着，<u>不如</u>出去走走。
   3. 遇到难题的时候，<u>与其</u>在网上到处搜索答案，<u>不如</u>自己认真思考一下。

    Working in pairs, take turns to talk about your plans for the summer vacation using 与其……（倒）不如……．

   A: 暑假我们……吧。
   B: ……（reason 1），与其……，不如……。
   B: ……（reason 2），与其……，不如……。

2. **Expressing concession: 即使……也……**

> Structure: **即使** + hypothetical statement + **也** + a state / situation that holds true

"<u>即使</u>对我这样的外国学生来说，这个名字<u>也</u>绝对不陌生。"

即使……也…… means "even if ..., ... still ...." The first clause with 即使 describes a hypothetical situation. The second clause with 也 describes a state or situation that holds true regardless of the condition in the first clause.

EXAMPLES:
1. <u>即使</u>在学习上取得优异的成绩，<u>也</u>不能骄傲自满。
2. <u>即使</u>遇上困难，我们<u>也</u>得勇往直前，千万不能放弃。
3. <u>即使</u>爸爸妈妈不同意，我<u>也</u>要学我自己喜欢的专业。

Describe the following situations using 即使……也…….

1. 你想出国，到中国念书，任何事情都无法改变你的决心。
2. 不管发生什么事，你都要参加龙舟比赛。
3. 你每天凌晨12点之前便上床睡觉，这是不会改变的习惯。

第二部分 融合中西的中国当代画家——吴冠中
PART 2　EAST MEETS WEST: CONTEMPORARY CHINESE PAINTER WU GUANZHONG

星期六，李静和宋杰一起参观798艺术区的吴冠中画展。

李静：我早就听说过20世纪的中国出现了很多大师，不管是在文学领域还是在艺术领域都群星璀璨。但是我没想到有吴冠中这样特殊的大师！他的画看起来是油画，却有中国画的美！

宋杰：是啊！我在美国的时候就看过吴冠中的画，他的几幅画现在还收藏在耶鲁大学美术馆。那时候我的艺术老师告诉我，吴冠中是一位"中西融合"的大师。

李静：所谓"中西融合"，指的就是他把中国水墨画的意境和西方油画的精神融合起来，对吗？

宋杰：没错！吴冠中1919年出生在中国江苏，1936年开始在杭州学画画，1946年他又去了巴黎学习艺术，这种经历让他对

吴冠中	p.n.	Wǔ Guànzhōng	Wu Guanzhong (1919-2010) (a renowned painter in contemporary China)
领域	n.	lǐngyù	area, field
璀璨	adj.	cuǐcàn	splendid, brilliant
特殊	adj.	tèshū	special
油画	n.	yóuhuà	oil painting
收藏	v.	shōucáng	collect and keep
耶鲁大学美术馆	p.n.	Yēlǔ Dàxué Měishùguǎn	Yale University Art Gallery
水墨画	n.	shuǐmòhuà	ink wash painting
江苏	p.n.	Jiāngsū	Jiangsu (a province in Eastern China)

中西方的艺术都有很深刻的见解。经过数十年的努力后，他画出了很多影响深远的作品。他的画现在已经被全球各地的博物馆收藏。由于他的艺术成就引起了全世界人民的重视，中国传统水墨艺术被带到了国际上，也就是说，吴冠中继承和发展了中国的传统水墨艺术。

李静：吴冠中真不愧是中西融合的大师！除了吴冠中以外，还有别的中国画家影响了现在的艺术世界吗？

宋杰：当然有啦！毕加索就喜欢用毛笔临摹中国画家齐白石的画，而且他说过"真正的艺术在中国"。梵高和莫奈其实都喜欢收集中国、日本等东方国家的艺术作品，他们的画里也有中国画的影子。

李静：当我看到西方现代画家的作品时，我觉得他们不再重视画一个东西画得像不像，而更重视他们的画是不是能反映他们的内心世界。这不就是我们李老师常常说的"物由心生"吗？这个变化肯定和中国画的影响有关。

宋杰：在过去的几百年，中国人把"物由心生"的意境传到了西方，西方的油画技术和焦点透视法也影响了东方，由此可见，世界艺术的进步离不开东西方的交流和融合。

李静：是啊！艺术不应该分国界，我们应该积极迎接来自不同文化的冲击和影响，我希望未来可以看到更多像吴冠中、齐白石一样的画家！

迎接	v.	yíngjiē	meet, welcome
冲击	n.	chōngjī	impact

宋杰：下周末有中央美术学院的毕业生艺术展，我相信我们在那里会发现更多的惊喜。下周末一起去吧！

中央美术学院	p.n.	Zhōngyāng Měishù Xuéyuàn	Central Academy of Fine Arts

李静：好啊！

China Highlights: East China

Jiangsu: Suzhou Garden

Zhejiang: West Lake, Hangzhou

Shanghai: Huangpu River

Shangdong: Qufu, hometown of Confucius

Anhui: Mount Huangshan

Jiangxi: The rural scene in Wuyuan

语言实践
LANGUAGE CONNECTION

1. Emphasizing the process of an experience: 经过……

   Structure: 经过 + event/time

   "经过数十年的努力后,他画出了很多影响深远的作品。"

   As a verb, 经过 is usually used in the first clause of a compound sentence to emphasize the process of an event, action, or experience, which is usually in the past. The second clause talks about the result of that event, action, or experience.

   EXAMPLES:
   1. 经过三个月的努力,他的数学成绩取得了很大的进步。
   2. 经过无数次的失败,雷军和他的公司获得了很多的经验,现在他们做手机的技术已经很成熟了。
   3. 经过这几场的篮球比赛以后,我们的队员都获得了丰富的经验。

Look at the following pictures and write down one sentence to describe the person or company shown in each picture using 经过.

EXAMPLE:

经过很多年在NBA的努力,姚明成为了在中国和美国都很有名的篮球明星。

❶

❷

❸

2. **Describing someone's accomplishments: 不愧是……**

Structure: subject + 不愧是 + accomplishment/reputation

"吴冠中真不愧是中西融合的大师！"

不愧是 means "worthy of" or "deserve to be called." It carries a positive connotation and is often used to give praise to someone's accomplishment or good reputation. It may not be used by the speaker to refer to his/her own accomplishment.

EXAMPLES:

1. 李向不愧是我们的队长，他在昨天的足球比赛中进了三个球！
2. 梵高不愧是世界著名的大画家，连我三岁的妹妹都喜欢欣赏他的画作《星空》。
3. 广州不愧是中国的美食之都，我们昨天在那里从早上吃到晚上，觉得每一道菜都好吃极了！

Choose one of the following fields and research online on one person from China who has had great accomplishments in the field. Write down one sentence to describe his/her contributions and accomplishments using 不愧是.

EXAMPLE:

张大千不愧是中国最有名的艺术家之一，世界很多著名的博物馆都收藏着他的画。

1. 演员　2. 企业家　3. 音乐家　4. 运动员　5. 科学家

第三部分 好莱坞电影里的中国元素
PART 3 CHINESE ELEMENTS IN HOLLYWOOD MOVIES

李静看了《疯狂的亚洲富豪》这部电影以后,在博客上跟朋友分享她对好莱坞电影里中国元素的看法。

我最近看了《疯狂的亚洲富豪》,这是好莱坞近25年来首次全用亚洲演员和亚洲导演拍摄的一部爱情喜剧,放映以来票房一直飙升,引起了媒体的关注和群众的热议。

其实我在小学和初中时代也看过不少和中国文化有关的好莱坞电影,其中包括我最喜欢的动画片:《花木兰》和《功夫熊猫》。

电影《花木兰》里不但有很多传统中国元素,比如建筑和服装,而且故事特别精彩动人。木兰是一个家喻户晓的民族英雄。她的父亲因为年纪大了,不能再去打仗。于是木兰就女扮男装,代父从军。她英勇善战,最后帮助她的军队赢得了战争,也获得了皇帝的奖励。

疯狂的亚洲富豪	p.n.	Fēngkuáng de Yàzhōu Fùháo	Crazy Rich Asians (a Hollywood movie)
导演	n.	dǎoyǎn	film director
拍摄	v.	pāishè	film (a movie)
放映	v.	fàngyìng	show (a film)
票房	n.	piàofáng	box office (earnings from a movie)
媒体	n.	méitǐ	media
群众	n.	qúnzhòng	the masses
热议	n.	rèyì	spirited discussion
动画片	n.	dònghuàpiàn	animation movie
花木兰	p.n.	Huā Mùlán	Mulan (a Hollywood movie)
功夫熊猫	p.n.	Gōngfu Xióngmāo	Kungfu Panda (a Hollywood movie)
家喻户晓	phr.	jiā yù hù xiǎo	widely known
民族英雄	phr.	mínzú yīngxióng	national hero
打仗	v.	dǎzhàng	fight a battle
女扮男装	phr.	nǚ bàn nán zhuāng	a female impersonating as a male
代父从军	phr.	dài fù cóng jūn	take one's father's place in the army
英勇善战	phr.	yīngyǒng shànzhàn	brave and good at fighting
赢	v.	yíng	win
奖励	n.	jiǎnglì	reward

后来我上高中修读中国历史，才开始明白《花木兰》故事里面所描写的"忠"、"孝"和"光宗耀祖"是儒家思想里非常重要的部分。木兰代父从军是"孝"，保卫国家是"忠"。"光宗耀祖"更是不容忽视的观念。就算是沏茶这样一个简单的家务，也要认真学习，千万不能有任何差错，因为你的一举一动都关系到你家族的光荣和耻辱。最后木兰战胜归来，给家族带来无上的荣耀。所以木兰在中国人心里一直是一位值得尊敬的女性，她不怕困难，冲破传统的束缚，为父亲、为国家出力，无疑是一位了不起的巾帼英雄。在美国的动画片中除了以家庭和国家为重的中国传统思想以外，还融入了西方对自我价值的追求。木兰在湖边一边思索，一边歌唱："我会向世界展示，我内心深处的一切，他们会珍惜这样一个真实的自我"❶。这部电影正好通过木兰这个角色，融合了中国人对家庭的重视和西方女性对独立和自我的追求。

我初中的时候，《功夫熊猫》一上映就受到观众热烈的欢迎。它把"功夫"和"熊猫"两个中国元素巧妙地结合在一起。影片塑造了一个武侠世界，通过

忠	n.	zhōng	loyalty
孝	n.	xiào	filial piety
光宗耀祖	phr.	guāngzōng yàozǔ	bring glory to one's ancestors
沏茶	v.o.	qī chá	make tea
任何	pron.	rènhé	any
差错	n.	chācuò	mistake
关系	v.	guānxì	concern, have a bearing on
家族	n.	jiāzú	clan, family
光荣	n.	guāngróng	glory
耻辱	n.	chǐrǔ	shame
战胜	v.	zhànshèng	defeat, triumph over
归来	v.	guīlái	return
束缚	n.	shùfù	fetters
巾帼	n.	jīnguó	heroine
自我价值	phr.	zìwǒ jiàzhí	value of self
思索	v.	sīsuǒ	think deeply, ponder
真实	adj.	zhēnshí	real

独立	n.	dúlì	independence
巧妙	adj.	qiǎomiào	ingenious, clever
塑造	v.	sùzào	portray
武侠	n.	wǔxiá	a martial artist with chivalrous conduct

❶ 《花木兰》主题曲《Reflection》
I will show the world
What's inside my heart
And be loved for who I am

仙鹤、宫殿、太极、阴阳、天书、面条和龙这些中国元素和传统哲理，以喜闻乐见的艺术形式给全世界的电影观众带来了惊喜。电影里蕴藏着深刻的中国哲理，把一个简单的故事变得更耐人寻味。

熊猫阿宝的五个师兄师姐分别是：虎、猴、螳螂、蛇和鹤。他们都有自己独特的武功。在我看来，这可能是从中国有名的"五禽戏"中得到了艺术创作灵感。

"五禽戏"是中国古代著名医学家华佗通过观察和模仿鸟兽的动作，设计出来的一套锻炼身体的方法。中国人相信人应该和自然界的万物和平共处，庄子说"天地与我并生，而万物与我为一"❷。而《功夫熊猫》里那种人与自然之间的和谐，就是道家思想所说的"天人合一"的境界。

电影中乌龟是和平谷最有威望的人物。他洞识天机，选择了憨厚的熊猫阿

仙鹤	n.	xiānhè	fairy crane
宫殿	n.	gōngdiàn	palace
太极	p.n.	Tàijí	Tai chi (a type of Chinese martial art)
阴阳	n.	yīnyáng	yin and yang (complementary forces in Chinese philosophy)
哲理	n.	zhélǐ	philosophy
形式	n.	xíngshì	format, pattern
蕴藏	v.	yùncáng	contain
耐人寻味	phr.	nài rén xún wèi	provide food for thought
师兄师姐	phr.	shīxiōng shījiě	senior fellow apprentices
螳螂	n.	tángláng	mantis
五禽戏	p.n.	Wǔqínxì	Five Animals Mimic Boxing (a kind of training which imitates the movements of the tiger, deer, bear, ape, and bird)
灵感	n.	línggǎn	inspiration
华佗	p.n.	Huà Tuó	Hua Tuo (140-208) (a famous Chinese physician of the late Eastern Han Dynasty)
模仿	v.	mófǎng	imitate
庄子	p.n.	Zhuāngzǐ	Zhuangzi (369-286 BC) (an influential Chinese philosopher of the Warring States period)
和谐	n.	héxié	harmony
天人合一	phr.	tiān rén hé yī	harmony between heaven and man
境界	n.	jìngjiè	state, realm
威望	n.	wēiwàng	prestige
洞识天机	phr.	dòngshí tiānjī	having a keen insight into nature's mysteries
憨厚	adj.	hānhòu	simple and honest

❷ "天地与我并生，而万物与我为一。"出自庄子的《齐物篇》。

宝为"神龙大侠",肩负起拯救和平谷的重任。熊猫阿宝的师傅很不理解为什么乌龟大仙会选择一点功夫都不懂的熊猫。龟大仙说无论你的徒弟是什么人,只要"引导"、"滋养"和"相信",都能让他把潜力发挥出来,最终获得成功。熊猫阿宝得到师傅的悉心教导,终于打败了敌人,让居民重新过上幸福的生活。成就自我、成就他人也是电影的主题之一。

我觉得有中国元素的电影一方面能迎合亚洲的新兴市场,一方面也能给西方观众带来新鲜感。这些都是好莱坞跨文化的一种尝试,这样融合中西文化的全球视野正是电影界的一个新方向。

肩负	adj.	jiānfù	undertake, shoulder
拯救	adj.	zhěngjiù	save
重任	n.	zhòngrèn	important task
师傅	n.	shīfu	master, teacher
徒弟	n.	túdì	protege
引导	v.	yǐndǎo	guide
滋养	v.	zīyǎng	nurture
发挥	v.	fāhuī	bring into play, give free rein to
悉心	adv.	xīxīn	devote all attention to
敌人	n.	dírén	enemy
成就	v.	chéngjiù	achieve, accomplish
主题	n.	zhǔtí	theme
迎合	v.	yínghé	cater to
新兴市场	phr.	xīnxīng shìchǎng	new and developing market
跨文化	v.o.	kuà wénhuà	cross-cultural
全球视野	phr.	quánqiú shìyě	global perspective

Did you know?

China has a vast film-going population and a fast growing box office revenue. Because of this, Hollywood has been paying more attention to the Chinese film market, eager to take a bite of this big pie. On the other hand, Chinese filmmakers are also keen to collaborate with Hollywood in order to break into the American market. What has resulted from this keenness in collaboration is the increasing number of Chinese films starring stars from Hollywood, which have been showing in both markets. This trend points to the fact that Asian scriptwriters, directors and actors are entering Hollywood on a scale larger than ever seen before. The smash hit *Crazy Rich Asians* is just one of the many examples. It is predicted that film ticket sales in China will surpass that in the United States by 2020.

语言实践
LANGUAGE CONNECTION

1. **Expressing relevance or connection: 关系到……**

   Structure: subject + 关系到 + object

   "因为你的一举一动都关系到你家族的光荣和耻辱。"

   关系 means "concern," "affect," or "have a bearing on." It is used to emphasize a relationship between two things. The word 到 is often added to 关系 to indicate the meaning of "having reached."

   EXAMPLES:
   1. 妈妈非常重视我们的起居饮食，因为这关系到我们的健康。
   2. 老师希望我们认真听讲，因为暑假作业的安排关系到我们每一位同学。
   3. 无人驾驶汽车的发展关系到城市的未来。

Use the following phrases to complete the sentences below. Each phrase can be used more than once.

优化公共交通系统	全球变暖	优异的成绩	暑期实习的机会
人工智能的研发	推动绿色出行	使用再生能源	提倡低碳生活

1. ……关系到你的前途。
2. ……关系到城市的发展。
3. ……关系到人类的未来。

2. Stating a way of doing something: 以……的形式

Structure: 以……的形式 + verb phrase

"影片以喜闻乐见的艺术形式给全世界的电影观众带来了惊喜。"

Similar to "in the form of," this is used to state how something was or is to be done.

EXAMPLES:

1. 快要到母亲节了，我想以画画的形式向妈妈表达我对她的爱。
2. 四川发生地震，全国各地的人们以不同的形式积极帮助灾区，有的人捐款，有的人捐衣物，还有的人亲自去当地救灾。
3. 这学期的中文课会以笔试和口头报告相结合的形式检查大家的学习情况。

Answer the following questions using 以……的形式.

1. 你的生日要到了，你想怎么庆祝？
2. 假设你的朋友生了重病，你要如何帮助他？

文化剪影
CULTURE ENRICHMENT

中国现当代文学家：鲁迅、莫言、刘慈欣
Modern and Contemporary Chinese Writers: Lu Xun, Mo Yan, and Liu Cixin

鲁迅、莫言及刘慈欣正好代表了中国现当代文学三个不同的阶段。鲁迅的作品代表着五四运动时代反传统的精神。莫言则是20世纪80年代乡土寻根❶文学的领军人物，他的小说描写了那时候农村的景象。21世纪，刘慈欣的科幻小说通过丰富的想象力，把读者带到未来的外星人世界。这三位作家都有自己独特的风格。

鲁迅和《阿Q正传》

鲁迅是有名的现代文学家。他曾经想当医生，但他发现文学比医学更能帮助当时的中国人。于是他开始写作，后来成为了著名作家。他最有名的作品是写于1921年的《阿Q正传》。故事以辛亥革命前后的农村为背景，描写了一个叫阿Q的贫穷流浪汉❷的故事。他每天被人欺负，但是他不知道反省和奋斗，只知道自尊自大，自欺欺人。他的这种"精神胜利法"❸，其实说的就是20世纪初期的中国人，在面对西方强国的挑战时，却不敢正视现实，只能自欺欺人的事实。

莫言和乡土小说

莫言的作品代表着20世纪80年代乡土文学的崛起。莫言融合了他在农村的生活经验、民间故事和历史，描写农民所遇到的困难。在《红高粱》❹里，他描写了20世纪30到40年代山东农民在中日战争中的英勇行为。他也在其他的小说里以独特的女性角度来看中国的大跃进❺运动。2012年，莫言获得了诺贝尔文学奖❻，诺贝尔奖评审团特别推荐了他的作品《天堂蒜薹之歌》❼。在这本长篇小说里，莫言支持弱势群体❽，为民请命，充分体现出作家的良知❾。莫言曾经说过：一个作家，一辈子其实只能干一件事：把自己的血肉，连同自己的灵魂，转移到自己的作品中去。

刘慈欣和《三体》

刘慈欣最有名的作品是《三体》三部曲系列，它们分别是《三体》、《黑暗森林》及《死神永生》，是目前中国最畅销的科幻小说，其中第一部在2015年获得雨果奖最佳小说奖。这三本书说的是地球文明和"三体文明"之间的交流与搏斗的故事。这部小说之所以非常受欢迎，有两个原因。第一，作者在小说里融入了大量现实中的先进物理学理论，特别吸引科学爱好者。第二，作者探索了很多读者感兴趣的"大问题"，比方说：太空是怎样的一个世界？外星人是否真的存在？如果真的有外星人，它们是否有跟人类一样的道德原则？

① 寻根 xúngēn trace one's roots
② 流浪汉 liúlànghàn the homeless
③ 精神胜利法 jīngshén shènglì fǎ spiritual victory
④ 红高粱 Hóng Gāo Liáng Red Sorghum
⑤ 大跃进 Dà Yuè Jìn The Great Leap Forward
⑥ 诺贝尔文学奖 Nuò Bèi'ěr Wénxuéjiǎng Nobel Prize in Literature
⑦ 天堂蒜薹之歌 Tiāntáng Suàntái zhī Gē The Garlic Ballads
⑧ 弱势群体 ruòshì qúntǐ vulnerable groups
⑨ 良知 liángzhī conscience
⑩ 雨果奖 Yǔ Guǒ Jiǎng Hugo Award

Interpersonal/Interpretive

1. In a pair, research online to find out information on the following writers and their representative works.

作家	国家	年代	代表作品	代表作品的重要性
海明威 (Ernest Hemingway)			老人与海 (The Old Man and the Sea)	
加夫列尔·加西亚·马尔克斯 (Gabriel Garcia Marquez)			百年孤独 (One Hundred Years of Solitude)	
罗琳 (J. K. Rowling)	英国			
艾莱娜·费兰特 (Elena Ferrante)			那不勒斯四部曲 (Neapolitan Quartet)	
詹姆斯·乔伊斯 (James Joyce)		1882–1941		
赛珍珠 (Pearl Buck)				她在中国长大，在1938年以《大地三部曲》获得诺贝尔奖。那是以中国农村为背景的小说，描写农民生活，是一本跨文化的作品。

2. In a pair, discuss and answer the following questions.

   1. 假如你有机会与一位作家会面，无论他/她是否还在世，你希望见到谁？你会跟他/她聊些什么？
   2. 如果你能变成一名文学家，你想变成谁？为什么？
   3. 如果你有时间，你打算阅读什么文学作品？

词汇拓展
VOCABULARY BUILDING

Reduplicated Words and Phrases (重叠词)

In writing, one way to make your description more vivid is to use reduplicated words and phrases. This is done by duplicating either single-character nouns or two-character adjectives, adverbs, verbs, measure words, and numerals.

In Chinese poetry, poets often use reduplication to intensify the emotions they want to convey. Some examples are shown below.

《登高》· 杜甫

风急天高猿啸哀，渚清沙白鸟飞回。
无边落木萧萧下，不尽长江滚滚来。
……

Du Fu, a Tang Dynasty poet considered by many to be best poet in China of all time, used reduplication and created some of his most memorable lines, as seen in this poem: 萧萧, 滚滚.

《声声慢》· 李清照

寻寻觅觅，冷冷清清，凄凄惨惨戚戚。
乍暖还寒时候，最难将息。
……

Song Dynasty lyricist Li Qingzhao made bold use of seven reduplicated words in succession to create a magnificent opening to 声声慢, one of her most well-known lyrics.

《乡愁》· 余光中

小时候，
乡愁是一枚小小的邮票，
……

长大后，
乡愁是一张窄窄的船票，
……

后来啊，
乡愁是一方矮矮的坟墓，
……

而现在，
乡愁是一湾浅浅的海峡，
……

Contemporary poet Yu Guangzhong used several reduplicated words to intensify his feelings in this emotional poem of yearning: 小小的, 窄窄的, 矮矮的, 浅浅的.

The most common formats of reduplication and some examples (with their root characters) are shown below.

AA format	AABB format	ABAB format
人：人人	三两：三三两两	一个：一个一个
天：天天	高兴：高高兴兴	享受：享受享受
件：件件	干净：干干净净	鼓励：鼓励鼓励
红：红红	热闹：热热闹闹	细长：细长细长的
高：高高	普通：普普通通	雪白：雪白雪白的

Words that are reduplicated usually sound rhythmic and thus help draw attention to the feeling you want to convey.

Work with a partner to complete the following activities.

1. Discuss how each word can be reduplicated and place it in the correct column according to the format of reduplication. Some words may fit into more than one format. For words classified under the AA format, you will need to think of a phrase or short sentence.

	白	蓝	绿	矮	粗	圆	方	长
	短	淡	酸	辣	甜	胖	瘦	找
冰凉	漂亮	安静	轻松	放松	认真	愉快	辛苦	老实
紧张	考虑	商量	顺利	调整	照顾	整理	准备	自然

AA format	AABB format	ABAB format
EXAMPLES:	**EXAMPLES:**	**EXAMPLES:**
❶ 大大的眼睛	❶ 热热闹闹	❶ 休息休息
❷ 人人都喜欢中国菜。	❷ 舒舒服服	❷ 尝试尝试

2. Use at least 10 of the words above to narrate a vivid story to your partner. Then, share your story with the class.

阅读理解
READING COMPREHENSION

Read the passage and answer the questions that follow.

偶像的诞生——看中国的流行文化
The Birth of an Idol: Chinese Pop Culture

流行文化不单是艺术的一种形式,也是生活很重要的一部分。让我们来认识几个在中国最受欢迎的电视节目,通过它们了解年轻人心目中的偶像是什么。

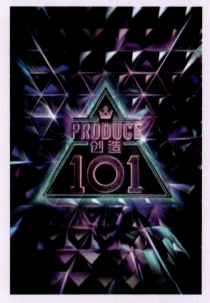

2018年夏天,中国最热门的节目就是《创造101》,这是一个以观众投票❶为主,从101位女生中选择11位女生,让她们成为明星的节目。这个节目只在网络上播放,首播当天的播放量已经达到2.1亿。同时,这个节目的选手也很快成为了年轻人的新偶像,比如孟美岐,她在两个月内就有了五百万个粉丝。

"偶像"这个词最早的意思和神有关,代表一种神秘、强大的力量。中国的流行偶像文化从20世纪80年代才开始,那时候中国人刚刚开始接触流行音乐,最容易买到的磁带❷和光盘❸都来自香港和台湾,邓丽君及四大天王(张学友、刘德华、郭富城、黎明)在中国非常受欢迎。但那时候,这些偶像们不常到中国,他们的粉丝只能通过磁带与电视了解他们,所以偶像们感觉很神秘也很完美。到了21世纪初,以周杰伦为代表的台湾流行歌手成为了新的偶像,他们唱歌、演戏,同时也到中国开演唱会,于是"去听演唱会"成为了一件让人很兴奋但也很奢侈的事情。然而,没有多少人真正想过,为什么中国没有自己的"偶像"。

到了2004年,一档叫《超级女声》的节目吸引了全中国人的关注,参赛者之一李宇春成为了当年最火的偶像。很多年轻人很开心,他们终于不用听着不熟悉的粤语❹或者韩语去"追星"了。到了2018年,《创造101》与《偶像练习生》这样的节目则代表了新的潮流——粉丝决定偶像。在节目播出的时候,偶像们要根据粉丝的要求不断改变自己。像孟美岐这样的新偶像,几乎每一天都要在微博上和粉丝互动。这时候，偶像不仅仅是一个让你学习的对象，他们还成为了和你一起成长的朋友。有不少观众都说，能看着一个平凡的女生成长为一个真正的明星，是《创造101》最吸引他们的地方。

由此可见，随着网络和社会的发展，偶像和粉丝的关系一直在改变，我们需要什么样的偶像，也许就能代表我们的文化改变的方向。

❶ 投票 tóu piào vote
❷ 磁带 cídài cassette tape
❸ 光盘 guāngpán compact disc
❹ 粤语 Yuèyǔ Cantonese

1. 中国从20世纪80年代开始有哪些流行音乐的偶像？查一查他们的代表作，选出你最喜欢的歌，和同学交流。

时间	20世纪80年代	2000年	2004年	2018年
偶像				
代表作				

2. 在中国，流行音乐偶像的变化有哪些原因？
3. 在美国，从20世纪60年代开始，在流行音乐方面，偶像经历了哪些变化？你觉得这是为什么？
4. 你最喜欢的歌手是谁？为什么？他／她有什么特别的地方？他／她有什么值得你学习的？

写作工坊
WRITING WORKSHOP

写一首诗——描述人或物 Writing a Poem: Describing a Person or a Situation

Visit this link http://www.360doc.com/content/16/1118/19/38312539_607611035.shtml to read the poem 妈妈 written by 刘声东[1]. Then read the following poem written by 白路知[2], who wrote it after reading the poem 妈妈.

《妈妈的爱》· 白路知

母亲的爱，就像影子。
你摸不到它，
但它是存在的。
你不可能总是看见它，
但它是存在的。
即使你，悲伤或沮丧，
它也永远在你身边。

[1] 刘声东 Liú Shēngdōng chief of the People's Liberation Army branch of the Xinhua News Agency
[2] 白路知 Bái Lùzhī a student who wrote this poem during her 5th semester of studying Chinese on the east coast of the United States

Write down the imageries you are able to spot in these two poems. Check with your teacher if you need help understanding these imageries. What format have the two poems been written in?

Choose someone or something you care deeply about. Then, using the imageries and formats found in these two poems, as well as those from other poems you have read, as references, create a poem of your own about this person or situation. There is no restriction on the number of lines and words to use in your poem.

学习总结
I CAN DO!

Interpretive Communication

- [ ] I can read a few classical and modern Chinese poems and analyze their imageries.
- [ ] I can understand when people talk about the influence of Chinese art, especially that of Wu Guanzhong and Qi Baishi, on Western painters such as Picasso and Monet.
- [ ] I can read and understand how Chinese elements are infused in American films.
- [ ] I can use some interpretive reading strategies while reading an article in Chinese.

Interpersonal Communication

- [ ] I can discuss the ways in which the American film industry has portrayed Chinese characters and represented Chinese elements for its audience.
- [ ] I can converse about the influence of Chinese art on Western painters.
- [ ] I can converse about and discuss how American films use Chinese elements in its storytelling.
- [ ] I can discuss the similarities and differences between Chinese painting and Western traditional painting.

Presentational Communication

- [ ] I can present on my analysis of a few classical and modern Chinese poems and talk about their cultural significance.
- [ ] I can present on my thoughts on the influence of Chinese art on modern Western painters.
- [ ] I can deliver an oral presentation explaining and justifying how Chinese elements are reflected in American films.
- [ ] I can write a short poem of my own, modelling it after examples taught.
- [ ] I can present on my favorite Chinese poem, analyze its poetic imageries, explain why it is my favorite and why I am recommending it to the class.

Cultural Knowledge

- [ ] I can describe and explain some basic characteristics of Chinese poetry with a few examples.
- [ ] I can talk about the key features of Chinese traditional painting.
- [ ] I can identify Chinese elements represented in American films.
- [ ] I can make a short presentation on a Chinese author, his/her representative works and his/her significance in Chinese literary history.

第七单元 UNIT 7
地球与我
THE EARTH AND US

学习目标
LEARNING OBJECTIVES

- ➤ Understand the environmental issues China and the world are facing today
- ➤ Read about eco-friendly practices in different countries
- ➤ Design a poster related to Earth Day
- ➤ Introduce an organic farm and explain how it can help us protect the environment

单元总览
CONTENTS AT A GLANCE!

导入 WARM UP

- **Part 1: 濒临绝种的动物** (Endangered Animals and Their Conservation)
  Language Connection:
  1. 那时候金丝猴离我们很近，<u>有的</u>在攀爬树枝，<u>有的</u>在互相追逐，<u>还有的</u>在吃野果和树叶。
  2. 熊猫数量<u>之所以</u>稀少，<u>是因为</u>它们不容易受孕。
  3. <u>为了</u>对外国表示友好，中国把国宝赠送给美国。

- **Part 2: 全球变暖：人类前所未有的威胁** (Global Warming: An Unprecedented Threat)
  Language Connection:
  1. <u>究竟</u>什么是"全球变暖"？
  2. 这是世界各国<u>为了</u>解决气候变化问题<u>而</u>达成的第一个国际协议。
  3. 人类必须把气温的变化控制在摄氏两度之内，<u>不然</u>"末日的时钟就要敲响了"。

- **Part 3: 可再生能源** (Developing Sources of Renewable Energy)
  Language Connection:
  1. <u>其实</u>北京的雾霾<u>并</u>没有想象中的那么严重。
  2. <u>其中</u><u>不乏</u>知名的公司，比如苹果、谷歌、微软、沃尔玛、星巴克等。

文化剪影：世界各地环保的不同方法
CULTURE ENRICHMENT: Eco-Friendly Practices Around the World

词汇拓展：与环保措施有关的词汇；有关环保的节日；与天灾有关的词汇；与赈灾有关的词汇
VOCABULARY BUILDING: Words Associated with Environmental Protection Measures; Special Days for Environmental Protection; Words Associated with Natural Disasters; Words Related to Disaster Relief

阅读理解：《来自2070年的一封信》观后感
READING COMPREHENSION: Reflections on a YouTube Video

写作工坊：撰写创意短文——宣传有机农场
WRITING WORKSHOP: Writing Creative Text – Promoting an Organic Farm

学习总结 I CAN DO!

导入
WARM UP

The National Low-carbon Day is observed in China on the 13th of June every year. To encourage students to adopt a low-carbon lifestyle, the environmental club of the high school you are studying at in Beijing is putting up posters like those below in the school compound. Work with a partner to come up with a slogan (标语, biāoyǔ) for each poster. The slogans should be crisp and persuasive.

节省用水
别让我们的眼泪成为世界上的最后一滴水

节省用电
为了明天的光明，请节约每一度电！

拒绝使用塑料袋
标语：_____

多吃蔬菜少吃肉
标语：_____

多乘坐公共交通
标语：_____

注意垃圾分类
标语：_____

Can you think of other practices you can adopt for a low-carbon lifestyle? Draw out your ideas or research online for images that can represent them. Think of a slogan for each idea.

标语：_____   标语：_____

第一部分 濒临绝种的动物
PART 1 ENDANGERED ANIMALS AND THEIR CONSERVATION

李静：听朋友说你去过香格里拉，真的吗？

宋杰：是的，我是去年跟学校的老师和同学一起去的。

李静：真羡慕你有那么好的机会。快跟我说说你的香格里拉行。

宋杰：我们到了香格里拉，从旅馆就能看见梅里雪山，雪山上终年积雪，是难得一见的美景。我们还坐了两个多小时的车到维西傈僳族自治县去看金丝猴。

李静：你看到金丝猴了！那可是濒临绝种的稀有动物！

宋杰：对！我们到了傈僳以后，走了一段特别惊险的小路到了金丝猴的国家自然保护区。跟我们一起去的有一位以前在国家地理杂志工作的科学家，还有一位藏族研究员，名叫卓玛。卓玛告诉我们，以

香格里拉	p.n.	Xiāng Gé Lǐ Lā	Shangri-La (a county-level city in Yunnan Province, China)
羡慕	v.	xiànmù	envy
旅馆	n.	lǚguǎn	hotel
梅里雪山	p.n.	Méilǐ Xuěshān	Meili Snow Mountains (a mountain range in Yunnan Province, China)
终年	n.	zhōngnián	throughout the year
维西傈僳族自治县	p.n.	Wéixī Lìsùzú Zìzhìxiàn	Weixi Lisu Autonomous County (an autonomous county in Diqing Prefecture, Yunnan Province, China)
金丝猴	n.	jīnsīhóu	snub-nosed monkey
濒临	v.	bīnlín	on the verge of
绝种	v.	juézhǒng	become extinct, die out
稀有动物	phr.	xīyǒu dòngwù	rare animal
惊险	adj.	jīngxiǎn	alarmingly dangerous
自然保护区	phr.	zìrán bǎohùqū	nature reserve
国家地理杂志	p.n.	Guójiā Dìlǐ Zázhì	National Geographic Magazine
藏族	p.n.	Zàngzú	Tibetan Ethnic Minority
研究员	n.	yánjiūyuán	researcher

前只能在100米以外看金丝猴，现在金丝猴跟人的关系越来越亲近，甚至可以近距离地观看。那时候金丝猴离我们很近，有的在攀爬树枝，有的在互相追逐，还有的在吃野果和树叶。它们身手矫健，动作灵活，经常三五成群地出没，在滇藏的雪山树林中形成一道风景线。

近距离	adj.	jìnjùlí	close range
攀爬	v.	pānpá	climb
追逐	v.	zhuīzhú	chase
矫健	adj.	jiǎojiàn	strong and vigorous
灵活	adj.	línghuó	agile
三五成群	phr.	sān-wǔ chéngqún	in groups of three or four
出没	v.	chūmò	roam about
滇藏	p.n.	Diān Zàng	Yunnan and Tibet
熊猫基地	phr.	xióngmāo jīdì	panda base

李静： 我虽然没有去过香格里拉，可是我去过成都，在那里参观过熊猫基地。

宋杰： 熊猫不但是中国的国宝，也是一种濒临绝种的动物。

李静： 熊猫基地是一个繁育、研究和保护熊猫的机构，里面完全模拟了熊猫在大自然的生活环境，不仅有竹林，还有湖泊和草地。我们进了基地，先看了一段关于熊猫生态和熊猫研究的视频，然后到繁育研究实验室参观。他们的实验室有一支强大的团队，包括遗传学、兽医学、繁殖学和生态学等各方面的专家。据我了解，熊猫数量之所以稀少，是因为它们不容易受孕，而且幼仔存活率低，专家们主

繁育	v.	fányù	breed
机构	n.	jīgòu	organization
模拟	v.	mónǐ	simulate
湖泊	n.	húpō	lake
实验室	n.	shíyànshì	laboratory
团队	n.	tuánduì	team
遗传学	n.	yíchuánxué	genetics
兽医学	n.	shòuyīxué	veterinary science
繁殖学	n.	fánzhíxué	reproductive science
生态学	n.	shēngtàixué	ecology
稀少	adj.	xīshǎo	few, rare
受孕	v.	shòuyùn	become pregnant
幼仔	n.	yòuzǎi	young animal
存活率	n.	cúnhuólǜ	survival rate

要的工作是用人工繁殖替熊猫配种，提高幼仔存活率，这样就能增加熊猫的数量了。

宋杰：我虽然没有去过成都，可是在华盛顿的动物园也看见过大熊猫。

李静：这是中国外交的一个策略，为了对外国表示友好，中国把国宝赠送给美国，让更多外国人观赏熊猫。

宋杰：除了熊猫以外，还有什么其他濒临绝种的动物？

李静：中国还有华南虎、藏羚羊和麋鹿等；当然众所周知，北极熊的处境也越来越危险了。

宋杰：北极熊有着白白的长毛和厚厚的脂肪层，可以抵御北极严寒的天气，它们一般在雪地和浮冰上猎食为生，可是近些年来因为全

球变暖，北极冰川融化速度加快，加上石油的开采严重破坏了生态系统，给它们的生存环境带来了极大的威胁。

石油	n.	shíyóu	petroleum, oil
开采	v.	kāicǎi	extract
威胁	n.	wēixié	threat

李静：因为全球变暖，夏季无冰期越来越长，它们没有地方去捕猎，因此脂肪层累积不够，生育率不断下降。除了北极熊以外，其他动物如海象、海豹和企鹅也都受到影响。

海象	n.	hǎixiàng	walrus
海豹	n.	hǎibào	seal
企鹅	n.	qǐ'é	penguin

宋杰：联合国已经采取行动，与当地社区合作，保护这些稀有动物。我们都希望大家提高环保意识，这样才可以维持地球上物种的多样性。

联合国	p.n.	Liánhéguó	United Nations
意识	n.	yìshí	awareness
地球	n.	dìqiú	earth
物种	n.	wùzhǒng	species
多样性	n.	duōyàngxìng	diversity

语言实践
LANGUAGE CONNECTION

1. **Referring to different groups:** 有的……，有的……，还有的……

   > Structure: 有的 + group 1，有的 + group 2，还有的 + group 3

   "那时候金丝猴离我们很近，<u>有的</u>在攀爬树枝，<u>有的</u>在互相追逐，<u>还有的</u>在吃野果和树叶。"

   有的 is used to refer to certain members of a group of people (e.g., 有的人), animals (e.g., 有的金丝猴), or objects (e.g., 有的树叶). The English equivalent is "some." It is often used several times in a sentence to refer to the different groups. The noun following 有的 may be omitted if it is clear from the context what the noun is.

   EXAMPLES:
   1. 今年我们打了很多比赛，<u>有的</u>打得特别精彩，<u>有的</u>打得很一般，<u>还有的</u>打得糟透了。
   2. 晚上六点以后，<u>有的</u>同学去自习室学习，<u>有的</u>去练钢琴，<u>还有的</u>回宿舍休息。
   3. 通过这次实习，我认识了很多人，<u>有的</u>是大公司的总裁，<u>有的</u>是大学教师，<u>还有的</u>是科学家，我觉得非常有意思！

 Write sentences describing what you see in the following pictures using 有的……，有的……，还有的…….

EXAMPLE:

今天下雨了，<u>有的</u>同学穿着雨衣，<u>有的</u>打着伞，<u>还有的</u>同学冒着雨跑回家。

2. **Stating the effect before the cause: 之所以……，是因为……**

> Structure: 之所以 + result + 是因为 + reason(s)

"熊猫数量<u>之所以</u>稀少，<u>是因为</u>它们不容易受孕。"

之所以……，是因为…… can be translated as "the reason why ... is because ...." It can be used when the speaker wishes to state the effect before the cause. It is normally used in formal speech.

EXAMPLES:
1. 妈妈<u>之所以</u>问这么多问题，<u>是因为</u>关心你。
2. 他<u>之所以</u>放弃那份工作，<u>是因为</u>他想回到学校去念博士学位。

With a partner, choose one of the following topics and have a debate on it.

1. 要保护环境，我们应该放慢经济发展。（正方：应该；反方：不应该）
2. 要学习好外语，我们必须到那个国家留学。（正方：必须去；反方：不必去）
3. 要确保信息安全，我们应该停止发展面部识别科技。（正方：应该停止；反方：应该继续）
4. 要保持健康，我们必须多吃有机食品（organic food）。（正方：必须；反方：不必）

Decide who will take the affirmative side and who will take the negative side. Then, prepare a short script giving your opinions.

EXAMPLE:
我们今天的辩论主题是……（topic）。我的观点是……（your position）。我之所以认为……（your position），首先是因为……（reason 1）；其次是因为……（reason 2）；最后是因为……（reason 3）。

3. Expressing a purpose: 为了……

Structure: 为了 + purpose

"<u>为了</u>对外国表示友好，中国把国宝赠送给美国。"

为了 is most often used to indicate the purpose of an action. It is similar to "in order to" or "for the purpose of," and usually acts as a preposition. The clause containing 为了 is placed before the verb in a sentence.

EXAMPLES:
1. <u>为了</u>让我们学校的交换生度过一个愉快的感恩节，老师们买了很多南瓜，让大家一起做南瓜灯和南瓜派（pumpkin pie）。
2. <u>为了</u>我的学习和未来，我的父母搬了家，而且每年夏天他们都会带我出国学外语。

Complete the following sentences.

1. 为了把中文学好，我们应该……。
2. 为了保护濒临灭绝的野生动物，我们高中生可以……。
3. 为了减轻中国的雾霾，中国政府……。
4. 为了促进中国和美国的交流，我们应该……。

China Highlights: South China (1)

Guangdong: Guangzhou, the capital city

Guangxi: Lijiang River, Guilin

Hainan: Beach of Sanya

第二部分 全球变暖：人类前所未有的威胁
PART 2 GLOBAL WARMING: AN UNPRECEDENTED THREAT

宋杰在美国学校的AP中文课上和同学一起搜索并讨论有关全球变暖的资料，然后在班上做了口头报告，以下是他们的报告的文本。

各位同学：

我们今天要谈的是"全球变暖"。**究竟**什么是"全球变暖"？"全球变暖"带来了什么问题？我们可以用什么方法来缓解全球变暖呢？

全球变暖是因为人类在**大气层**中排放大量的**温室气体**，其中主要是二氧化碳，造成了**温室效应**，从而导致**温度**上升的一种**气候**变化。全球变暖给人类带来了前所未有的威胁。

究竟	adv.	jiūjìng	exactly
大气层	n.	dàqìcéng	atmosphere
温室气体	phr.	wēnshì qìtǐ	greenhouse gas
温室效应	phr.	wēnshì xiàoyìng	greenhouse effect
温度	n.	wēndù	temperature
气候	n.	qìhòu	climate

　　由于气候变暖，冰原和冰川融化，导致海平面不断上升。很多岛屿和沿海地区都可能被水淹没，比方说马尔代夫、太平洋岛国、加尔各答、达卡等，甚至像纽约曼哈顿和上海这样的大城市，都会受到影响。同时，空气中的二氧化碳也会造成天气极端化、物种濒临灭绝等连锁反应。

　　由此可见，由于全球变暖，人类生存的环境也遭到了严重的破坏。世界各国都在寻求解决的方法，希望通过控制人类自己的行动来减少对气候变化的影响。1997年在日本京都召开了全球气候变化大会，制定了《京都协定书》(The Kyoto Protocol)，这是世界各国为了解决气候变化问题而达成的第一个国际协议。2009年的《哥本哈根协议》(The Copenhagen Accord)，194个国家达成了升温不超过摄氏两度的共识。2015年在法国巴黎举行了第21届联合国气候变化大会COP21，最后195个国家签署了《巴黎协定》(The Paris Agreement)，确立了2020年后的目标：除了把全球升温控制在摄氏两度之内，还会极力争取不超过摄氏1.5度的目标。

冰原	n.	bīngyuán	ice field
海平面	n.	hǎipíngmiàn	sea level
岛屿	n.	dǎoyǔ	island
淹没	v.	yānmò	flood, submerge
马尔代夫	p.n.	Mǎ'ěrdàifū	Maldives (a tropical nation in the Indian Ocean)
太平洋	p.n.	Tàipíngyáng	Pacific Ocean
加尔各答	p.n.	Jiā'ěrgèdá	Kolkata (the capital city of the state of West Bengal, India)
达卡	p.n.	Dákǎ	Dhaka (the capital of Bangladesh)
极端化	n.	jíduānhuà	becoming extreme
灭绝	v.	mièjué	die out
连锁反应	phr.	liánsuǒ fǎnyìng	chain reaction
遭到	v.	zāodào	suffer, encounter
破坏	n.	pòhuài	damage
寻求	v.	xúnqiú	seek
京都	p.n.	Jīngdū	Kyoto (the capital city of Kyoto Prefecture, Japan)
召开	v.	zhàokāi	convene
达成	v.	dáchéng	reach (a consensus or agreement)
协议	n.	xiéyì	agreement
共识	n.	gòngshí	consensus, agreement
签署	v.	qiānshǔ	sign (an agreement)
确立	v.	quèlì	establish
极力	adv.	jílì	do one's utmost
争取	v.	zhēngqǔ	strive for

各国将努力降低温室气体的排放，希望能在本世纪下半叶达成碳排放和碳吸收的平衡。

我们向大家推荐一部非常有价值的纪录片，叫做《±2℃》。《±2℃》是台湾拍摄的一部环保纪录片，名字源自2009年联合国在哥本哈根举行的气候变化大会。会议的结论是人类要挽救地球，就必须把气温的变化控制在摄氏两度之内，不然"末日的时钟就要敲响了"。纪录片里一再强调，因为人类没有好好保护地球，所以地球已经遭到毁灭性的破坏，导致很多反常的现象，比方说：飓风、暴雨、干旱、水灾、热浪、森林野火、冰川融化、海平面上升等等。自1970年以来，全球自然灾害数量增加近三倍，这些都是地球给我们发出的警告。

工业越是发达的国家，环境问题越是严重，因为温室气体排放主要是因为工业生产活动。中国、美国、印度、俄罗斯、日本和德国是二氧化碳排放量最大的几个国家。我们生活在这些国家，不仅有义务，更有责任去减排。如果我们不改变自己的生活方式，后果不堪设想。请大家一起行动起来，保护地球——我们唯一的家园。

叶	n.	yè	a time period
碳	n.	tàn	carbon
吸收	n.	xīshōu	absorption
纪录片	n.	jìlùpiàn	documentary
源自	v.	yuánzì	originate from
会议	n.	huìyì	conference
结论	n.	jiélùn	conclusion
挽救	v.	wǎnjiù	save
末日	n.	mòrì	doomsday
强调	v.	qiángdiào	emphasize
毁灭性	adj.	huǐmièxìng	destructive
反常	adj.	fǎncháng	abnormal
飓风	n.	jùfēng	hurricane
暴雨	n.	bàoyǔ	rainstorm
干旱	n.	gānhàn	drought
水灾	n.	shuǐzāi	flood
热浪	n.	rèlàng	heat wave
森林野火	phr.	sēnlín yěhuǒ	forest fire
灾害	n.	zāihài	disaster
倍	m.w.	bèi	times (multiplier)
警告	n.	jǐnggào	warning
俄罗斯	p.n.	Éluósī	Russia
义务	n.	yìwù	duty
不堪设想	phr.	bùkān shèxiǎng	too ghastly to contemplate
唯一	adj.	wéiyī	only

语言实践
LANGUAGE CONNECTION

1. **Pressing for an exact answer: 究竟……**

   Structure: 究竟 + question word

   "究竟什么是"全球变暖"？"

   究竟 means "exactly or actually." It is used by the speaker to intensify the question, so as to get to the bottom of a problem or issue.

   EXAMPLES:
   1. 我们想知道究竟是什么导致了全球变暖。
   2. 马上就要比赛了，他们究竟会什么时候到？
   3. 明天我们究竟要不要去打篮球呢？

   Complete the following dialogs with 究竟.

   1. A：小李，你在哪儿？我都等你等了一个小时了！
      B：哎呀，不好意思，我刚刚才起床。
      A：……？
      B：对不起！我差不多半小时以后到！

   2. A：请问你找谁？
      B：我想找张老师。张老师说明天要春游，但是我听说明天会下雨。……？
      A：好的，我帮你问问吧！

   3. A：今天我们要一起研究丝绸之路！
      B：……？
      A：问得好！我们要研究丝绸之路是怎么发展起来的。

2. **Useful verb:** 达成……

> **Structure:** 达成 + object

"这是世界各国为了解决气候变化问题而达成的第一个国际协议。"

达成 means "reach." As a transitive verb, it is often used with objects such as 协议, 共识, and 目标. 达成 should be used in formal speech or writing.

EXAMPLES:
1. 现在，各国对于如何保护环境和野生动物这个问题达成了协议。
2. 昨天，中国和美国政府对于共同建设新的科技基地的问题达成了共识。
3. 为了达成赢得全国冠军的目标，这个篮球队正在加紧练习。

Write to-do lists for three of your goals.

EXAMPLE: 为了达成学好数学的目标，我一定要

- 每天做50道数学题
- 每个星期去找数学老师问问题
- 每天上课都认真做笔记
- 每天花一个小时做数学作业

Pattern: 为了达成……的目标，我一定要……

China Highlights: South China (2)

Hong Kong: Victoria Harbor

Macau: Ruins of St. Paul's

3. Expressing a consequence: 不然 / 要不然……

Structure: condition, (要) 不然 + Result

"人类必须把气温的变化控制在摄氏两度之内，不然"末日的时钟就要敲响了"。"

The conjunction 不然 / 要不然 means "if not, or else, otherwise." It is used in the second clause to indicate a consequence, usually negative, if the condition in the first clause is not fulfilled.

1. 你今天一定要好好复习，不然明天考试你又要不及格了。
2. 请你帮我叫个车，要不然我就赶不上我的班机了！
3. 我们一定要时时注意科技的发展，要不然我们就会被淘汰了。

Write a suggestion or warning based on the information in each of the following pictures.

EXAMPLE:

请不要再吸烟了，要不然你的肺会受不了的！

❶

❷

❸

❹

❺

第三部分 可再生能源
PART 3 DEVELOPING SOURCES OF RENEWABLE ENERGY

李静在中国生活了一段时间了，她最近写了一篇博客，跟美国的同学分享了她在中国的一些体验。

　　我去年准备来中国的时候，家人一方面为我高兴，因为我有那么难得的机会到中国学习中文，可是另一方面又担心北京严重的雾霾会影响我的健康。幸好到了北京以后，迎接我的是一连好几天的蓝天白云，我拍了很多照片给爸妈看，他们才放下心来。其实北京的雾霾并没有想象中的那么严重。北京的朋友告诉我近几年治理雾霾取得了一些成绩。空气PM2.5浓度明显下降。冬天取暖用的煤炭、工业污染和汽车废气是造成雾霾的三大原因。政府鼓励人民用天然气和电力来取代煤炭，同时也正在积极地把大工厂搬离京城，而且严格地控制汽车的数量。

难得	adj.	nándé	rare, hard to come by
幸好	adv.	xìnghǎo	fortunately
治理	v.	zhìlǐ	control
浓度	n.	nóngdù	concentration
明显	adj.	míngxiǎn	obvious
取暖	v.	qǔnuǎn	warm oneself
煤炭	n.	méitàn	coal

在过去的100多年里，能源发生了不少的变革，从20世纪初期人们主要使用煤炭，到了六七十年代变成石油。不过，煤炭、石油这样的化石燃料现在仍然占主导地位。这种传统的能源因为经过燃烧所以有排放物，这样就造成了空气的污染。全球变暖、空气污染都跟化石燃料有关系，所以现在大家都在找清洁的能源。清洁能源也被称为绿色能源，或者可再生能源，也就是说，它们在被开发和利用的过程里不产生或者产生较少的污染物。清洁能源包括太阳能、水力发电、风力发电和潮汐能等。

化石燃料	phr.	huàshí ránliào	fossil fuel
主导	v.	zhǔdǎo	leading
燃烧	v.	ránshāo	burn
排放物	n.	páifàngwù	emission
可再生	adj.	kězàishēng	renewable
开发	v.	kāifā	exploit
产生	v.	chǎnshēng	produce
包括	v.	bāokuò	include
太阳能	n.	tàiyángnéng	solar energy
水力发电	phr.	shuǐlì fādiàn	hydroelectricity
风力发电	phr.	fēnglì fādiàn	wind power generation
潮汐能	n.	cháoxīnéng	tidal energy

我接待家庭的妹妹在北京念高中，他们学校在2014年开始了"阳光校园"工程，那是世界银行与北京市合作的创建绿色城市的其中一个项目。在几百所学校的楼顶都安装了太阳能光伏发电装置，供应空调、取暖和教室照明的电力，这样不但大量减少了电费的开支，而且让学生认识到发展清洁能源和减少碳足迹的重要性，希望他们在以后的生活中能够积极倡导使用清洁能源。

工程	n.	gōngchéng	project
世界银行	p.n.	Shìjiè Yínháng	World Bank (an international financial institution)
楼顶	n.	lóudǐng	the roof of a building
光伏发电装置	phr.	guāngfú fādiàn zhuāngzhì	photovoltaic system, solar power system
供应	v.	gōngyìng	supply
照明	n.	zhàomíng	lighting
开支	n.	kāizhī	expenses
倡导	v.	chàngdǎo	advocate

上个星期我的接待家庭请了张叔叔一家来吃饭。张叔叔是中国宜家家居的高管。他说宜家家居最近加入了"RE100"(RE: Renewable Energy)项目。"RE100"是气候组织 The Climate Group 发起的跨国合作项目，号召全球最具影响力的企业，承诺百分百利用可再生能源。其中不乏知名的公司，比如苹果、谷歌、微软、沃尔玛、星巴克等。他说宜家的目标是在2020年，在全球投资数百座风力发电机，在店面与仓库全面使用太阳能板，生产清洁能源。同时他说在北欧地区的自产量甚至比需求还多。

　　我们饭后谈到世界什么时候才能达到碳排放量负增长。他们表示恐怕道路还很长。中国和美国都是温室气体的排放大国，中国计划2030年二氧化碳排放达到峰值，并且希望能尽量提早实现这个目标。王阿姨说除了"RE100"，还有"EV100"(EV: Electric Vehicles) 计划，这是企业实现百分百汽车电动化的誓约。看来这些大企业已经开始合作推动清洁能源的发展。我觉得这些都是令人鼓舞的消息。实现碳排放负增长，真是指日可待呢。

宜家	p.n.	Yíjiā	IKEA
高管	n.	gāoguǎn	executive
发起	v.	fāqǐ	initiate
跨国	adj.	kuàguó	transnational
号召	v.	hàozhào	call, appeal
承诺	v.	chéngnuò	promise
不乏	v.	bùfá	there is no lack of
微软	p.n.	Wēiruǎn	Microsoft
沃尔玛	p.n.	Wò'ěrmǎ	Walmart
星巴克	p.n.	Xīngbākè	Starbucks
店面	n.	diànmiàn	shop front
仓库	n.	cāngkù	warehouse
太阳能板	phr.	tàiyángnéng bǎn	solar panel
北欧	p.n.	Běi Ōu	Northern Europe
自产量	phr.	zìchǎnliàng	volume of self-production
峰值	n.	fēngzhí	peak value
尽量	adv.	jǐnliàng	to the greatest extent
提早	v.	tízǎo	be sooner than planned
誓约	n.	shìyuē	pledge, promise
鼓舞	adj.	gǔwǔ	encouraging
指日可待	phr.	zhǐrì kědài	just around the corner

语言实践
LANGUAGE CONNECTION

1. **Expressing an actual situation: 其实……**

   "<u>其实</u>北京的雾霾并没有想象中的那么严重。"

   其实 means "actually" or "in fact," and is used in a similar way to its English equivalents. 其实 can also be used with 并不 / 并没有 to express negation, which takes this structure: 其实 + subject + 并不 / 并没有 + sentence.

   EXAMPLES:
   1. 你们以为她只会说中文，<u>其实</u>她的日语也说得很好。
   2. 别看老师常批评你，<u>其实</u>老师是很关心你的。
   3. 我妈妈希望我可以在大学学习数学，<u>其实</u>我并不喜欢数学。

 Complete the following dialogs using 其实.

EXAMPLE:

A: 我听说中国人的主食只有米饭，对吗？

B: <u>其实</u>北方的中国人也把面食当作主食。

A: 我下个星期要去北京了，我担心在北京只能吃中餐，我会很想念家乡的食物。

B: ……

A: 你的中文说得真好！我听说中文很难学，你一定很聪明！

B: ……

A: 我今年夏天要去美国康州做交换生，但是我听说美国的小城市生活很无聊。

B: ……

2. **Useful verb: 不乏……**

> Structure: category/group/context + 不乏 + something

"其中不乏知名的公司，比如苹果、谷歌、微软、沃尔玛、星巴克等。"

不乏 means "no lack of." It is often used to emphasize that something exists in certain amounts.

EXAMPLES:
1. 我们班数学考试考得很好，其中不乏拿满分的同学。
2. 在美国，尤其在加州，不乏追求绿色投资的新公司。
3. 现在越来越多年轻人在买房的时候会选择使用清洁能源的房子，我身边不乏这样的例子。

 Look at the following pictures and complete the sentences using 不乏.

EXAMPLE:

最近几年，在中国出现了很多有名的电商，其中不乏阿里巴巴这样全球知名的大公司。

1. 为了保护环境，许多汽车公司都推出了电动汽车，……。

2. 中国有许多手机公司，……。

3. 现在有很多提供住宿的网站，……。

文化剪影
CULTURE ENRICHMENT

世界各地环保的不同方法
Eco-Friendly Practices Around the World

每年的4月22日是世界地球日(Earth Day)，这是特别为保护世界环境而订立的节日。现在庆祝活动已经拓展到接近200个国家，有10亿人参与。世界地球日每年都有不同的主题，如空气污染、避免沙漠化❶、拯救❷海洋、珍惜资源、倡导绿色简约生活等。让我们来看看世界各地是如何保护环境的。

伦敦：用100%绿色能源为城市供电

从2018年10月开始，伦敦的金融城将通过在建筑物上安装太阳能板、投资大型太阳能和风力发电电厂以及购买绿电，实现100%可再生能源供电。这个计划将让伦敦市民用上绿色能源。

负责制定这个计划的是伦敦金融城政策与资源委员会，其主席孟珂琳表示，通过生产自己的电力和投资可再生能源，他们正在努力帮助英国达到节能减排的目标。

荷兰❸：漂浮❹城市成为新家园

"漂浮城市"是荷兰建筑师Koen Olthuis和他的工作室提出的一个构想❺。他们认为，人类应该停止和海洋斗争❻，相反地，应该与海洋共存❼，为人类争取更多的居住空间。因此，工作室现在正在荷兰设计"漂浮屋"，这些房子的下面是特别的材料，可以让房子漂浮在水上；同时，漂浮屋

也利用支柱，把房子固定❽在水边。漂浮屋和一般的房子一样，可以在里面进行装修，而且漂浮屋会随着水位升降，比一般的房屋更安全。

印度：不再使用一次性塑料用品

印度是现在经济发展最快的国家之一，但是随着经济发展，印度也必须面对一系列❾的环境问题，其中塑料滥用❿就是一个严重的问题。在2018年的世界环境日(World Environment Day)，印度总理莫迪宣布：印度将在2022年全面禁止⓫使用一次性的塑料用品，同时印度还将打造100个无垃圾的国家名胜古迹。

莫迪表示每个人都有责任⓬，在追求发展的同时不给我们的环境带来灾难，我们应该共同努力战胜塑料污染，让这个地球成为更好的居所。

❶ 沙漠化 shāmòhuà desertification
❷ 拯救 zhěngjiù save
❸ 荷兰 Hélán Netherlands
❹ 漂浮 piāofú floating
❺ 构想 gòuxiǎng idea, concept
❻ 斗争 dòuzhēng battle
❼ 共存 gòngcún co-exist
❽ 固定 gùdìng fix
❾ 一系列 yíxìliè a series of
❿ 滥用 lànyòng abuse
⓫ 禁止 jìnzhǐ forbid
⓬ 责任 zérèn responsibility

Interpretive/Interpersonal

1) In groups, research online to complete the following activity.

为了响应地球日，你的学校正在举办制作宣传海报的比赛。学校将选出最好的五个作品，放在学校礼堂展示。你想展示什么？你可以参考以下内容：

1. 你认为地球日的意义是什么？
2. 地球日应该讨论哪些课题？为什么？
3. 这些课题应该如何宣传？

Presentational

2) Compile your research into a poster. You may also prepare a presentation of 10-15 slides on your research.

3) In pairs, complete the following activity.

认识了这些环境政策和措施以后，你有没有得到新的启发？你认为自己作为年轻人，能为保护环境作出什么贡献？把你的想法写成一份"保护环境誓言（pledge）"。

词汇拓展
VOCABULARY BUILDING

1. **Words Associated with Environmental Protection Measures**

   There are many words associated with environmental protection, which has become a hot topic in the whole world. Can you guess the meaning of each term or phrase below?

节能减排	植树造林	倡导绿色出行	倡导低碳生活
发展环境友好型社会	保护自然资源	保持生态平衡	提高环保意识

   1) Use an online dictionary to find out the *pinyin* and meaning of these terms and phrases. Find out a few examples of what each term or phrase refers to.
   2) Search online to find out what 低碳生活 refers to. List a few examples.
   3) Write an e-mail to a professor in the field of environmental studies. Choose two of the environmental protection measures above and ask the professor to recommend some relevant reading materials to you.

2. **Special Days for Environmental Protection**

   There are some special days observed annually worldwide to remind people of the importance of environmental protection. Search online for the dates of these special days below and give a brief introduction to each day. Think about what you can do on these days to make them meaningful.

世界一小时	国际生物多样性日	世界海洋日	世界水日

3. **Words Associated with Natural Disasters**

   The character 灾 means "disaster." Different characters may be placed before it to form words that refer to different types of disasters. Some examples are 火灾, 水灾 and 旱灾.

   Search online for other words related to disasters.

4. **Words Related to Disaster Relief**

   What should the government and society do after a natural disaster to alleviate the harm and suffering it has brought about? These are some words related to disaster relief:

   - 救灾 (provide disaster relief)
   - 赈灾 (emergency relief supplies)
   - 灾民 (victims of a disaster)
   - 灾情 (condition of a disaster)

   Search online for a news article on a natural disaster. Describe how you would provide relief for the people affected by it using the words above.

阅读理解
READING COMPREHENSION

Follow this link https://www.youtube.com/watch?v=W2tGE1w-8ds to watch the video 来自 2070 年的一封信. Then read the passage and answer the questions that follow.

《来自2070年的一封信》观后感
Reflections on a YouTube Video

这个短视频扩大了我的眼界，对我有很深刻的影响。视频的作者用一些很严峻的现象描写了我们地球在2070年的景象。比如，作者说，在2070年，他50岁，但看起来像85岁的老人。他是世界上最老的人之一，因为那时地球上的平均寿命只有35岁。不仅如此，作者也强调那时世界上的水资源非常有限，一个人平均一天只能喝半杯水；甚至因为水资源很有限，水就变成了工人的薪水；女孩都理光头，因为没有水洗头发。地球的臭氧层❶也几乎完全不见了。

2070年，人类的生活都完全改变了，因为生态的节奏都乱了。我觉得令我感到非常害怕的是当作者的孩子问："爸爸，我们为什么没有水呢？"人们总是觉得有水喝、有水用是<u>天经地义</u>的事情。由于有这种想法，我们常常浪费水。如果我们继续这样做，未来的孩子都不能在外面游泳，也看不到五颜六色的花朵，更看不到茂盛的森林。这些设想都会成为现实：如果现在的我们不保护环境，未来的孩子必将付出极大的代价。他们会失去真正的童年，不能健康地成长。

❶ 臭氧层 chòuyǎngcéng ozone layer

我觉得视频的作者想告诉我们：我们还有时间找到解决办法。他希望这些关于2070年的想象能启发我们，<u>让我们行动起来，不再沉默</u>。虽然我们常常听到"全球变暖"这四个字，但大多数人对于全球变暖对人类和动物的影响都知道得太少了。我觉得作者要让我们了解，如果我们继续浪费水，继续过着高碳生活，这个视频所描述的未来世界将变成真实的。

冯丽佳 Erica Vandenbulcke（美国高中十年级的学生，小学六年级开始学中文，这是她AP®中文班上的作业）

1. 从下面的词语中找出可以代替"天经地义"的词。

   Ⓐ 非常正确　　Ⓑ 非常有用　　Ⓒ 非常自然　　Ⓓ 非常危险

2. 想象一下：如果"地球的臭氧层也完全不见了"，我们的生活会发生什么变化？

3. 你认为"让我们行动起来，不再沉默"（第三段）这句话是什么意思？如果你有机会，你会怎么解决文章里提到的环境问题？

写作工坊
WRITING WORKSHOP

写创意短文——宣传有机农场
Writing Creative Text – Promoting an Organic Farm

In this section, you will practice writing promotional text for a website.

Imagine that you have been tasked with writing for the website of an organic farm. You need to use the text to encourage people to switch to a healthier lifestyle by eating less meat and more fruit and vegetables. The text should also promote choosing local produce over those from overseas, with the purpose of reducing one's carbon footprint.

Follow these three suggested steps in completing the task. Your text should be at least 400 words in length.

1. **Understanding the background of the farm**

   Read the following introduction of the farm.

北京的郊区有不少的绿色生态有机农场。他们不用转基因❶的产物，也不采用化学合成的农药、化肥❷、生长调节剂❸及饲料。农场周围的水源和空气都必须无污染，这样才能让蔬菜及水果自然地生长。李静和宋杰周末参观了一个在房山的有机农场，农场的主人是一名素食者，他认为每个人都应该选择可持续的食物并支持有机农业。他说，这样不但能让大家身体更健康，而且可以减少碳足迹，创造可持续的绿色未来。

❶ 转基因 zhuǎnjīyīn genetically modified
❷ 化肥 huàféi chemical fertilizer
❸ 生长调节剂 shēngzhǎng tiáojiéjì growth regulator

Unit 7 The Earth and Us · 地球与我

2. **Understanding the big ideas**

Look at the following poster to understand the reasons why the farm encourages people to eat less meat and more fruit and vegetables.

3. **Structuring your text**

As you are writing for a website, you should categorize your text to aid in readers' understanding. To help you decide what you should use as your categories, think about what you would like to know about a company that sells products you want to buy. Create a short header for each category. You may use the following example as a guide.

- 我们的理念：创建有机农场的目的是什么？我们通过什么方式达到这个目的？
- 我们的选择：我们的饮食习惯对环境有什么影响？我们应该如何减轻这些影响？
- 我们的产品：有机农场生产些什么？
- 近期活动：我们会举办什么活动来推广绿色低碳生活方式？

学习总结
I CAN DO!

Interpretive Communication

- [ ] I can read about endangered wild animals in China and the polar bear, as well as some causes of their predicament and current protection measures to prevent them from going extinct.
- [ ] I can read and understand basic information on global warming, as well as a brief history of the United Nations' climate change conferences and the international collaboration in combating global warming.
- [ ] I can read about and understand the effort and commitment from several big multinational companies in using 100% renewable energy resources.

Interpersonal Communication

- [ ] I can talk about the work of the scientists at the Chengdu Panda Base in creating a natural environment for pandas to breed and live, so as to increase the number of pandas in the world.
- [ ] I can discuss the extreme weather and climate conditions, as well as the economic and environmental losses that global warming has caused.
- [ ] I can converse about the commitment from some big companies to reducing carbon dioxide emission.

Presentational Communication

- [ ] I can describe the measures that have been taken in China and other countries to protect endangered wild animals.
- [ ] I can make a poster for Earth Day, detailing how to lead a greener life to protect the Earth, the only home for all of us.
- [ ] I can make a brief presentation on the benefits of replacing traditional energy resources with renewable energy resources such as solar energy, hydraulic power, wind-generated power, and tidal energy.
- [ ] I can create promotional text for the website of an organic farm to support its operation and promote a healthier lifestyle, which will reduce our carbon footprint and create a sustainable green future.

Cultural Knowledge

- [ ] I can name and talk about several endangered wild animals in China and briefly discuss their present predicament.
- [ ] I can describe briefly the content of Taiwanese environmental protection documentary ±2C and discuss its significance in raising awareness about global warming.
- [ ] I can talk about the Sunshine Campus Project, a collaborative project between Beijing and the World Bank, under which solar panels are installed on the rooftop of schools to generate power and the use of solar energy in society is promoted.

第八单元 UNIT 8
科技与生活
TECHNOLOGY IN OUR LIVES

学习目标
LEARNING OBJECTIVES

- Learn about the impact of technology on life in China
- Read about how fast food companies embrace technology to enhance the dining experience of their customers
- Understand the functions of face recognition technology
- Describe how life would be like in the next five years based on current and projected developments in artificial intelligence

单元总览
CONTENTS AT A GLANCE!

导入 WARM UP

- **Part 1: 无现金社会** (Cashless Society in China)
  Language Connection:
  1. 出租车为了<u>迎合</u>中国游客的<u>需要</u>，都可以使用支付宝了。
  2. 移动支付最大的好处就是能<u>在</u>顾客<u>和</u>商家<u>之间</u>搭建起桥梁。

- **Part 2: 人工智能** (Artificial Intelligence and Its Role in Society)
  Language Connection:
  1. 每年春运铁路、公路、航空等客流量<u>高达</u>30亿人次。
  2. 机器人<u>就算</u>24小时不间断地工作，<u>也</u>不会觉得累。

- **Part 3: 互联网重塑现代生活** (How the Internet Has Changed Our Lives)
  Language Connection:
  1. <u>可不是吗</u>？我不敢想象没有网络的生活。
  2. 以前<u>一旦</u>外国有了新事物，中国<u>就</u>出现模仿它们的东西。

文化剪影：快餐智能化：科技给我们带来新的体验
CULTURE ENRICHMENT: The Use of High Technology in the Fast Food Industry in China

词汇拓展：与"网"有关的词语；与"智能"有关的词语；智能管家
VOCABULARY BUILDING: Words Associated with 网; Words Associated with 智能; Smart Home Products

阅读理解：面部识别
READING COMPREHENSION: Face Recognition

写作工坊：写文章——未来的智能化生活
WRITING WORKSHOP: Writing an Essay – Toward a Smart Life in the Future

学习总结 I CAN DO!

导入
WARM UP

The era of artificial intelligence (AI) has descended upon us. Which traditional jobs are likely to be affected by AI? Are there jobs where human beings are being replaced by robots? Which jobs are unlikely to see such a drastic change?

1. Work in small groups to share ideas and respond to the following questions.

   a) 图里的人在什么地方工作？为什么他们的工作容易被取代？
   b) 有哪些工作在未来几年里还不太可能被人工智能取代？为什么？
   c) 在未来，许多职业可能会被人工智能取代，这会对你选择大学的专业带来什么影响？

收银员

保安人员

翻译员

驾驶员

2. Interview your English teacher for his/her opinion on the following situation and report to the class in Chinese.

2017年，一家工作室通过人工智能来重新写了一部分的《哈利·波特》，连原作者罗琳（J. K. Rowling）都对它表示了很大的兴趣。大家都很好奇如何通过人工智能写作，写出来的作品又有怎样的水平。

第一部分 无现金社会
PART 1 CASHLESS SOCIETY IN CHINA

海文：你们来中国已经好几个月了，觉得中国和美国在生活上有什么不一样？

李静：我觉得最大的**差别**就是**移动支付**了。在中国我简直不用带钱包。

| 差别 | n. | chābié | difference |
| 移动支付 | phr. | yídòng zhīfù | mobile payment |

宋杰：我也觉得在中国太方便了！我来中国学习以前看过一个新闻报道，一个CNN的记者在中国生活，24小时之内没有用**现金**。我当时觉得不可思议，可是我去年来北京学习中文，刚到的第二个星期，我们项目的**岳**老师就设计了几个活动，让我们体验**无现金**社会。

现金	n.	xiànjīn	cash
岳	n.	Yuè	Yue (Chinese surname)
无现金	adj.	wú xiànjīn	cashless

李静：那你比我还先进，一年前就体验到了！

宋杰：那得**归功**于我们的老师。因为我们未满18岁，所以在中国不能有银行**账户**，岳老师就用微信的红包把学校给我们的餐费、交通费等打到我们的微信上。这样我们就可以在北京吃饭和坐地铁了。

| 归功 | v. | guīgōng | give the credit to |
| 账户 | n. | zhànghù | account |

李静：是呀！我们每天上班以前都在家附近买早点，用手机扫一下二维码就可以结账了。我下载了易通行，到了地铁站把二维码对着验票口，地铁门就会打开。从五道口到东直门只要五元。如果要打车就在"滴滴出行"应用上输入目的地，专车不到五分钟就到。到达目的地以后就会自动结算。

海文：我们最常见的两种移动支付方法就是支付宝和微信支付。一般来说，你只需要跟这两家绑定你的银行账户，就可以使用了。

结帐	v.	jiézhàng	pay the bill
易通行	p.n.	Yìtōngxíng	Yitongxing (an app for payment)
验票口	n.	yàn piào kǒu	fare gate, ticket barrier
五道口	p.n.	Wǔdàokǒu	Wudaokou (a neighborhood in Beijing)
东直门	p.n.	Dōngzhímén	Dongzhimen (a subway station in Beijing, China)
自动	adj.	zìdòng	automatic
结算	v.	jiésuàn	settle a bill
支付宝	p.n.	Zhīfù Bǎo	Alipay (a mobile and online payment platform)
微信支付	p.n.	Wēixìn Zhīfù	WeChat Pay (a mobile payment platform)
绑定	v.	bǎngdìng	link

宋杰：我四处都能看见支付宝，朋友告诉我，现在大部分纽约的出租车为了迎合中国游客的需要，都可以使用支付宝了。

海文：除了你们刚才提到的便捷以外，移动支付最大的好处就是能在顾客和商家之间搭建起桥梁，把你所有的消费资料给商家，为他们提供了更多赚钱的机会。

顾客	n.	gùkè	customer
搭建	v.	dājiàn	build
赚钱	v.o.	zhuànqián	make money

李静：能说得具体一点吗？

海文：比方说我姐姐去练瑜伽，就可以先在线上预约教练，然后去健身房练习，最后在网上付钱。这样健身房就有了她的资料，了解她的健身习惯。商家掌握了你的资料，了解你的消费习惯，就能更好地提供服务。你想想中国人口那么多，如果大家都是用移动支付，这些大数据是非常有价值的。

| 教练 | n. | jiàoliàn | instructor, coach |

| 大数据 | n. | dà shùjù | big data |

宋杰：移动支付也比较安全，大家都不带现金出门。我前几天看新闻说，劫匪去杭州三家便利店抢劫才得到1800多元的现金。

海文：如果我们真的进入无现金社会，应该能避免偷窃和抢劫。如果每次交易都留下痕迹，这样贪污就不那么容易了。由此可见，移动支付的确能防止一些犯罪行为。也不用浪费钱来印钞票了。

劫匪	n.	jiéfěi	robber
抢劫	v.	qiǎngjié	rob
偷窃	v.	tōuqiè	steal
交易	n.	jiāoyì	transaction
痕迹	n.	hénjì	trace, mark
贪污	v.	tānwū	embezzle
防止	v.	fángzhǐ	prevent
犯罪	v.	fànzuì	commit a crime
印	v.	yìn	print
钞票	n.	chāopiào	bank note

李静：我也觉得一部手机能解决很多事，以后真的不必带钱包了！

海文：当然凡事都有利有弊，为了便捷，我们就得牺牲个人的隐私，因为所有的消费活动都会被记录下来。不过只要商家和政府负责任地使用数据，立法控制与保护数据，我相信推行无现金的生活将会是利大于弊的。

凡事	n.	fánshì	everything
利	n.	lì	advantage
弊	n.	bì	disadvantage
牺牲	v.	xīshēng	sacrifice
隐私	n.	yǐnsī	privacy
负责任	v.o.	fù zérèn	take responsibility
立法	v.	lìfǎ	make laws, legislate
保护	v.	bǎohù	protect
推行	v.	tuīxíng	promote, advocate

语言实践
LANGUAGE CONNECTION

1. **Catering to certain needs:** 迎合……需求／需要／口味

   Structure: 迎合 + X + 的需求/需要/口味

   "出租车为了迎合中国游客的需要，都可以使用支付宝了。"

   This structure has a connotation of intentionally adapting one's speech or action so as to suit the desires, demands, needs, or tastes of others.

   EXAMPLES:
   1. 全新设计的购物中心为了迎合年轻家庭的需求，提供一站式购物和娱乐。
   2. 如今电视节目五花八门，迎合了不同性别、不同年龄的观众的需要。
   3. 肯德基迎合中国人的口味，推出了中式早餐、老北京鸡肉卷等，在中国市场大获成功。

   Imagine that the student population of your school is becoming increasingly diverse. Think of three different needs of the students and the changes that the school can make to accommodate these needs. Write them down by completing the following sentences that use 迎合.

   1. 学校为了迎合学生不同的饮食习惯，……。
   2. 学校为了迎合……。
   3. 学校为了迎合……。

China Highlights: Southwest China

Chongqing: Wulong Karst

Sichuan: Jiuzhaigou Valley

Yunnan: Black Dragon Pool, Lijiang

2. **Establishing a connection between two items:**
   在……和…… / 他们之间搭建起桥梁 / 联系 / 平台

   Structure: 在 A 和 B 之间搭建起桥梁/联系/平台

   "移动支付最大的好处就是能在顾客和商家之间搭建起桥梁。"

   搭建 means to build a temporary shelter or structure. It can be figuratively used to refer to the setting up of an organization, a connection, a system, or a platform.

   EXAMPLES:
   1. 中国学生和美国学生在夏令营中一起学习和生活，他们之间搭建起友谊的桥梁。
   2. 我们的校园网络在学校和社区之间搭建起有效的平台。
   3. 校长鼓励学生努力学习，将来在美国与其他国家之间搭建起沟通的桥梁，促进文化的交流。

   Complete the following sentences using 在 A 和 B 之间搭建起桥梁 / 联系 / 平台.

   1. 社交软件（shèjiāo ruǎnjiàn networking app）……。
   2. 在中国的美国大使……。
   3. 社区活动中心……。
   4. 我们高中的学生会（xuéshēnghuì student council）……。

Guizhou: Terraced rice terraces

Tibet: The Potala Palace, Lhasa

PART 2 人工智能
ARTIFICIAL INTELLIGENCE AND ITS ROLE IN SOCIETY

第二部分

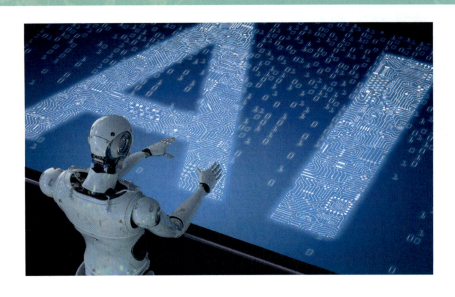

海文： 我来给你们介绍一下，这位是李先生，他是我爸爸的好朋友。在硅谷工作了一段时间，现在回国了，对人工智能非常有研究。

（大家打招呼）

宋杰： 我对人工智能非常感兴趣，特别是最近阿尔法围棋（AlphaGo）以3比0的成绩打败了世界冠军，让人工智能这个话题再度引起关注。

李静： 我寄宿家庭的妈妈是做科学研究的。她也常常谈到这个问题，究竟什么是"人工智能"呢？

李先生：人工智能简单来说就是人造的智慧。它通过海量的数据和强大的运算方法，让机器模仿人类的工作，优化我们的生活。

人工智能	phr.	réngōng zhìnéng	artificial intelligence
阿尔法围棋	p.n.	Ā'ěrfǎ Wéiqí	AlphaGo (a computer program that plays the board game Go)
冠军	n.	guànjūn	champion
话题	n.	huàtí	topic
再度	adv.	zàidù	once again
引起	v.	yǐnqǐ	give rise to
人造	adj.	rénzào	man-made, artificial
智慧	n.	zhìhuì	intelligence, wisdom
海量	adj.	hǎiliàng	massive
强大	adj.	qiángdà	powerful
运算	v.	yùnsuàn	carry out an (mathematical) operation
机器	n.	jīqì	machine
优化	v.	yōuhuà	optimize

宋杰： 请问什么是"海量的数据"？

李先生： 海量的数据又称为"大数据"，就是说数据多得像在一个数据的海洋里。大数据可以说是人工智能的催化剂，互联网和云计算是它的基础。

| 催化剂 | n. | cuīhuàjì | catalyst |
| 云计算 | n. | yún jìsuàn | cloud computing |

海文： 能解释一下什么是"云计算"吗？

李先生： 云是一个比喻，它就代表互联网，计算就是不同的运算方法。随着互联网、社交媒体和移动支付的急剧增长，管理和分析这些数据的方法——"云计算"也有很大的发展。

比喻	n.	bǐyù	metaphor
急剧	adj.	jíjù	rapid
增长	v.	zēngzhǎng	increase, grow
分析	v.	fēnxī	analyze

李静： 我最想知道的是，人工智能怎样影响到我们的生活呢？

李先生： 我举个简单的例子，春运的网上订票，用的就是云计算。每年春运铁路、公路、航空等客流量高达30亿人次，那就是快接近中国人口的两倍了。为了解决春节网络订票的问题，采用云计算的方法，一次交易只需要0.5秒，每天售票能力高达1500万张。除了中国以外，恐怕世界上没有别的国家有这样巨大的数据。所以中国庞大的人口、先进的互联网和海量的数据，都是发展人工智能的优势。

订票	v.o.	dìng piào	book tickets
公路	n.	gōnglù	highway
航空	n.	hángkōng	aviation
客流量	n.	kèliúliàng	volume of passenger traffic
亿	num.	yì	hundred million
人次	m.w.	réncì	person (referring to passenger traffic volume)
采用	v.	cǎiyòng	use, employ
巨大	adj.	jùdà	huge
庞大	adj.	pángdà	huge

宋杰： 我听说亚马逊的仓库也是使用机器人来操作的，一般的工人只能做8个小时，而且人的体力是有限的。机器人就算24小时不间断地工作，也不会觉得累。

亚马逊	p.n.	Yàmǎxùn	Amazon
体力	n.	tǐlì	physical strength
有限	adj.	yǒuxiàn	limited

李静： 最近美国的Domino's披萨也可以用语音下订单了。我想知道除了我们刚才所举的例子以外，人工智能还可以应用到哪些方面。

语音	n.	yǔyīn	voice (message)
订单	n.	dìngdān	(purchase) order
应用	v.	yìngyòng	apply
广泛	adj.	guǎngfàn	extensive
医疗	n.	yīliáo	medical treatment

李先生： 人工智能的应用是非常广泛的，可以在农业、医疗、金融、汽车制造等各方面使用。

宋杰： 我爸爸说目前谷歌有一个"深度学习"医疗研究项目，叫DeepMind Health。DeepMind Health研发了Streams软件，能帮助医生及时了解病人的病史和检查报告，更快更准确地优化对病人的医疗方案。

深度学习	phr.	shēndù xuéxí	deep learning
研发	v.	yánfà	develop
及时	adv.	jíshí	promptly, without delay
病史	n.	bìngshǐ	medical history
准确	adj.	zhǔnquè	accurate

海文： 人工智能也能帮助农业生产，自从城镇化开始，农村人口越来越少，可是对农业生产的需要却不断地增加，很需要人工智能推动农业的发展。

生产	n.	shēngchǎn	production

李静： 我担心人工智能发展得那么快，会不会有一天机器人取代了我们的工作？

海文： 我想收银员、保安、制造业工人，甚至律师、记者的工作，都会受到一定的影响。可是人工智能同时也能增加很多工作的机会。

| 保安 | n. | bǎo'ān | security guard |

李先生： 人工智能可以说是一个"工业革命"。它会打破目前的经济格局。也就是说，只要一个国家掌握了人工智能的技术，它就能在世界经济舞台上扮演重要的角色。

| 工业革命 | phr. | Gōngyè Gémìng | Industrial Revolution |
| 打破 | v. | dǎpò | break |

海文： 希望人工智能可以给我们带来更美好的生活。

宋杰： 我常常在想，有一天我们有无人驾驶的汽车，那多好呀！我开车到学校的时候就可以一路玩手机和看电影了。

| 驾驶 | v. | jiàshǐ | drive (a vehicle) |

李静： 我真期待这一天早点到。

李先生： 2017年是人工智能元年，有着很多划时代的变化。我想人工智能时代已经到来了，我们得准备好去迎接这个新的机遇。

| 元年 | n. | yuánnián | first year |

语言实践
LANGUAGE CONNECTION

1. **Expressing an amount:** ……高达 / 长达 / 多达……

   Structure: subject + 高达/长达/多达 + amount

   "每年春运铁路、公路、航空等客流量高达30亿人次。"

   Using 高达, 长达, or 多达 is a formal way to emphasize that the height, length, or number of a subject has reached a certain amount. It is often used to stress that something is especially tall, long, or numerous.

   EXAMPLES:
   1. 每年春运期间，离开北京的人多达848万！
   2. 高铁现在成为了人们最喜欢的出行工具之一，它高速快捷，时速可以高达350公里。
   3. 为了能进入篮球队，他非常努力地训练，每天练习的时间长达8个小时。

    In pairs, use the Guinness World Records website to find out the answers to the following statements. Then complete each sentence using 高达, 长达 or 多达.

   1. 中国最高的大楼是……，……米。
   2. 亚洲最高的大楼是……，……米。
   3. 美国最高的山是……，……米。
   4. 中国最长的河流是……，……公里。
   5. 美洲最长的河流是……，……公里。
   6. 世界上最长的铁路是……，……公里。
   7. ……是中国人口最多的城市，人口……。
   8. ……是推特上粉丝最多的人，粉丝……。
   9. ……是美国学生人数最多的大学，人数……。
   10. ……是中国用户最多的网站，用户……。

2. **Emphasizing that something will still be true even if another thing happens: 就算……也……**

> Structure: 就算 + hypothetical statement or subject + 也

"机器人<u>就算</u>24小时不间断地工作，<u>也</u>不会觉得累。"

就算 is an informal way of saying "even if," and is used to introduce a hypothetical statement. However, unlike 即使, 哪怕, and 就是, 就算 expresses more of the speaker's feeling that he/she does not believe that the hypothetical statement is reasonable or has much chance of being realized.

EXAMPLES:

1. <u>就算</u>会失败，我<u>也</u>不会后悔！
2. <u>就算</u>你成绩好，你<u>也</u>不一定会被名牌大学录取。

 Write letters of encouragement to your friends based on the following scenarios using 就算……也…….

EXAMPLE:
亲爱的小李：
　　我知道现在你正在申请实习，这份工作竞争非常激烈。我觉得你非常优秀，我相信你一定可以成功。<u>就算</u>你没有获得这个工作，我<u>也</u>觉得你是最棒的！
小张

SCENARIOS:

1. 写给正在准备考大学的朋友
2. 写给正在准备体育比赛的朋友
3. 写给正在申请工作的朋友

第三部分 互联网重塑现代生活
PART 3 HOW THE INTERNET HAS CHANGED OUR LIVES

宋杰：前两天在我们的办公楼，网络出现了一点问题，工作全面停顿，可想而知，我们多么依赖网络。

海文：可不是吗？我不敢想象没有网络的生活。互联网是1994年进入中国的，在这短短20多年间带来了革新性的影响：从收发邮件、阅读新闻、搜索资料到交友聊天、网络游戏、网上购物等等，都是通过互联网。它不但渗透到我们生活每一个层面，而且改变了我们的经济模式和对政治的参与方式。

网络	n.	wǎngluò	network
全面	adj.	quánmiàn	entire, total
停顿	v.	tíngdùn	halt
可想而知	phr.	kě xiǎng ér zhī	it is obvious that
想象	v.	xiǎngxiàng	imagine
革新性	adj.	géxīnxìng	innovative
邮件	n.	yóujiàn	mail
阅读	v.	yuèdú	read
渗透	v.	shèntòu	pervade
层面	n.	céngmiàn	level

李静：互联网的发展实在是太快了。我美国高中的朋友告诉我《纽约时报》最近报道了中国最大的社交平台——微信，称它为一个"超级"的应用程序。外国人感到很惊讶，因为微信可以用文字、语音、图片和视频来沟通。它的功能比脸书还要多。

超级	adj.	chāojí	super
应用程序	n.	yìngyòng chéngxù	application
文字	n.	wénzì	writing
图片	n.	túpiàn	image

海文：是的，以前一旦外国有了新事物，中国就出现模仿它们的东西，比方说谷歌对百度，推特对新浪微博，YouTube对优酷，都是很好的例子。现在中国已经超越了模仿外国的时代，中国创造的东西更符合中国人的需要。比方说用汉字发信息比较花时间，微信就有利用语音信息来取代文字，现在已经变成一种非常普遍的沟通方式。

一旦	conj.	yídàn	once
优酷	p.n.	Yōukù	Youku (a video hosting service based in Beijing, China)
创造	v.	chuàngzào	create
符合	v.	fúhé	fit
汉字	n.	hànzì	Chinese characters

宋杰：微信很多功能是脸书没有的。比方说在网上挂号、预约看病，上周我寄宿家庭的弟弟发烧了，李阿姨就马上替他预约。看完病后就可以直接在微信上支付药费和检查费。以前没有微信的时候要一次又一次地排队呢！现在有微信节省了不少时间。

挂号	v.	guàhào	register
替	prep.	tì	on behalf of

排队	v.	páiduì	queue, line up

李静：互联网的高效与便捷正迎合我们时代的快速步伐，而且能把我们联系在一起。随着中国城镇化，很多人跟我们留学生一样，从小镇来到了一个陌生的大城市，怎么样跟家人沟通，怎么样认识新朋友，都成了迫切的问题。微信朋友圈的功能就应运而生了。据微信的统计，他们的用户已经超过了10亿人！

高效	adj.	gāoxiào	efficient
步伐	n.	bùfá	pace
迫切	adj.	pòqiè	urgent
应运而生	phr.	yìngyùn ér shēng	emerge as the times demand
统计	n.	tǒngjì	statistics

海文：沟通是很重要的。以前我们看电视，只是安静地坐着，等候电视媒体给我们传送消息，可是现在我们可以摇摇手机给我们喜欢的演员投票，甚至决定歌手下一次音乐会的演出节目。这样观众已经跟电视互动交流了。互联网可以说是颠覆了"沟通"这个词的定义了。

等候	v.	děnghòu	wait
投票	v.	tóupiào	cast a vote
颠覆	v.	diānfù	overturn, subvert
定义	n.	dìngyì	definition

李静：你们刚才谈到互联网最重要的一个功能是"沟通"。我觉得正是因为这种沟通的功能，让世界变得越来越小。我们现在随时随地可以跟不同国家、不同种族、不同宗教和文化背景的人在网上沟通，从资讯到思想上进行交流，所以互联网是开放的也是有包容性的。比方

种族	n.	zhǒngzú	race
文化背景	phr.	wénhuà bèijǐng	cultural background
资讯	n.	zīxùn	information
包容性	n.	bāoróngxìng	tolerance

说最近"我也是"的标签，引起了大家对性骚扰的关注。这些都是通过网民的支持来改革社会上一些不平等、不合理的现象。

标签	n.	biāoqiān	hashtag
性骚扰	n.	xìngsāorǎo	sexual harassment
网民	n.	wǎngmín	web user, netizen
平等	adj.	píngděng	equal, fair
合理	adj.	hélǐ	reasonable

海文：你说得真好，互联网不但影响了我们的生活，改变了我们的商业模式，同时也促进了我们的政治参与。这是一股非常巨大的、前所未有的力量，在推动我们前进。

| 股 | m.w. | gǔ | a stream of |
| 前进 | v. | qiánjìn | go forward |

语言实践
LANGUAGE CONNECTION

1. **Expressing agreement: 可不是吗**

   "<u>可不是吗</u>？我不敢想象没有网络的生活。"

   可不是吗 means "Isn't it?" or "Isn't it true?" in English. It is a colloquial phrase used to express one's agreement with the words just spoken by someone else in a conversation. It is usually used to begin a response and is similar to the expressions "Tell me about it." and "That's very true."

   EXAMPLES:

   ❶ A: 今天的数学考试真难啊！
      B: <u>可不是吗</u>？我昨晚复习了三个小时，结果今天只完成了一半的题！

   ❷ A: 现在的移动支付太方便了。
      B: <u>可不是吗</u>？现在坐公交车都不用刷卡，直接刷手机就好了，我出门都不用带钱包。

   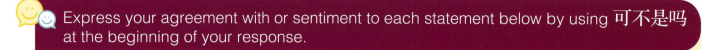
   Express your agreement with or sentiment to each statement below by using 可不是吗 at the beginning of your response.

   EXAMPLE:
   Statement: 今年的春天真的好冷啊！
   Response: 可不是吗？现在都五月了，我每天出门还要穿很厚的大衣！

   ❶ 今天路上真的太堵了！
   ❷ 今天的空气污染好严重啊！
   ❸ 现在用手机订外卖真的太方便了！
   ❹ 我觉得这几年智能手机的发展太快了！
   ❺ 现在坐高铁真是方便！

2. **Expressing a consequence when something happens: 一旦……就……**

Structure: 一旦 + condition + 就 + consequence

"以前一旦外国有了新事物，中国就出现模仿它们的东西。"

一旦 is used to express what would happen after a certain condition is met. It is usually used with 就. It expresses that once something happens, another thing will happen too. It is similar to the structure "once ..., then ...."

EXAMPLES:
1. 人工智能一旦发展起来，很多工作就会被取代。
2. 你一旦迷上了电脑游戏，成绩就会受到影响。

What are some important things you value in your life? Use 一旦……就…… to talk about the importance of the following aspects to you.

EXAMPLE:
一旦没有家人的关爱，我就会觉得生活没有意思。

1. 朋友的支持
2. 家人的关爱
3. 准备考试的时间
4. 珍惜用水

China Highlights: Northwest China (1)

Shaanxi: Ancient tower on the city wall of Xi'an

Gansu: Mogao Grottoes, Dunhuang

文化剪影
CULTURE ENRICHMENT

快餐智能化：科技给我们带来新的体验
The Use of High Technology in the Fast Food Industry in China

麦当劳是美国最受欢迎的快餐店之一，可以说是伴随着很多人长大的地方。很多人小时候不但喜欢在麦当劳吃开心乐园餐❶，还喜欢在店里的游乐场玩耍。麦当劳成了童年回忆的一部分。在中国，现代生活节奏紧张，快餐也成了人们喜爱的选择。在大城市里，麦当劳、肯德基、赛百味等快餐店应运而生。其中麦当劳的分店就多达2500家，到2022年底计划增加到4500家。

最近麦当劳推出"未来2.0"项目，利用高科技来提高服务水平并吸引顾客。这个项目包括触屏自助点餐机、送餐到桌和移动支付的服务。这样就方便多了。麦当劳的点餐页面甚至可以缩小到屏幕❷的右下角❸，这样家庭点餐的时候孩子也可以自己选择。点餐之后，顾客可以用手机上的移动支付来付钱，然后就可以坐下，等候服务员上菜了。麦当劳广告上写着"把陪伴留给孩子"。这样多好呀，父母不用排队，有更多时间在孩子身边享受一家人在一起的美好时光。

除了麦当劳以外，肯德基也在杭州的一间K Pro推出了面部支付。顾客只要在自动点餐机上选好餐，然后让点餐机扫描❹自己的脸，最后输入手机号就行了。这样一来，不用手机，只需要通过"刷脸"就可以付钱了，这是全球面脸支付的第一个试点，顾客都觉得又新奇又方便。

也许有一天，我们出门时不但不用带现金，就连手机也可以不带了。

❶ 开心乐园餐 Kāixīn Lèyuán Cān Happy Meal
❷ 屏幕 píngmù screen
❸ 右下角 yòuxiàjiǎo lower right corner
❹ 扫描 sǎomiáo scan

课堂活动
CLASS ACTIVITIES

Interpersonal:

Discuss the answers to the following questions with the classmate seated next to you.

1. 在快餐业利用这些科技有什么好处？

新科技	好处
电子餐牌 (touch screen menu kiosk)	1. 不浪费纸，环保 2. 3.
面部识别 (face recognition)	1. 2. 3.
移动支付 (mobile payment)	1. 2.
网上订餐—到店取餐 (online order and pick up at the store)	1. 2.
网上订餐—外卖 (online order and take out)	1. 2.

2. 美国最近有什么新的科技给人们带来新的体验？亚马逊推出了无人超市 Amazon Go。这家店用了什么新科技？它为顾客提供了什么样的新体验？

词汇拓展
VOCABULARY BUILDING

1. Words Associated with 网

网 means "net" or "web" and can refer to concrete things such as 蜘蛛网 (spider web) and 渔网 (fish net). It also conveys a more abstract meaning of "network." A website is called 网站 in Chinese. Websites are usually named according to the functions or roles they play. For example, two popular dating websites in the US are named "eharmony" (eharmony.com) and "Match" (Match.com). A similar dating website in China is 百合网 (www.baihe.com), named with the hope of helping people to 百分百地找到适合你的朋友.

1) The following words relate to the abstract meaning of 网. Use an online dictionary to find out the *pinyin* and meaning of these words:

> 网络　互联网　网购　网页　网民　网红　网友　交通网　人际关系网

2) Imagine that the following organizations are setting up their own websites. How would you name their websites in Chinese? Why?

1. 学校环保学会设立一个网站，鼓励大家保护环境。
2. 学生高中部设立一个网站，组织高中学生暑期到海外游学。
3. 社区组织设立一个健身的网站，鼓励大家锻炼身体。

2. Words Associated with 智能

With the development of science and technology, the word 智能 (intelligence, smart) is frequently used. There are a lot of "smart" products in our daily lives. Here are some of them:

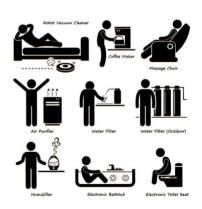

> 智能手机　　智能电脑　　智能音响
> 智能冰箱　　智能家居　　智能交通

1) Use an online dictionary to find out the *pinyin* and meaning of the words above. Research these products to find out their functions.

2) What other smart products do you know? Complete the table below by stating the names of the products and their functions in Chinese. Note that the names do not necessarily contain 智能.

Smart Products	Functions
虚拟个人助理 Cortana, Alexia	告诉你今天的天气，日程有什么安排
	能计算你一天走了多少步
智能汽车	
	可以写新闻报道，美联社(Associated Press)和福克斯(FOX)都已经在用这种方法报道新闻

3. **Smart Home Products 智能管家**

   Mark Zuckerberg has created a smart housekeeper (智能管家) called Jarvis. This name draws reference from Edwin Jarvis, a loyal household butler of the Stark family in *Iron Man*. Watch this clip "马克·扎克伯格亲自打造人工智能家庭管家" from Tencent Video: https://v.qq.com/x/cover/u6mg72vf7z99ujv/k0358xbnwll.html

   1) Complete the table below based on the video. What do you think of these products?

Smart Products	Functions
智能门锁	
智能窗帘	
	• 能调节光暗 • 吃饭的时候就开灯 • 睡觉的时候就关灯

   2) Imagine you are developing a smart wardrobe. What functions do you want it to have?

阅读理解
READING COMPREHENSION

Read the passage and answer the questions that follow.

面部识别
Face Recognition

我今天为大家介绍一下面部识别❶。面部识别是一种先进的科技，使用起来又快又方便。苹果手机就有面部识别功能，你不但可以用面部识别让你的手机解锁，而且可以通过面部识别在App商店买东西。我特别喜欢这个功能，因为有了面部识别，我用手机上校园网的时候，就不用一次又一次地输入密码了。

面部识别还可以帮助老师点名❷。中国传媒大学就有老师用这个方法，因为要是他们的课一班有一两百个学生，点名就很花时间。有了面部识别，老师只需要一个iPad，然后学生站在屏幕前，就能完成签到，这样老师就知道谁没有来上课了。这个方法非常有效，因为再也没有学生可以互相帮对方"签到"了。

面部识别不仅能识别人的脸，还能识别动物的脸。苹果App商店有一个新的应用，叫Finding Rover。Finding Rover能用来帮助你找回丢失的宠物。这个app可以识别你宠物的脸，然后告诉你，你的宠物在哪里。

很多警察也喜欢面部识别，因为面部识别可以帮他们知道谁在使用毒品❸。如果你吸过毒，你的资料就会被记录在政府的数据库里。比如在去年中国的啤酒❹节上，警察逮捕❺了10多个人，因为警察的处理器❻可以辨认❼数据库名单❽上的人。虽然面部识别非常有用，但是如果你是一个双胞胎❾，手机就区分❿不了了。比如说，我的同学Anne和Alexa是双胞胎姐妹。我可以通过跟她们聊天知道她们谁是谁，但是手机没办法区别她们的脸。因此我觉得苹果手机还需要解决这个问题。

李明威 William Raccio（美国高中十二年级的学生，在美国东部高中选修了四年的中文课，这是他学习"人工智能"单元以后作的报告的其中一部分）

❶ 面部识别 miànbù shíbié face recognition
❷ 点名 diǎnmíng roll call
❸ 毒品 dúpǐn drugs
❹ 啤酒 píjiǔ beer
❺ 逮捕 dàibǔ arrest
❻ 处理器 chǔlǐqì processor
❼ 辨认 biànrèn identify, recognize
❽ 名单 míngdān list
❾ 双胞胎 shuāngbāotāi twins
❿ 区分 qūfēn distinguish

1. 根据文章，完成以下表格。

人群	面部识别带来的好处
学生	上网不用输入密码，上网更快更方便
老师	
养宠物的人	
警察	

2. 请用自己的话说一说，"签到"是什么意思。

3. 在你看来，面部识别科技还需要在哪些地方改进？

4. 如果你可以发展面部识别的科技，你最想用面部识别来帮助哪些人？为什么？

写作工坊
WRITING WORKSHOP

写文章 Writing an Essay

Write an essay on the following topic. Your essay should be about 400 words in length.

未来的智能化生活
Toward a Smart Life in the Future

1. Analyzing the topic

The topic is about events that are happening now and will shape life in the future. How would artificial intelligence affect or influence your life and work over the next five years? It thus requires you to predict the developments in artificial intelligence based on current technology and imagine what things might be invented, or how it might be used to do things in new, different ways, and how your life might be affected by these inventions and new ways of doing things. Would your life be made more convenient by artificial intelligence, or would you face some challenges and disadvantages?

2. Structuring your essay

Begin your essay with the following sentences.

我早上起来打开了手机，房间就亮起了柔和的灯光。我问小助手Siri今天的天气如何，并要它提醒我一整天的日程安排……

As a schedule is mentioned in the opening sentences, you are required to write about the things you would likely do in the course of a day. Whichever things you write about, remember that they must be related to artificial intelligence.

As an ending, you may write about your thoughts on the things that you have encountered or done in the course of the day.

3. **Deciding on what to write about**

You may use the following examples in your essay.

- Google Home 播放你最喜欢的歌曲。
- 你乘坐无人驾驶的汽车到学校。
- 你在写文章时用"与书对话❶"搜索资料。
- 你回到家时看到门口放着一个由无人机❷送来的包裹。
- 你找不到心爱的小狗,打开应用 Finding Rover,看到小狗跑到邻居的院子里去了。
- 你用面部识别进入你的银行账户。
- 你饿的时候用 Uber Eats 来订外卖。
- 你出门忘了带钱包,用苹果支付来买东西。
- 你在时装店用增强现实❸来试穿衣服,可以转换衣服的颜色。
- 你到上海的星巴克烘培工坊❹喝咖啡,用增强现实看咖啡的制作过程。

❶ 与书对话 Yǔ Shū Duìhuà Google Talk to Books
❷ 无人机 wúrénjī drone
❸ 增强现实 zēngqiáng xiànshí augmented reality
❹ 星巴克烘培工坊 Xīngbākè Hōngbèi Gōngfáng Starbucks Reserve Roastery

学习总结
I CAN DO!

Interpretive Communication

- [ ] I can read about the advancements in mobile technology that have enabled cashless consumption and the vast amount of data collected through mobile payment in China.
- [ ] I can understand when people talk about the development and application of artificial intelligence in different professions and industries.
- [ ] I can understand when people talk about how the Internet has changed our lives.

Interpersonal Communication

- [ ] I can discuss the advantages and disadvantages of cashless consumption and the vast amount of data collected through mobile payment in China.
- [ ] I can converse about the rapid development of artificial intelligence, its applications and impact on our lives now and in the near future.
- [ ] I can talk about how the Internet has changed our lives, by asking and answering a series of questions.
- [ ] I can talk about the similarities and differences of WeChat and Facebook, by asking and answering a series of questions.

Presentational Communication

- [ ] I can describe briefly the advancements in mobile technology that have enabled cashless consumption in China, the vast amount of data collected during the process, and the advantages and disadvantages of this trend.
- [ ] I can talk about the development and application of artificial intelligence in different professions and industries, and their impact on our lives now and in the near future.
- [ ] I can deliver an oral presentation on how the Internet has changed our lives.
- [ ] I can deliver an oral or written presentation on the daily lives of people now and over the next five years based on current and projected developments in artificial intelligence.

Cultural Knowledge

- [ ] I can describe and explain how mobile technology has enabled cashless consumption in China.
- [ ] I can name some examples of cashless mobile transactions.
- [ ] I can describe the functions of WeChat and other commonly used apps in China.

第九单元 UNIT 9
中国的经济发展
CHINA'S ECONOMY

学习目标
LEARNING OBJECTIVES

- Learn about how China is leading the world in business innovations
- Read about famous Chinese brands and the shift from e-commerce to "New Retail"
- Discuss some new trends in health and diet
- Write a cover letter for a job application

单元总览
CONTENTS AT A GLANCE!

导入 WARM UP

- **Part 1:** 全球第二大经济体——先进还是落后？富裕还是贫穷？
  The Chinese Economy: What It Really Is

  Language Connection:
  1. <u>不管</u>黑猫白猫，能捉老鼠的<u>都</u>是好猫。
  2. 那<u>到底</u>中国是先进的还是落后的？是富裕的还是贫穷的？
  3. <u>如果</u>这些差距现象得不到缓解，<u>就</u>会造成分化和对立。

- **Part 2:** 从电子商务到新零售 From E-Commerce to the New Retail Model of O2O

  Language Connection:
  1. 现在网购人群<u>不再</u>局限于年轻人<u>了</u>，连中老年人也加入其中。
  2. 这<u>基本上</u>是一个O2O（online to offline）的商业模式，实现了线上线下的完美结合。

- **Part 3:** 从中国制造到中国创造 From Made-in-China to Created-in-China

  Language Connection:
  1. 除了我们熟悉的谷歌、脸书以外，还有<u>不可不</u>知的中国三巨头——百度、阿里巴巴和腾讯，简称为BAT。
  2. 她们凭着<u>敏锐的触觉</u>，<u>活跃的思维</u>，<u>充沛的精力</u>，成为了初创企业的领军人物。

文化剪影：健康与饮食的新热潮
CULTURE ENRICHMENT: Hot New Trends in Health and Diet

词汇拓展：与经济有关的词语
VOCABULARY BUILDING: Words Associated with the Economy

阅读理解：阿里巴巴的企业文化
READING COMPREHENSION: The Corporate Culture of Alibaba

写作工坊：写说明短文——为应聘推销自己
WRITING WORKSHOP: Writing Informative Text: Promoting Oneself In a Job Application

---

学习总结　I CAN DO!

导入
WARM UP

With the rapid development of China's economy, some Chinese brands have gained international recognition and popularity. Research online and find out some of the products each of these seven must-know Chinese brands is famous for. What is an equivalent brand from your country or a western brand that you know for each of them?

产品：_____

你的国家相等的品牌：_____

其他西方品牌：_____

产品：_____

你的国家相等的品牌：_____

其他西方品牌：_____

产品：_____

你的国家相等的品牌：_____

其他西方品牌：_____

产品：_____

你的国家相等的品牌：_____

其他西方品牌：_____

产品：_____

你的国家相等的品牌：_____

其他西方品牌：_____

产品：_____

你的国家相等的品牌：_____

其他西方品牌：_____

产品：_____

你的国家相等的品牌：_____

其他西方品牌：_____

Research online to find out the international rankings by total revenue of these seven brands.

品牌	海尔	联想	小米	华为	百度	比亚迪汽车	李宁
排名							

第一部分 世界第二大经济体——
先进还是落后？富裕还是贫穷？
PART 1 THE CHINESE ECONOMY: WHAT IT REALLY IS

陈教授：宋杰，听说你们今天又到三里屯去了，对吗？

宋杰：是的，今天我们去看了特斯拉的新车展，那里真是人山人海，现在电动车已经变成中国人的新宠。

三里屯	p.n.	Sānlǐtún	Sanlitun (a popular destination for shopping, dining and entertainment in Beijing, China)
特斯拉	p.n.	Tèsīlā	Tesla
车展	n.	chēzhǎn	car show
人山人海	phr.	rén shān rén hǎi	full of people
新宠	n.	xīnchǒng	new favorite
大街小巷	phr.	dà jiē xiǎo xiàng	streets and lanes

陈教授：现在和以前不一样了，30年前我上大学的时候，北京大街小巷都是自行车，没有几家人是有汽车的。

宋杰：中国是怎么样从一个发展中国家变成全球第二大经济体的？

发展中国家	phr.	fāzhǎn zhōng guójiā	developing country
经济体	n.	jīngjìtǐ	economy

陈教授：真是一个很好的问题。这也是让很多美国学生感到很困惑的一个问题。20世纪80年代中国的领导人邓小平倡导改革开放政策，推动农业、工业、科技和国防四个现代化，让中国经济迅速发展。他曾经说过两句挺有意思的话，也许可以回答你的问题。

国防	n.	guófáng	national defense
现代化	n.	xiàndàihuà	modernization

宋杰：　　　是哪两句话？

陈教授：　第一句是"不管黑猫白猫，能捉老鼠的都是好猫"，是说不管是社会主义还是资本主义，不管是计划经济还是市场经济，只要能改善人民生活，让中国强大起来，那就是最好的。这句话反映实用主义的思想。第二句话是"摸着石头来过河"。中国现代化的路怎么走，当时没有现成的经验可以学习，没有一个很明确的方案，只能走一步算一步，在不断摸索中前进。这句话反映了中国经济发展的探索精神。中国自改革开放以来的发展颠覆了很多传统的观念，我们可以说这是弯道超车或者是跨越式发展。你们现在使用的微信钱包就是一个很好的例子。因为中国信用卡的使用没有美国普及，所以干脆就直接进入无现金社会了。世界上很多新兴经济的崛起，正在构建一个新的世界秩序。

社会主义	n.	shèhuì zhǔyì	socialism
资本主义	n.	zīběn zhǔyì	capitalism
计划经济	phr.	jìhuà jīngjì	planned economy
市场经济	phr.	shìchǎng jīngjì	market economy
实用主义	n.	shíyòng zhǔyì	pragmatism
摸	v.	mō	feel, touch
方案	n.	fāng'àn	solution
摸索	v.	mōsuǒ	try to find out
探索精神	phr.	tànsuǒ jīngshén	exploratory spirit
弯道超车	phr.	wāndào chāochē	overtaking at a turn
跨越式发展	phr.	kuàyuè shì fāzhǎn	leapfrog development
微信钱包	p.n.	Wēixìn Qiánbāo	WeChat Wallet

宋杰：　　　您的解释回答了我的疑惑，在中国这段日子让我深刻地体会到中国现代化的一面，但是当我到陕西帮助那些贫困山区的孩子时，又看到了落后的一面。中国的城市和农村好像是两个完全不同的世界。那到底中国是先进的还是落后的？是富裕的还是贫穷的？我有时候也糊涂了。

崛起	n.	juéqǐ	rise
构建	v.	gòujiàn	build, construct
秩序	n.	zhìxù	order
疑惑	n.	yíhuò	doubt
陕西	p.n.	Shǎnxī	Shaanxi (a province in Northwest China)
到底	adv.	dàodǐ	what on earth (used in a question for emphasis)
富裕	adj.	fùyù	rich
贫穷	adj.	pínqióng	poor

陈教授：你今天问了两个很值得讨论的问题。我上个月在纽约华尔街看见附近米其林星级的饭馆和顶尖的时尚，体会到了美国的财富；可是走了几个街区却看见好几个流浪汉，那你说美国是富裕的还是贫穷的？我恐怕在别的国家也不难找到这些例子。其实每个经济发达的国家都有这种不协调的现象。先进与落后，富裕和贫穷，同时存在于一个大城市里。很多人虽然住在一个城市，却生活在两个不同的世界。这是贫富的差距，也是科技进步和全球化必然的结果，你现在实习的公益项目，当然可以通过"扶贫"帮助一些贫困的孩子，可是不能完全解决这些问题。如果这些差距现象得不到缓解，就会造成分化和对立，引发很多严重的社会和政治问题。这些都是有待解决的问题，值得我们一再思考。

华尔街	p.n. Huá'ěrjiē	Wall Street
米其林星级	phr. Mǐqílín xīngjí	Michelin-starred
顶尖	adj. dǐngjiān	best, top
财富	n. cáifù	wealth
街区	n. jiēqū	district
流浪汉	phr. liúlàng hàn	homeless people
不协调	phr. bù xiétiáo	not in harmony

必然	adj. bìrán	inevitable
结果	n. jiéguǒ	outcome, result
扶贫	v. fúpín	help the poor
分化	n. fēnhuà	division
对立	n. duìlì	opposition
引发	v. yǐnfā	cause, lead to
有待	v. yǒudài	await
思考	v. sīkǎo	think deeply, ponder over

语言实践
LANGUAGE CONNECTION

1. **Emphasizing a result that remains unchanged: 不管……都……**

   > Structure: 不管 + condition + 都 + unchanged result/action

   "不管黑猫白猫，能捉老鼠的都是好猫。"

   不管 means "no matter." It is used in the first part of a sentence to introduce possible conditions, while 都, whose meaning is "all," is used in the second part of the sentence to emphasize that an action or result will not be changed by the preceding conditions.

   EXAMPLES:
   1. 不管你是中国人，还是外国人，只要在中国生活，都要遵守中国的法律。
   2. 不管是三岁的小孩，还是三十岁的大人，在妈妈眼里，都是孩子。
   3. 不管你在哪个国家旅游，你都要学会入乡随俗。
   4. 不管别人怎么想，你都要坚持下去。

   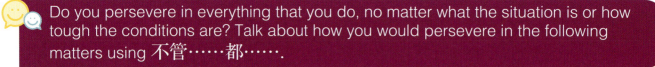

   Do you persevere in everything that you do, no matter what the situation is or how tough the conditions are? Talk about how you would persevere in the following matters using 不管……都……．

   1. 每天早上跑步
   2. 参与社区服务工作
   3. 坐公共交通工具上学
   4. 不用一次性的塑料吸管
   5. 用中文跟中国朋友交流

2. **Emphasizing puzzlement or doubt: 到底……**

   "那到底中国是先进的还是落后的？是富裕的还是贫穷的？"

   到底 can mean "what on earth" and is used to emphasize puzzlement in a situation through a question. It can also mean "in reality," and is used to express one's doubt in a situation or outcome.

EXAMPLES:

① 他说我们九点见面,你说我们十点见面,我们到底几点见面?
② 中国到底有没有实现真正的男女平等?
③ 现在中国的无现金支付方式到底会不会完全取代传统支付方式,还是个没有答案的问题。

Imagine your friend did not show up for his appointment with you. You have tried but failed to reach him. Write down some questions that you want to ask him when you see him using 到底.

3. **Expressing supposition: 如果……就……**

Structure: 如果 + condition + 就 + outcome or required action for the condition to successfully occur

"如果这些差距现象得不到缓解,就会造成分化和对立。"

This structure is equivalent to the English form of "if …, then, …," where a condition or situation is expressed in the first clause, while the outcome of or required action for the preceding condition or situation is expressed in the second clause.

EXAMPLES:

① 如果你想要参加演讲比赛,你现在就要报名。
② 如果没有家人的支持和朋友的关心,我就不会有今天的成绩。
③ 如果你想写中国历史方面的论文,你就去找张老师谈谈,他一定会提供一些有用的材料。

Imagine you are faced with the following situations. Talk about what you would do using 如果……就…….

① 你有机会到中国去
② 你要在暑期找到实习工作
③ 你中国的朋友来美国旅游
④ 人们不好好地保护地球

第二部分 从电子商务到新零售
PART 2 FROM E-COMMERCE TO THE NEW RETAIL MODEL OF O2O

李静在她的高中社团非常活跃，特别是在经济学会。这次学会希望她在微信视频上跟同学讨论一下中国的经济发展，把她在中国的所见所闻跟大家分享。李静邀请了宋杰一起参与。以下是这次分享的中文记录。

| 活跃 | adj. | huóyuè | active |

大家好！

我和宋杰对经济的课题特别感兴趣。在高中一年级的时候就选修了经济学。我觉得经济不仅是书本上的理论，更是生活中可以观察到的活动。简单来说，从生产到消费的过程，也就是商品如何从商家到消费者的手上，其中包括设计、制造、分销、零售、物流等等。在中国留学和实习期间给了我们很多了解中国经济的机会。

消费者	n.	xiāofèizhě	consumer
分销	n.	fēnxiāo	distribution
零售	n.	língshòu	retail
物流	n.	wùliú	logistics

消费能力的提升

最让我感到惊讶的是中国人的消费能力。随着人们收入提高，消费也在不断提升。以前中国人总是觉得要存钱，可是现在的中国人开始舍得花钱去追求美好的生活了。从20世纪80年代追求的冰箱、洗衣机、彩色电视机到"有车有房"，再到海外旅游。现在中国是全

| 收入 | n. | shōurù | income |

| 彩色 | n. | cǎisè | color |

世界汽车和奢侈品的主要消费国之一。大企业如大众汽车、波音公司以及苹果公司，很大部分的市场份额都是来自中国的。这就足以说明中国人消费力非常强劲。

网购热潮

互联网正在改变中国人的消费习惯。中国4G用户已经接近10亿，这构成了世界上最大的移动互联网。现在网购人群不再局限于年轻人了，连中老年人也加入其中。网购的热潮正在形成一股非常强大的力量，推动着中国的经济发展。双十一光棍节慢慢演变成了一个网购狂欢节，规模超越了"黑色星期五"和"网络星期一"。阿里不但引进外国商品，也向全球推销中国的产品，已达到"货通全球"的程度。这种跨境的商务，俗称"海淘"❶，正好说明了全球化的经济趋势。

马云倡导"新零售"

马云近期指出：纯电商时代很快就会结束。网购方便是方便，可是给实体店造成了巨大的挑战。比方说，我小时候最喜欢的"玩具

---

❶ "海淘"就是境外购物。"淘宝"是阿里巴巴的一个著名网购平台，所以售卖海外的货物称为"海淘"。

与我"已经倒闭了。我家附近的梅西也关门了。究竟怎么样才能让网购和实体店共存呢?

马云提出的"新零售"模式也许是打破两者对立格局的一个好方法:结合线上(网购)和线下(实体店)两方面的优势,打通所有的渠道来提升客户的体验,增加服务的效率。我趁着周末跟朋友到代表"新零售"的"盒马鲜生"超市参观。这基本上是一个O2O(online to offline)的商业模式,实现了线上线下的完美结合。我们在超市购物只需要扫码,用支付宝结账。超市里面还有餐饮服务和星巴克咖啡,这种超市+餐饮的服务受到不少白领的青睐,性价比远远超过一般的超市和饭馆。盒马除了是超市加餐厅以外,同时也是一个仓库,所以货物配送特别方便。我听说亚马逊最新推出了"亚马逊Go",不用排队结账,他们的宣传片的口号是"拿了就走Just walk out!",不用去收银台。我觉得盒马鲜生和亚马逊Go这种线上线下一体化的融合,也就是用随时随地、触手可及的购物方式,为未来商务发展提供了一个新方向。

倒闭	v.	dǎobì	close down
梅西	p.n.	Méixī	Macy's
渠道	n.	qúdào	channel
客户	n.	kèhù	customer, client
盒马鲜生	p.n.	Hémǎ Xiānshēng	Hema Xiansheng (a supermarket chain by Alibaba that integrates physical retail and e-commerce)
商业	n.	shāngyè	business
餐饮	n.	cānyǐn	food and beverage
青睐	n.	qīnglài	favor
性价比	n.	xìngjiàbǐ	price-performance ratio
宣传片	phr.	xuānchuán piàn	promotional film
随时随地	phr.	suíshí suídì	anytime and anywhere
触手可及	phr.	chù shǒu kě jí	within reach

中国的经济发展真是瞬息万变,我们得多关注新闻,这样才能跟得上时代的步伐。相信这些经济新浪潮很快会传到世界各地去。让我们拭目以待吧!

瞬息万变	adj.	shùnxī wàn biàn	fast changing
浪潮	n.	làngcháo	tide, wave (figurative)
拭目以待	phr.	shì mù yǐ dài	wait expectantly

语言实践
LANGUAGE CONNECTION

1. Expressing the discontinuation of a situation: 不再……了

   Structure: subject + 不再 + verb + object + 了

   "现在网购人群<u>不再</u>局限于年轻人<u>了</u>，连中老年人也加入其中。"

   This structure can be used to express that something will never be done again, or that a situation will never happen again.

   EXAMPLES:

   ❶ 从今年10月开始，苹果公司要开发新的手机，<u>不再生产iPhone X了</u>。

   ❷ 李文马上要转学了，从下个月开始他<u>不再</u>是我们的辩论队队长<u>了</u>。

   ❸ 自从有了手机支付之后，我就<u>不再</u>带钱包出门<u>了</u>！

    Search online about the changes in people's lives after the economic reforms launched in China in 1978. Write down a statement about the changes in the following aspects using 不再……了.

   EXAMPLE:

   衣：改革开放以后，人们<u>不再</u>只穿单调的黑、白、灰色衣服<u>了</u>，大家穿得越来越好看，颜色越来越鲜艳。

   ❶ 食
   ❷ 住
   ❸ 行（交通）

2. Expressing the meaning of "basically": 基本上……

> Structure: subject + 基本上 + verb + object

"这基本上是一个O2O (online to offline) 的商业模式，实现了线上线下的完美结合。"

基本 means "basic" and 基本上 means "basically." Similar to how the word "basically" is used, 基本 may be placed at the beginning of a sentence or before the verb in the sentence.

EXAMPLES:

1. 我们基本上已经完成课程理论的部分，马上就可以进入实习阶段了。
2. 他的哥哥在商学院主修亚洲经济，基本上对亚洲的各大企业都有一定的认识。
3. 通过接待家庭和学习的帮助，我已经基本上适应了在北京的生活。

Working with a partner, write down five things that are currently trending among teenagers using 基本上.

EXAMPLE:

现在最热门的服装零售店是Urban Outfitter，我的同学们基本上都买过他们的衣服。

China Highlights: Northwest China (2)

Ningxia: Golden Mosque

Xinjiang: Pasture in autumn

Qinghai: Yaks by the Qinghai Lake

第三部分 从中国制造到中国创造
PART 3 FROM MADE-IN-CHINA TO CREATED-IN-CHINA

宋杰到中国留学期间，常常在博客上跟朋友分享他的所见所闻。以下是他在博客上谈到中国经济的一篇文章。

我的亲友知道我去中国留学以后，常对我说："中国东西很便宜，多买一些纪念品回来。""小心点，别买假货。"中国给他们的印象就是：廉价和仿造。可是我来到中国以后看到了很多的新事物，完全改变了我对中国的看法。

20世纪80年代改革开放以后，中国经济飞速发展。庞大的人口、廉价的劳动力加上对外来文化的兴趣，让中国不但成为了世界工厂，而且也成为欧美商品竞争的一个新兴市场。很多大企业纷纷进入中国，包括可口可乐、大众汽车、摩托罗拉、麦当劳、肯德基、雀巢和星巴克。早期中国人对这些外国品牌都感到很新鲜，可是近几年中国不再是只会加工制造的世界工厂，不再模仿欧美的技术。这意味着中国的经济在全球产业链中的地位发生了巨大的变化。目前世界排名前十的互联网公司里，除了我们熟悉的谷歌、脸书以外，还有不可不知的中国三巨头——百度、阿里巴巴和腾讯，简称为BAT。在手机和智能产品方面，华为❶、小米❷、海尔和联想等中国企业也发展得非常迅猛。让我最意想不到的是一个由中国人开发和运营

假货	n.	jiǎhuò	counterfeit goods
廉价	adj.	liánjià	cheap
仿造	v.	fǎngzào	copy, imitate
纷纷	adv.	fēnfēn	one after another, in succession
可口可乐	p.n.	Kěkǒu Kělè	Coca Cola
摩托罗拉	p.n.	Mótuō luólā	Motorala
麦当劳	p.n.	Màidāngláo	McDonald's
肯德基	p.n.	Kěndéjī	Kentucky Fried Chicken
雀巢	p.n.	Quècháo	Nestle
品牌	n.	pǐnpái	brand
产业链	phr.	chǎnyè liàn	industry chain
熟悉	v.	shúxī	be familiar with
巨头	n.	jùtóu	magnate
阿里巴巴	p.n.	Ālǐbābā	Alibaba (a Chinese multinational e-commerce, retail, Internet, AI and technology conglomerate)
腾讯	p.n.	Téngxùn	Tencent (a Chinese multinational investment holding conglomerate specializing in Internet-related services and products, entertainment, AI, and technology)
华为	p.n.	Huáwéi	Huawei (a Chinese multinational networking, telecommunications equipment, and services company)
小米	p.n.	Xiǎomǐ	Xiaomi (a Chinese electronics company)
海尔	p.n.	Hǎi'ěr	Hai'er (a Chinese collective multinational consumer electronics and home appliances company)
联想	p.n.	Liánxiǎng	Lenovo (a Chinese multinational technology company)
迅猛	adj.	xùnměng	swift and strong
意想不到	phr.	yìxiǎng búdào	unexpected

❶ 2018年全球四大手机生产商排名为：三星、华为、苹果、小米。
❷ 小米已经于2018年7月在香港交易所上市。

的音乐应用musical.ly在欧美青少年群体中风靡一时。这些企业都代表了中国的创新力。

如果我们要进一步了解创造力，最好的方法就是观察初创公司。一提到初创公司，大家都想到优步、爱彼迎、Slack团队协作工具和Dropbox云端储存公司等。成立不到10年，市值超过10亿美元且还没有上市的初创公司我们称之为"独角兽"。全球有两百多家独角兽，而中国占百分之三十左右，其中市值最高的是来自中国的蚂蚁金服和滴滴出行。

初创公司	phr.	chūchuàng gōngsī	start-up (company)
云端储存	phr.	yúnduān chǔcún	cloud storage
市值	n.	shìzhí	market capitalization
上市	v.	shàngshì	become a publicly owned company
独角兽	n.	dújiǎoshòu	unicorn (a start-up that is valued at one billion dollars or more)
蚂蚁金服	p.n.	Mǎyǐ Jīnfú	Ant Financial (a fintech company which is affiliated to Alibaba)

有一些独角兽是新一代创业5年以下的公司。其中有VIPKID和瑞幸咖啡。VIPKID是一个一对一儿童在线学习英语的平台，服务的对象是4到12岁的孩子。他们成立不到4年就完成了2亿美元的D轮融资。VIPKID在海外聘请教师，充分发挥他们的潜能，同时也结合了中国成千上万学习英语的学生。这样良好的资源配合给教育界带来了一个新气象，让他们成为了创投领域的新宠。

中国本土初创公司瑞幸咖啡试图挑战在中国已经有20年历史和3000多家门店的星巴克。瑞幸咖啡在短短几个月内就开设了超过1000家门店，他们的咖啡售价低于星巴克百分之二十左右，成功把咖啡这种生活享受带入大众化的市场。顾客只能通过他们的应用买咖啡，这样他们就掌握了大量珍贵的数据。同时瑞幸加设了星巴克以前没有的外卖服务❸。他们是用网络+低价+外卖来获得飞速的成长，以至于他们成立不到一年就已经成为中国唯一的咖啡店独角兽。这是一个"新零售"线上线下一体化的成功案例。

---

❸ 星巴克跟阿里巴巴合作，2018年秋季开始外卖服务。

这些初创公司的成功都有相似的地方。他们掌握市场的动态，找到痛点和问题，通过解决这些问题来赢得用户和顾客。这就是为什么他们会成功的原因：因为打出租车越来越困难，于是有了优步和滴滴；因为星巴克太贵而且没有外卖，于是有了瑞幸咖啡。成功的企业都善于捕捉新市场的机遇，满足客户的需求。

在这些初创的独角兽中，VIPKID的创始人米雯娟和瑞幸的钱治亚都是女性。创业圈不乏能干的女性，她们凭着敏锐的触觉，活跃的思维，充沛的精力，成为了初创企业的领军人物。虽然很多人说女性在工作中会遇上玻璃天花板，其实只要你有能力，一定有很多人会给你机会发挥所长。中国有一句话"妇女能顶半边天❹"，也正好说明女性在职场上的地位。

我在中国的实习很快就要结束了，我打算到"小米之家"买一个智能音箱给爸妈，至于弟弟，我会选择一个大疆的无人机，这样下次家庭聚会的时候我们就可以用它来航拍。我相信我的家人一定会喜欢这些来自中国的创新产品。

动态	n.	dòngtài	trends, developments
痛点	n.	tòngdiǎn	pain point (a specific problem that prospective customers of a business are experiencing)
善于	v.	shànyú	be good at
捕捉	v.	bǔzhuō	capture
满足	v.	mǎnzú	satisfy

凭	v.	píng	rely on
敏锐	adj.	mǐnruì	sharp
触觉	n.	chùjué	sense
思维	n.	sīwéi	thinking
充沛	adj.	chōngpèi	abundant
玻璃天花板	phr.	bōli tiānhuābǎn	glass ceiling
职场	n.	zhíchǎng	workplace
音箱	n.	yīnxiāng	speaker
大疆	p.n.	Dàjiāng	Dà-Jiāng Innovations (DJI) (a Chinese technology company)
无人机	n.	wúrénjī	drone
航拍	v.	hángpāi	take photographs from a flying object (aerial photography)

---

❹ 妇女能顶半边天，就是说妇女在工作上跟男性一样重要。

语言实践
LANGUAGE CONNECTION

1. **Expressing double negation: 不可不……**

   Structure: 不可不 + verb

   "除了我们熟悉的谷歌、脸书以外，还有不可不知的中国三巨头——百度、阿里巴巴和腾讯，简称为BAT。"

   不可 means "cannot." 不可不 is usually used with a verb to form a verb phrase emphasizing something that cannot be missed or must be done. This verb phrase has two negative elements that are combined for a positive connotation that is more forceful. Commonly used verb phrases containing 不可不 are:

   - 不可不看 must see/ must watch/ must read
   - 不可不做 must do
   - 不可不知 must know
   - 不可不谈 must talk about
   - 不可不尝 must taste

   EXAMPLES:
   1. 这部电影讲的是我老家的故事，对我来说，是不可不看的电影。
   2. 如果你想成为一个企业家，这本书里有一些你不可不知的知识。
   3. 《三体》是现在最火的科幻小说，也是年轻人不可不谈的话题。
   4. 如果想学好中文，你不可不做的事情就是练习听力和写汉字。
   5. 最近几年，喜茶成为了中国年轻人最喜欢的饮料连锁店，他们的特色茶也成为了外国人来中国大城市不可不尝的饮料。

Write a tour guide for visitors to your hometown. Introduce some activities they must do using 不可不看 / 不可不做 / 不可不知 / 不可不尝. You may start your guide with "如果你下个月来我的家乡，……"

2. Parallelism

"她们凭着敏锐的触觉，活跃的思维，充沛的精力，成为了初创企业的领军人物。"

Parallelism in Chinese can refer to the use of the components in a sentence or sentences that have the same grammatical structures, or are similar in their construction. Parallelism is found in literary works as well as ordinary conversations. Parallelism can make one's writing more forceful, interesting, and clear. It helps to link related ideas and to emphasize the relationships between them.

EXAMPLES:

❶ 我最喜欢的季节是夏天，因为夏天有蔚蓝的天空，碧绿的大海，美味的冰淇淋。

❷ 现在申请大学的竞争越来越激烈，想要上好大学，我们需要优秀的成绩，丰富的社交经验，强大的自信心。

 Answer the following questions using parallelism.

EXAMPLE:
Question: 你最喜欢什么样的餐厅？
Answer: 我喜欢的餐厅，要有美味的食物，贴心的服务，优美的环境。

❶ 你以后想住在大城市还是小城市？为什么？
❷ 你为什么爱你的家乡？你的家乡什么时候最美？
❸ 如果你想学好中文，有什么事情是不得不做的？

文化剪影
CULTURE ENRICHMENT

健康与饮食的新热潮
Hot New Trends in Health and Diet

随着经济的发展和收入的提高,中国人开始追求生活的品质——健康成了大家关注的课题。越来越多年轻人喜欢健身,他们也喜欢在周末去郊游,享受阳光和清新的空气,也喜欢购买绿色的有机食品。这一股潮流带动了体育用品和健康饮食行业的发展。在大城市里,有越来越多的健身房和瑜伽馆,很多人成为健身房会员,一有空就锻炼。街上随处可以看见体育用品的广告。耐克❶和亚迪达斯❷在中国非常受欢迎。瑜伽服装品牌Lululemon也通过阿里巴巴的新零售科技迅速地进入中国市场。中国当地品牌李宁、安踏、特步及361°也很受欢迎。

李宁是中国人十分尊崇❸的退役体操运动员,曾为中国夺得许多奖牌和冠军。他也是有名的企业家,他开创的运动服装品牌的口号是"一切皆有可能"。最近,李宁把运动服装和时尚结合在一起,推出设计新颖的运动休闲服,迎合了年轻人的品味,获得一致好评。

新产品智能跑鞋"赤兔"则走向科技化,实现了"从中国制造到中国创造"。这款跑鞋将鞋底的智能芯片❹与小米的运动应用结合,给出统计数据,让人们更容易掌握自己的跑步情况,备受欢迎。

在饮食方面,中国人越来越重视食物安全,关心卡路里❺的摄入❻,碳酸饮料❼与高糖零食❽的销售量正往下降。初创企业乐纯(Le Pur,法文纯粹的意思)的酸奶应运而生。在运动后喝酸奶来补充体力,最为理想。乐纯在打通渠道和宣传❾两方面做得非常成功。他们也使用新零售的模式，让顾客除了可以在线上订购以外，还可以在半岛酒店❿、华尔道夫⓫及柏悦⓬等高端酒店品尝到，也可以在大众化的7-11和全家超市买得到。位于三里屯的体验店曾经举办过一个"飞放自我"的活动。年轻人在店里领取贴有自己个性标签的红色气球，然后飞放。三里屯上空飘满了红色气球，很有节日的气氛，收到了很好的宣传效果。乐纯在短短两年的时间，凭着新鲜、健康及好吃三个重要的因素打进了健康饮食的市场，还获得可口可乐千万元的融资。

　　中国人的消费期望不断在上升，对运动和健康的追求带动了不少新企业的发展。这是令人鼓舞的现象。

❶ 耐克 Nài Kè Nike
❷ 亚迪达斯 Yà Dí Dá Sī Adidas
❸ 尊崇 zūnchóng respect
❹ 芯片 xīnpiàn chip
❺ 卡路里 kǎlùlǐ calorie
❻ 摄入 shèrù intake
❼ 碳酸饮料 tànsuān yǐnliào carbonated beverage
❽ 高糖零食 gāo táng língshí high-glucose snacks
❾ 宣传 xuānchuán publicity
❿ 半岛酒店 Bàndǎo Jiǔdiàn Peninsula Hotel
⓫ 华尔道夫 Huá Ěr Dào Fū Waldorf Astoria
⓬ 柏悦 Bóyuè Park Hyatt

课堂活动
CLASS ACTIVITIES

Interpersonal

In pairs, research online to complete the following activities.

1. 为了推广产品，让品牌形象鲜明，容易记住，品牌都纷纷设计出简单易记的口号来鼓励运动员。请利用互联网，找出以下运动品牌的口号。

运动品牌	口号
李宁	一切皆有可能
安踏	
特步	
361°	
耐克	
阿迪达斯	
锐步❶	

❶ 锐步 Ruì Bù Reebok

2. 你的学校要举办国际文化节，其中一项活动是体育竞赛。学校希望有不同语言的口号和标语，来代表来自不同国家与文化的学生。请为中国同学会设计一个口号。

Presentational

Answer the following questions individually.

1. 你喜欢什么零食？
2. 你觉得什么样的零食最健康？
3. 你吃过 Halo Top 冰淇淋和 KIND 零食棒吗？这两个品牌的零食为什么那么受欢迎？

词汇拓展
VOCABULARY BUILDING

Words Associated with the Economy

In this unit, we have learned about the Chinese economy and how some Chinese companies and entrepreneurs are revolutionizing the way business is conducted and contributing to China's vision of becoming a creator of goods and services. Today, the Chinese economy is the second largest in the world.

1) When we discuss the economy, we will often use the following words.

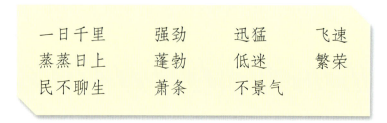

一日千里　强劲　迅猛　飞速
蒸蒸日上　蓬勃　低迷　繁荣
民不聊生　萧条　不景气

Use a dictionary to find out the *pinyin* and meaning of those words you find unfamiliar. Then, place them into the categories below.

形容经济发展好或快的词语	形容经济发展不好或缓慢的词语

2) We will also often come across two terms that describe the stock exchange and how well an economy is doing: 牛市 and 熊市. Both are loan words from English. Make a guess what the original terms in English are.

3) Some other words that describe the economy or workplace are also loan words from English. Write down their original terms in English.

- 黑色星期五
- 网络星期一
- 玻璃天花板
- 独角兽

4) In Part 3 of this unit, we learned about the word 痛点, which means "用户最想解决的问题." It is often talked about in the business world in China. There are some other Chinese words that are suffixed with 点.

a) Match each term that has 点 in it to its meaning.

热点 •	• 跑步或一件事的开始
要点 •	• 做事应该注意的部分
重点 •	• 跑步或一件事的结束
终点 •	• 事情很重要的一部分
起步点 •	• 社会上大家都在热烈讨论的事情

b) Complete the following activity.

你的家庭、社区或学校里有什么痛点？比方说，学校吃饭的时候队伍很长、社区夏天泳池开放时间太短等等。请你说出一个痛点，并谈谈有什么解决方法。

阅读理解
READING COMPREHENSION

Read the passage and answer the questions that follow.

阿里巴巴的企业文化
The Corporate Culture of Alibaba

今年夏天李一山跟着他的高中去杭州参观了阿里巴巴的总部。李一山对阿里巴巴的成功很感兴趣。在参观的时候,很多阿里巴巴的员工一直在说:"这是我们的企业文化。"当李一山问到:"到底什么是阿里巴巴的企业文化?"很多员工都笑了笑,请李一山和他们一起来感受。

目前阿里巴巴有超过7万名员工,所有的员工在入职前都在杭州进行培训,工作后也要继续学习,他们一直要学习和讨论的就是阿里巴巴的价值观。阿里巴巴的价值观是"客户第一,员工第二,股东第三"。拿"客户第一"来说,阿里巴巴的总部园区里有一部大电话,用来听用户意见,所有的员工都能随时听到用户的声音,马云自己也常常去听。马云鼓励员工们学会倒立❶,这样可以用不同的角度看世界。阿里巴巴就是用这样实际的方式帮助用户,也帮助企业成长。

说到"员工第二",每个阿里巴巴的员工都有自己的"花名"❷,这些花名多数都来自中国的武侠小说❸,比如马云叫自己"风清扬"。每年阿里巴巴都有"武林大会"❹,大家会在一起谈论怎么更好地帮助用户,就像武侠世界的英雄一样去拯救❺世界。同时,阿里巴巴每年也通过集体婚礼、阿里好声音等活动来帮助员工找到归属感。阿里巴巴的员工都觉得这里像一个家一样,而且就算他们以后离开了,阿里巴巴的精神也会被他们带去不同的地方。

一个大企业的健康运转离不开强大的企业文化，强大的企业文化会促进员工跟着公司一起成长。马云在港大演讲时说："未来不是知识的竞争，而是创造力和想象力的竞争，是学习能力的竞争，是独立思考的竞争。"李一山相信在阿里巴巴工作一定能让他更加有创造力和想象力。他准备明年夏天就申请阿里巴巴的实习！

❶ 倒立 dàolì stand upside down
❷ 花名 huāmíng nickname
❸ 武侠小说 wǔxiá xiǎoshuō swordsman fiction
❹ 武林大会 wǔlín dàhuì meeting in the martial arts circle
❺ 拯救 zhěngjiù save

1. 阿里巴巴的价值观是什么？员工要怎么样才能明白阿里巴巴的价值观？

2. 请上网查一查，阿里巴巴"客户第一"的企业文化还有什么表现？

3. 请用自己的话说一说，什么叫"归属感"。

4. 美国也有像阿里巴巴一样的大公司，他们有什么特别的企业文化？请举一两个例子。

5. 你觉得马云的这段话说得对不对？请结合自己的经历，谈一谈你对这段话的理解。

　　"未来不是知识的竞争，而是创造力和想象力的竞争，是学习能力的竞争，是独立思考的竞争。"

写作工坊
WRITING WORKSHOP

写说明短文——为应聘推销自己
Writing Informative Text – Promoting Oneself in a Job Application

Have you ever applied or thought of applying to be an intern at a local company during your summer vacation? What about a job at a company in another country?

In this section, you will practice writing informative text to promote yourself in an application for an intern position at a company in China. Read the two hiring advertisements below and complete the activity that follows.

深圳华为集团夏季实习生招聘信息

实习职位：项目管理
基本要求：年龄不限、性别不限
工作地点：深圳

职位描述：
1. 负责项目运营，确保项目按照公司相关管理制度和规定来进行
2. 保证项目的质量，以满足客户的要求

职位要求：
1. 具备良好的沟通能力和人际交往能力
2. 统计、微积分❶、计算机、软件、信息技术等理工科专业优先考虑
3. 拥有丰富的学生会和社会实践经验会更有优势
4. 喜欢挑战，希望在不同国家不同文化中积累跨国工作经验

真格基金夏季实习生招聘信息

实习职位： 投资分析
基本要求： 年龄不限、性别不限
工作地点： 北京

职位描述：
1. 为真格基金夏季的梦想日演唱会做项目分析
2. 为真格基金的梦想中心发展做项目分析

职位要求：
1. 具有强大的分析能力与数据收集能力
2. 学习过宏观经济学❷和微观经济学❸等专业优先考虑
3. 熟悉经济形势，并且可以通过统计分析经济形势

❶ 微积分 wēijīfēn calculus
❷ 宏观经济学 hóngguān jīngjìxué macroeconomics
❸ 微观经济学 wēiguān jīngjìxué microeconomics

Choose one of the two positions to apply to. Write a 500-word cover letter to the company. Follow the guide below.

1. First 200 words: Explain why you wish to apply for this position. You may approach it from aspects such as the job requirements and location, and your strengths and objective.

2. Next 300 words: Introduce your educational background and work experience. Then, explain why you are the ideal candidate for this position and talk about how you can contribute to the company through this position.

学习总结
I CAN DO!

Interpretive Communication

- [ ] I can read about the new world economic order brought about by four decades of changes in the Chinese society arising from its Reform and Opening-up policy.
- [ ] I can understand when people talk about the online shopping trend and rise in consumption power of the Chinese over the past few decades.
- [ ] I can understand when people talk about Baidu, Alibaba and Tencent, and their business models.

Interpersonal Communication

- [ ] I can discuss and talk about the two most famous sayings of Deng Xiaoping that are related to his Reform and Opening-up policy for China.
- [ ] I can converse about some Chinese O2O (online to offline) companies and their modus operandi, as well as their significance in both the traditional and emerging markets.
- [ ] I can talk about how some Chinese companies are leading the world in innovation and the maximization of human and market potential in order to serve customer needs.

Presentational Communication

- [ ] I can write a cover letter for a job application based on a hiring advertisement, explaining my strengths, experience and how I can contribute to the company.
- [ ] I can make an oral presentation on the two stages of economic development in China since the implementation of the Reform and Opening-up policy, from "Made in China" to "Chinese-Created."
- [ ] I can make a brief presentation comparing Chinese and American companies, for example, between Alibaba and Amazon, and between Luckin Coffee and Starbucks.

Cultural Knowledge

- [ ] I can name some famous Chinese brands from various industries and talk about their representative products and their branding slogans.
- [ ] I can describe the enterprise culture of Alibaba with some examples.
- [ ] I can explain some major changes in the Chinese society over four decades of reforms and opening-up, and their significance.

APPENDICES

1. 生词索引（汉英） Vocabulary Index (Chinese to English) *page 262*
2. 生词索引（英汉） Vocabulary Index (English to Chinese) *page 276*
3. 语法点 Language Use *page 292*
4. 中国地图 Map of China *page 296*

1. 生词索引（汉英）VOCABULARY INDEX (CHINESE TO ENGLISH)

A

阿尔法围棋	p.n.	Ā'ěrfǎ Wéiqí	AlphaGo (a computer program that plays the board game Go)	210
阿里巴巴	p.n.	Ālǐbābā	Alibaba (a Chinese multinational e-commerce, retail, Internet, AI and technology conglomerate)	245
爱彼迎	p.n.	Àibǐyíng	Airbnb	45
安全	adj.	ānquán	safe	35
安稳	adj.	ānwěn	stable	69
案件	n.	ànjiàn	case	102
案例	n.	ànlì	case (example)	247

B

白帝城	p.n.	Báidìchéng	Baidi City (an ancient temple complex in Chongqing, China)	146
白话文运动	p.n.	Báihuàwén Yùndòng	Vernacular Language Movement	96
百度	p.n.	Bǎidù	Baidu (a Chinese multinational technology company)	128
百分	n.	bǎifēn	percent	64
百闻不如一见	phr.	bǎi wén bù rú yí jiàn	seeing is believing	73
绑定	v.	bǎngdìng	link	206
包括	v.	bāokuò	include	189
包容性	n.	bāoróngxìng	tolerance	218
保安	n.	bǎo'ān	security guard	213
保护	v.	bǎohù	protect	207
保守	adj.	bǎoshǒu	conservative	63
暴雨	n.	bàoyǔ	rainstorm	184
北极熊	n.	běijíxióng	polar bear	176
北欧	p.n.	Běi Ōu	Northern Europe	190
北漂一族	phr.	běi piāo yì zú	(a term describing people working in Beijing who are not registered residents there)	72
倍	m.w.	bèi	times (multiplier)	184
背道而驰	phr.	bèi dào ér chí	go against	63
背景	n.	bèijǐng	background	147
贝聿铭	p.n.	Bèi Yùmíng	Ieoh Ming Pei (a Chinese American architect)	102
比方	v.	bǐfang	for example	44
比例	n.	bǐlì	ratio	64
比喻	n.	bǐyù	metaphor	211
弊	n.	bì	disadvantage	207
毕加索	p.n.	Bìjiāsuǒ	Pablo Ruiz Picasso (1881-1973) (a famous Spanish painter)	152
必然	adj.	bìrán	inevitable	237
编写	v.	biānxiě	write	74
边缘	n.	biānyuán	verge, brink, edge	74
变革	n.	biàngé	reform, transformation	45
变化	n.	biànhuà	change	35
便捷	adj.	biànjié	convenient	35
标签	n.	biāoqiān	hashtag	219
飙升	v.	biāoshēng	soar, surge	68
标题	n.	biāotí	headline	123
表示	v.	biǎoshì	express, say	118
濒临	v.	bīnlín	on the verge of	174
冰原	n.	bīngyuán	ice field	183
并非	adv.	bìngfēi	is not	129
病史	n.	bìngshǐ	medical history	212
波	n.	bō	wave	45
玻璃金字塔	p.n.	Bōli Jīnzìtǎ	the Louvre Pyramid	103
玻璃天花板	phr.	bōli tiānhuābǎn	glass ceiling	248
波士顿	p.n.	Bōshìdùn	Boston	89
波音公司	p.n.	Bōyīn Gōngsī	Boeing Company	241
波折	n.	bōzhé	twists and turns, setbacks	68
不断	adv.	búduàn	continuously	45
不愧	adv.	búkuì	worthy of, deserve to be called	152
捕捉	v.	bǔzhuō	capture	248
不乏	v.	bùfá	there is no lack of	190
步伐	n.	bùfá	pace	218
不堪	adj.	bùkān	unbearable	45
不堪设想	phr.	bùkān shèxiǎng	too ghastly to contemplate	184
不可思议	adj.	bù kě sī yì	unimaginable, inconceivable	89
不协调	phr.	bù xiétiáo	not in harmony	237
不足为奇	phr.	bù zú wéi qí	be nothing strange	69

C

财富	n.	cáifù	wealth	237
采光	v.	cǎiguāng	natural lighting (for an indoor space)	73
彩色	n.	cǎisè	color	240
采用	v.	cǎiyòng	use, employ	211
参观	v.	cānguān	visit, look around	123
餐饮	n.	cānyǐn	food and beverage	242
仓库	n.	cāngkù	warehouse	190
藏	v.	cáng	hide	103
操作	v.	cāozuò	operate	44
草堂	n.	cǎotáng	thatched cottage	146
策略	n.	cèlüè	tactics	176
层面	n.	céngmiàn	level	216
差别	n.	chābié	difference	205
差错	n.	chācuò	mistake	157
茶余饭后	phr.	chá yú fàn hòu	at one's leisure	44
产生	v.	chǎnshēng	produce	189
产业	n.	chǎnyè	industry	90
产业链	phr.	chǎnyè liàn	industry chain	245
长江三角洲	p.n.	Chángjiāng Sānjiǎo Zhōu	Yangtze River Delta (a metropolitan region)	124
长江中游	p.n.	Chángjiāng Zhōngyóu	Yangtze River Valley (a metropolitan region)	124
尝试	v.	chángshì	try	102
长途	adj.	chángtú	long-distance	130
倡导	v.	chàngdǎo	advocate	189

倡议	v.	chàngyì	propose, initiate	15
超级	adj.	chāojí	super	217
钞票	n.	chāopiào	bank note	207
朝代	n.	cháodài	dynasty	4
潮汐能	n.	cháoxīnéng	tidal energy	189
车展	n.	chēzhǎn	car show	235
沉重	adj.	chénzhòng	heavy	63
衬托	v.	chèntuō	be a foil to	147
城邦	n.	chéngbāng	city-state	124
成本	n.	chéngběn	cost	45
承担	v.	chéngdān	bear	64
成都	p.n.	Chéngdū	Chengdu (the capital city of Sichuan Province, China)	39
程度	n.	chéngdù	extent, degree	39
成就	v.	chéngjiù	achieve, accomplish	159
成立	v.	chénglì	establish	95
承诺	v.	chéngnuò	promise	190
城市群	n.	chéngshì qún	city cluster	123
城乡差距	phr.	chéngxiāng chājù	urban-rural gap	119
成渝	p.n.	Chéngyú	Cheng Yu (a metropolitan region)	124
城镇化	n.	chéngzhènhuà	urbanization	124
耻辱	n.	chǐrǔ	shame	157
充分	adv.	chōngfèn	as fully as possible	147
冲击	n.	chōngjī	impact	153
憧憬	n.	chōngjǐng	yearning	74
充沛	adj.	chōngpèi	abundant	248
重庆	p.n.	Chóngqìng	Chongqing (a city in Southwest China)	130
重新	adv.	chóngxīn	again	45
抽象	adj.	chōuxiàng	abstract	148
初步	adv.	chūbù	initially	63
初创公司	phr.	chūchuàng gōngsī	start-up (company)	246
出色	adj.	chūsè	outstanding	102
出世	n.	chūshì	renounce the world, keep aloof from worldly affairs	148
出行	v.	chūxíng	get around	34
出没	v.	chūmò	roam about	175
处境	n.	chǔjìng	unfavorable situation, plight	176
触觉	n.	chùjué	sense	248
触手可及	phr.	chù shǒu kě jí	within reach	242
传播	v.	chuánbō	spread, teach	10
船队	n.	chuánduì	fleet	9
传入	v.	chuánrù	be brought into	5
船只	n.	chuánzhī	ship	10
创立	v.	chuànglì	found	40
创始人	n.	chuàngshǐrén	founder	45
创投	phr.	chuàngtóu	venture capital investment (an abbreviated form of 创业投资)	247
创新	v.	chuàngxīn	innovate	45
创业	v.	chuàngyè	start a business	45
创造	v.	chuàngzào	create	217
春田市	p.n.	Chūntián Shì	Springfield (a city in Massachusetts)	89
春运	n.	chūnyùn	passenger transportation during or around the Spring Festival	128
纯电商	p.n.	chún diànshāng	pure e-commerce	241
辍学	v.	chuòxué	drop out of school	117
词根	n.	cígēn	root word	124
瓷器	n.	cíqì	porcelain	5
促进	v.	cùjìn	promote	4
催化剂	n.	cuīhuàjì	catalyst	211
璀璨	adj.	cuǐcàn	splendid, brilliant	151
存活率	n.	cúnhuólǜ	survival rate	175
存在	v.	cúnzài	exist	64
寸金寸土	phr.	cùn jīn cùn tǔ	worth a lot of money	69

D

D轮融资	phr.	D lún róngzī	Series D funding	247
搭乘	v.	dāchéng	take (a mode of transportation)	34
搭建	v.	dājiàn	build	207
达成	v.	dáchéng	reach (a consensus or agreement)	183
达·芬奇的密码	p.n.	Dá Fēnqí de Mìmǎ	the Da Vinci Code	103
达卡	p.n.	Dákǎ	Dhaka (the capital of Bangladesh)	183
打败	v.	dǎbài	defeat	94
打工子弟	phr.	dǎgōng zǐdì	children of migrant workers	119
打工族	n.	dǎgōngzú	the working class	35
打拼	v.	dǎpīn	work hard in one's job	35
打破	v.	dǎpò	break	213
打造	v.	dǎzào	make, create	123
打仗	v.	dǎzhàng	fight a battle	156
大规模	n.	dà guīmó	big scale	128
大疆	p.n.	Dàjiāng	Dà-Jiāng Innovations (DJI) (a Chinese technology company)	248
大街小巷	phr.	dà jiē xiǎo xiàng	streets and lanes	235
大气层	n.	dàqìcéng	atmosphere	182
大使	n.	dàshǐ	ambassador	10
大数据	n.	dà shùjù	big data	207
大约	adv.	dàyuē	approximately	103
大众化	adj.	dàzhònghuà	popular	34
大众捷运系统	p.n.	dàzhòng jiéyùn xìtǒng	mass rapid transit system	34
大众汽车	p.n.	Dàzhòng Qìchē	Volkswagen	241
代表作	n.	dàibiǎozuò	masterpiece	103
带动	v.	dàidòng	spur on	124
代父从军	phr.	dài fù cóng jūn	take one's father's place in the army	156
代驾	n.	dàijià	designated driver service (a Didi service)	40
带来	v.	dàilái	bring	45
带领	v.	dàilǐng	lead	102
代码	n.	dàimǎ	code	74
单独二孩	phr.	dān dú èr hái	(a term that refers to the condition in China's two-child policy, where a couple is allowed to have a second child if either of them is an only child)	63
担任	v.	dānrèn	hold a post	74
当时	adv.	dāngshí	at that time	10

倒闭	v.	dǎobì	close down	242
导演	n.	dǎoyǎn	film director	156
岛屿	n.	dǎoyǔ	island	183
到底	adv.	dàodǐ	what on earth (used in a question for emphasis)	236
道教	p.n.	Dàojiào	Daoism	148
道路	n.	dàolù	road, route	4
德州	p.n.	Dézhōu	Texas	68
登录	v.	dēnglù	log in	44
等候	v.	děnghòu	wait	218
邓小平	p.n.	Dèng Xiǎopíng	Deng Xiaoping (1904-1997) (former leader of the People's Republic of China who is widely credited with the economic reforms of the 1980s which propelled China to the economic powerhouse it is today)	96
滴滴	p.n.	Dīdī	Didi (a Chinese ride-sharing company)	40
滴滴顺风车	phr.	Dīdī shùnfēngchē	hitch-riding service by Didi	130
敌人	n.	dírén	enemy	159
抵御	v.	dǐyù	withstand	176
地理学家	n.	dìlǐ xuéjiā	geographer	5
地球	n.	dìqiú	earth	177
地区	n.	dìqū	area, district	117
第五大道	p.n.	Dì Wǔ Dàdào	Fifth Avenue	123
地中海	p.n.	Dìzhōnghǎi	Mediterranean Sea	5
颠覆	v.	diānfù	overturn, subvert	218
滇藏	p.n.	Diān Zàng	Yunnan and Tibet	175
点亮眼睛	p.n.	Diǎnliàng Yǎnjing	Education in Sight (an NGO in China that seeks to improve the eyesight of children in rural areas)	118
典雅	adj.	diǎnyǎ	elegant	147
电报	n.	diànbào	telegram	90
电动车	n.	diàndòng chē	electric car	39
店面	n.	diànmiàn	shop front	190
电视剧	n.	diànshìjù	TV series	68
调查	v.	diàochá	investigate	102
顶尖	adj.	dǐngjiān	best, top	237
订单	n.	dìngdān	(purchase) order	212
订票	v.o.	dìng piào	book tickets	211
定期	adv.	dìngqī	at regular intervals	118
定位	n.	dìngwèi	location	128
定义	n.	dìngyì	definition	218
东南亚	p.n.	Dōngnányà	Southeast Asia	9
东直门	p.n.	Dōngzhímén	Dongzhimen (a subway station in Beijing, China)	206
动画片	n.	dònghuàpiàn	animation movie	156
洞识天机	phr.	dòngshí tiānjī	having a keen insight into nature's mysteries	158
动态	n.	dòngtài	trends, developments	248
独角兽	n.	dújiǎoshòu	unicorn (a start-up that is valued at one billion dollars or more)	246
独立	n.	dúlì	independence	157
独生子女	phr.	dúshēng zǐnǚ	only child	62
堵塞	n.	dǔsè	traffic jam	39
杜甫	p.n.	Dù Fǔ	Du Fu (712-770) (a prominent Chinese poet of the Tang Dynasty)	146
短途	n.	duǎntú	short distance	44
对话	n.	duìhuà	dialog	4
对立	n.	duìlì	opposition	237
对象	n.	duìxiàng	target audience	247
多哈伊斯兰艺术博物馆	p.n.	Duōhā Yīsīlán Yìshù Bówùguǎn	Museum of Islamic Art, Doha	103
多样性	n.	duōyàngxìng	diversity	177

E

俄罗斯	p.n.	Éluósī	Russia	184
二胎	n.	èr tāi	second child	62
二维码	n.	èrwéimǎ	QR code	44

F

发达	adj.	fādá	developed	124
发挥	v.	fāhuī	bring into play, give free rein to	159
发起	v.	fāqǐ	initiate	190
发生	v.	fāshēng	take place	35
发展中国家	phr.	fāzhǎn zhōng guójiā	developing country	235
罚款	v.	fákuǎn	impose a fine on	39
番	m.w.	fān	(measure word) turn	69
翻译	v.	fānyì	translate	34
梵高	p.n.	Fángāo	Vincent Willem van Gogh (1853-1890) (a famous Dutch Post-Impressionist painter)	152
烦恼	adj.	fánnǎo	worried, vexed	72
凡事	n.	fánshì	everything	207
繁育	v.	fányù	breed	175
繁殖学	n.	fánzhíxué	reproductive science	175
反常	adj.	fǎncháng	abnormal	184
反思	v.	fǎnsī	reflect	45
反映	v.	fǎnyìng	reflect	68
反正	adv.	fǎnzhèng	all the same, in any case	69
犯罪	v.	fànzuì	commit a crime	207
方案	n.	fāng'àn	solution	236
方针	n.	fāngzhēn	policy	62
房价	n.	fángjià	price of housing	68
防止	v.	fángzhǐ	prevent	207
访问	v.	fǎngwèn	interview	90
仿造	v.	fǎngzào	copy, imitate	245
放映	v.	fàngyìng	show (a film)	156
非洲	p.n.	Fēizhōu	Africa	4
纷纷	adv.	fēnfēn	one after another, in succession	245
分化	n.	fēnhuà	division	237
分离	n.	fēnlí	separation	148
分析	v.	fēnxī	analyze	211
分销	n.	fēnxiāo	distribution	240
坟墓	n.	fénmù	tomb	148
奋斗	v.	fèndòu	strive	74
封建	adj.	fēngjiàn	feudalistic	95
风景线	n.	fēngjǐngxiàn	scenery	44

Chinese	Type	Pinyin	English	Page
疯狂的亚洲富豪	p.n.	Fēngkuáng de Yàzhōu Fùháo	Crazy Rich Asians (a Hollywood movie)	156
风力发电	phr.	fēnglì fādiàn	wind power generation	189
风靡一时	phr.	fēngmí yì shí	be all the rage	44
风味	n.	fēngwèi	local flavor	124
风险	n.	fēngxiǎn	risk	16
峰值	n.	fēngzhí	peak value	190
佛教	p.n.	Fójiào	Buddhism	5
否则	conj.	fǒuzé	otherwise, else	39
夫妻	n.	fūqī	husband and wife	68
浮冰	n.	fúbīng	drift ice	176
符合	v.	fúhé	fit	217
扶贫	v.	fúpín	help the poor	237
福气	n.	fúqì	good fortune	63
幅员	n.	fúyuán	the extent of a country	35
覆盖	v.	fùgài	cover	35
付款	v.o.	fùkuǎn	pay (a sum of money)	44
富强	adj.	fùqiáng	prosperous and strong	94
富裕	adj.	fùyù	rich	236
负责任	v.o.	fù zérèn	take responsibility	207

G

Chinese	Type	Pinyin	English	Page
改编	v.	gǎibiān	adapt from	68
改革	v.	gǎigé	reform	45
改革开放	phr.	gǎigé kāifàng	Chinese economic reform	124
改良	v.	gǎiliáng	improve	94
干旱	n.	gānhàn	drought	184
甘肃	p.n.	Gānsù	Gansu (a province in Northwest China)	5
高达	phr.	gāo dá	reach up to	117
高管	n.	gāoguǎn	executive	190
高科技	n.	gāo kējì	high technology	44
高铁	n.	gāotiě	high-speed rail	35
高效	adj.	gāoxiào	efficient	218
哥伦布	p.n.	Gēlúnbù	Christopher Columbus	9
格局	n.	géjú	structure, format	147
革新性	adj.	géxīnxìng	innovative	216
庚子赔款	p.n.	Gēngzǐ Péikuǎn	Boxer Rebellion Indemnity (1900)	95
工程	n.	gōngchéng	project	189
宫殿	n.	gōngdiàn	palace	158
功夫熊猫	p.n.	Gōngfu Xióngmāo	Kungfu Panda (a Hollywood movie)	156
公共	adj.	gōnggòng	public	123
公立	adj.	gōnglì	public	119
公路	n.	gōnglù	highway	211
工业革命	phr.	Gōngyè Gémìng	Industrial Revolution	213
公益	n.	gōngyì	public welfare	4
公寓	n.	gōngyù	apartment	45
共鸣	n.	gòngmíng	sympathetic response	68
共识	n.	gòngshí	consensus, agreement	183
贡献	n.	gòngxiàn	contribution	10
共享单车	phr.	gòngxiǎng dānchē	bicycle sharing	44
供应	v.	gōngyìng	supply	189
构建	v.	gòujiàn	build, construct	236
购买	v.	gòumǎi	purchase	45
估计	v.	gūjì	estimate	64
股	m.w.	gǔ	a stream of	219
古代	n.	gǔdài	ancient time	9
谷歌	p.n.	Gǔgē	Google	74
鼓舞	adj.	gǔwǔ	encouraging	190
顾客	n.	gùkè	customer	207
固然	adv.	gùrán	admittedly, it is true that	119
挂号	v.	guàhào	register	217
挂念	n.	guàniàn	miss	147
关怀	v.	guānhuái	care for	147
观念	n.	guānniàn	idea	63
关系	v.	guānxì	concern, have a bearing on	157
冠军	n.	guànjūn	champion	210
光伏发电装置	phr.	guāngfú fādiàn zhuāngzhì	photovoltaic system, solar power system	189
光荣	n.	guāngróng	glory	157
光宗耀祖	phr.	guāngzōng yàozǔ	bring glory to one's ancestors	157
广东人	n.	Guǎngdōngrén	Cantonese	89
广泛	adj.	guǎngfàn	extensive	212
广阔	adj.	guǎngkuò	broad	69
广州	p.n.	Guǎngzhōu	Guangzhou (a city in Guangdong Province, China)	69
归功	v.	guīgōng	give the credit to	205
硅谷	p.n.	Guīgǔ	Silicon Valley	74
归来	v.	guīlái	return	157
规模	n.	guīmó	scale	241
轨迹图	n.	guǐjì tú	route map	128
国策	n.	guócè	national policy	63
国防	n.	guófáng	national defense	235
国家地理杂志	p.n.	Guójiā Dìlǐ Zázhì	National Geographic Magazine	174

H

Chinese	Type	Pinyin	English	Page
海尔	p.n.	Hǎi'ěr	Hai'er (a Chinese collective multinational consumer electronics and home appliances company)	245
海豹	n.	hǎibào	seal	177
海淀区	p.n.	Hǎidiànqū	Haidian District (a district in Beijing)	68
海量	adj.	hǎiliàng	massive	210
海平面	n.	hǎipíngmiàn	sea level	183
海上丝绸之路	p.n.	Hǎishang Sīchóu zhī Lù	Maritime Silk Road	9
海淘	p.n.	Hǎitáo	Haitao (a cross-border e-commerce platform by Alibaba)	241
海峡	n.	hǎixiá	straits	148
海象	n.	hǎixiàng	walrus	177
憨厚	adj.	hānhòu	simple and honest	158
罕见	adj.	hǎnjiàn	rare	128
汉代	p.n.	Hàndài	Han Dynasty (202 B.C. - 220 A.D.)	5
汉字	n.	hànzì	Chinese characters	217

航海家	n.	hánghǎijiā	navigator		9
航空	n.	hángkōng	aviation		211
航路	n.	hánglù	sailing route		9
航拍	v.	hángpāi	take photographs from a flying object (aerial photography)		248
杭州	p.n.	Hángzhōu	Hangzhou (the capital city of Zhejiang Province, China)		39
号召	v.	hàozhào	call, appeal		190
河北	p.n.	Héběi	Hebei (a province in Northern China)		124
合并	v.	hébìng	merge		40
合肥	p.n.	Héféi	Hefei (capital city of Anhui Province)		72
合理	adj.	hélǐ	reasonable		219
盒马鲜生	p.n.	Hémǎ Xiānshēng	Hema Xiansheng (a supermarket chain by Alibaba that integrates physical retail and e-commerce)		242
和平共处	phr.	hépíng gòngchǔ	co-exist peacefully		10
和谐	n.	héxié	harmony		158
合作	v.	hézuò	collaborate		16
赫胥黎	p.n.	Hè Xūlí	Thomas Henry Huxley (1825-1895) (English biologist)		95
黑色星期五	p.n.	Hēisè Xīngqīwǔ	Black Friday		241
痕迹	n.	hénjì	trace, mark		207
红海	p.n.	Hónghǎi	the Red Sea		9
后人	n.	hòurén	later generations		90
胡椒	n.	hújiāo	pepper		5
胡乱	adv.	húluàn	casually, carelessly		45
胡萝卜	n.	húluóbo	carrot		5
湖泊	n.	húpō	lake		175
胡适	p.n.	Hú Shì	Hu Shi (1891-1962) (a scholar widely credited with language reform by advocating the use of written vernacular Chinese)		95
胡同	n.	hútòng	hutong (a type of narrow street or alley in northern Chinese cities)		124
互补	v.	hùbǔ	complement one another		16
户籍	n.	hùjí	household registration		119
户口	n.	hùkǒu	registered residence		73
互联网包车	phr.	hùliánwǎng bāochē	online car charter		130
花木兰	p.n.	Huā Mùlán	Mulan (a Hollywood movie)		156
华尔街	p.n.	Huá'ěrjiē	Wall Street		237
华南虎	n.	Huánánhǔ	South China tiger		176
华盛顿	p.n.	Huáshèngdùn	Washington, D.C. (the capital of the United States of America)		176
华为	p.n.	Huáwéi	Huawei (a Chinese multinational networking, telecommunications equipment, and services company)		245
华裔	n.	huáyì	foreign citizen of Chinese origin		103
划时代	adj.	huàshídài	epoch-making		96
化石燃料	phr.	huàshí ránliào	fossil fuel		189
话题	n.	huàtí	topic		210
华佗	p.n.	Huà Tuó	Hua Tuo (140-208) (a famous Chinese physician of the late Eastern Han Dynasty)		158
换取	v.	huànqǔ	exchange something for		118
黄金	n.	huángjīn	gold		147
回教	p.n.	Huíjiào	Islam		5
回民	n.	Huímín	Muslim		5
茴香	n.	huíxiāng	fennel		5
回忆	n.	huíyì	memory		90
毁灭性	adj.	huǐmièxìng	destructive		184
会议	n.	huìyì	conference		184
活跃	adj.	huóyuè	active		240
货通全球	phr.	huò tōng quánqiú	worldwide distribution		241

J

基础建设	phr.	jīchǔ jiànshè	infrastructure		16
基督教	p.n.	Jīdūjiào	Christianity		5
机构	n.	jīgòu	organization		175
基金会	n.	jījīn huì	foundation		118
机器	n.	jīqì	machine		210
机械制造	phr.	jīxiè zhìzào	manufacture of machinery		90
极端化	n.	jíduānhuà	becoming extreme		183
急剧	adj.	jíjù	rapid		211
极力	adv.	jílì	do one's utmost		183
及时	adv.	jíshí	promptly, without delay		212
集中	v.	jízhōng	concentrate		129
继承	v.	jìchéng	carry on		152
计划	v.	jìhuà	plan		129
计划经济	phr.	jìhuà jīngjì	planned economy		236
纪录片	n.	jìlùpiàn	documentary		184
寄情	v.	jìqíng	give expression to one's feelings		148
技术	n.	jìshù	technology		10
加尔各答	p.n.	Jiā'ěrgèdá	Kolkata (the capital city of the state of West Bengal, India)		183
加班	v.	jiābān	work overtime		74
加深	v.	jiāshēn	deepen		90
家乡	n.	jiāxiāng	home		148
家喻户晓	phr.	jiā yù hù xiǎo	widely known		156
家族	n.	jiāzú	clan, family		157
假货	n.	jiǎhuò	counterfeit goods		245
甲午战争	p.n.	Jiǎwǔ Zhànzhēng	First Sino-Japanese War (1894-1895) (launched by Japanese imperialism to annex Korea and invade China)		94
驾驶	v.	jiàshǐ	drive (a vehicle)		213
肩负	adj.	jiānfù	undertake, shoulder		159
检查	n.	jiǎnchá	inspection		118
简称	n.	jiǎnchēng	the abbreviated form of a name		69
简单	adj.	jiǎndān	simple		34
简直	adv.	jiǎnzhí	simply, at all		69
间隔	v.	jiàngé	have an interval		63
见解	n.	jiànjiě	view, opinion		152
建立	v.	jiànlì	build		10
见仁见智	phr.	jiànrén jiànzhì	a matter of opinion		69
建设	n.	jiànshè	construction		35
江苏	p.n.	Jiāngsū	Jiangsu (a province in Eastern China)		151
奖励	n.	jiǎnglì	reward		156
奖项	n.	jiǎngxiàng	award		89

讲座	n.	jiǎngzuò	lecture	123	橘色	n.	júsè	orange (color)	44
焦点透视法	phr.	jiāodiǎn tòushì fǎ	focus perspective (an art technique)	152	局限	v.	júxiàn	limit	241
交换	v.	jiāohuàn	exchange	10	巨大	adj.	jùdà	huge	211
交易	n.	jiāoyì	transaction	207	飓风	n.	jùfēng	hurricane	184
角度	n.	jiǎodù	angle, perspective	16	巨头	n.	jùtóu	magnate	245
矫健	adj.	jiǎojiàn	strong and vigorous	175	绝对	adv.	juéduì	absolutely	148
教会学校	phr.	jiàohuì xuéxiào	mission school	89	崛起	n.	juéqǐ	rise	236
教练	n.	jiàoliàn	instructor, coach	207	绝种	v.	juézhǒng	become extinct, die out	174
教授	n.	jiàoshòu	professor	4	君主制度	n.	jūnzhǔ zhìdù	monarchy	95
教学	n.	jiàoxué	teaching	119	**K**				
接待	v.	jiēdài	receive (visitors, guests, etc.)	89	卡塔尔	p.n.	Kǎtǎ'ěr	Qatar	103
街区	n.	jiēqū	district	237	开采	v.	kāicǎi	extract	177
劫匪	n.	jiéfěi	robber	207	开创	v.	kāichuàng	start, create	10
结果	n.	jiéguǒ	outcome, result	237	开发	v.	kāifā	exploit	189
结论	n.	jiélùn	conclusion	184	开放	v.	kāifàng	lift a ban or restriction	62
结束	v.	jiéshù	end	241	开支	n.	kāizhī	expenses	189
结算	v.	jiésuàn	settle a bill	206	康州	p.n.	Kāng Zhōu	Connecticut	89
捷运	n.	jiéyùn	rapid transit	34	烤肉	v.o.	kǎoròu	grill meat, barbecue	68
结帐	v.	jiézhàng	pay the bill	206	考验	n.	kǎoyàn	test	64
解读	v.	jiědú	analyze, interpret	129	可口可乐	p.n.	Kěkǒu Kělè	Coca Cola	245
解释	v.	jiěshì	explain	15	可谓	v.	kěwèi	it can be said that …	35
解说	v.	jiěshuō	explain	102	可想而知	phr.	kě xiǎng ér zhī	it is obvious that	216
解锁	v.o.	jiěsuǒ	undo a lock, unlock	44	可再生	adj.	kězàishēng	renewable	189
巾帼	n.	jīnguó	heroine	157	克服	v.	kèfú	overcome	90
金丝猴	n.	jīnsīhóu	snub-nosed monkey	174	客户	n.	kèhù	customer, client	242
尽量	adv.	jǐnliàng	to the greatest extent	190	客流量	n.	kèliúliàng	volume of passenger traffic	211
进化论	n.	jìnhuàlùn	theory of evolution	95	肯德基	p.n.	Kěndéjī	Kentucky Fried Chicken	245
近郊	n.	jìnjiāo	suburbs, outskirts	35	肯定	adv.	kěndìng	definitely	129
近距离	adj.	jìnjùlí	close range	175	肯尼亚	p.n.	Kěnníyà	Kenya	9
近视	n.	jìnshì	myopia, short-sightedness	118	口号	n.	kǒuhào	slogan	40
京城	n.	jīngchéng	capital	147	跨国	adj.	kuàguó	transnational	190
京都	p.n.	Jīngdū	Kyoto (the capital city of Kyoto Prefecture, Japan)	183	跨文化	v.o.	kuà wénhuà	cross-cultural	159
经济带	phr.	jīngjì dài	economic zone	15	跨越式发展	phr.	kuàyuè shì fāzhǎn	leapfrog development	236
经济体	n.	jīngjìtǐ	economy	235	快车	n.	kuàichē	an express ride (a Didi service)	40
京津冀	p.n.	Jīngjīnjì	Jingjinji (a metropolitan region)	123	跨境	phr.	kuàjìng	cross-border	241
精练	adj.	jīngliàn	succinct	148	宽敞	adj.	kuānchang	spacious	73
精武门	p.n.	Jīngwǔmén	Fist of Fury (Hong Kong martial arts film starring Bruce Lee)	101	矿冶	n.	kuàngyě	mining and metallurgy	90
惊险	adj.	jīngxiǎn	alarmingly dangerous	174	昆明	p.n.	Kūnmíng	Kunming (capital city of Yunnan Province)	74
惊讶	adj.	jīngyà	surprised	35	困惑	adj.	kùnhuò	bewildered	74
经验	n.	jīngyàn	experience	123	**L**				
晶莹剔透	adj.	jīngyíng tītòu	crystal clear	103	拉丁文	n.	Lādīngwén	Latin	124
警告	n.	jǐnggào	warning	184	浪潮	n.	làngcháo	tide, wave (figurative)	242
景象	n.	jǐngxiàng	scene, sight	147	浪漫主义	n.	làngmàn zhǔyì	romanticism	148
竟	adv.	jìng	unexpectedly	123	朗诵	n.	lǎngsòng	recitation	148
境界	n.	jìngjiè	state, realm	158	劳动力	n.	láodònglì	labor force	63
纠结	v.	jiūjié	be tangled, torn between	69	劳动人口	n.	láodòng rénkǒu	work force	64
究竟	adv.	jiūjìng	exactly	182	老百姓	n.	lǎobǎixìng	ordinary people	68
90后	phr.	jiǔlínghòu	post-90s generation (a Chinese term referring to people born between 1990 and 2000)	45	老龄化	n.	lǎolínghuà	aging	64
居住	v.	jūzhù	reside	68	烙印	n.	làoyìn	mark, imprint	148

Chinese	Type	Pinyin	Definition	Page
李白	p.n.	Lǐ Bái	Li Bai (701-762) (a prominent Chinese poet of the Tang Dynasty)	146
李昌钰	p.n.	Lǐ Chāngyù	Henry Chang-Yu Lee (a Chinese American forensic scientist)	102
里弄	n.	lǐlòng	lanes and alleys in Shanghai	68
理论	n.	lǐlùn	theory	95
理念	n.	lǐniàn	idea	96
李小龙	p.n.	Lǐ Xiǎolóng	Bruce Lee (1940-1973) (a martial arts actor and martial artist)	101
李政道	p.n.	Lǐ Zhèngdào	Tsung-Dao Lee (an Asian American physicist)	103
利	n.	lì	advantage	207
立法	v.	lìfǎ	make laws, legislate	207
历史	n.	lìshǐ	history	4
联合国	p.n.	Liánhéguó	United Nations	177
廉价	adj.	liánjià	cheap	245
连接	v.	liánjiē	link	4
连锁反应	phr.	liánsuǒ fǎnyìng	chain reaction	183
联想	v.	liánxiǎng	associate with	45
联想	p.n.	Liánxiǎng	Lenovo (a Chinese multinational technology company)	245
两	m.w.	liǎng	tael (a unit of weight)	147
量	n.	liàng	capacity	130
猎食	v.	lièshí	hunt for food	176
辽阔	adj.	liáokuò	vast	35
灵感	n.	línggǎn	inspiration	158
灵活	adj.	línghuó	agile	175
零售	n.	língshòu	retail	240
领导人	n.	lǐngdǎorén	leader	96
领军	adj.	lǐngjūn	leading	90
领域	n.	lǐngyù	area, field	151
楼顶	n.	lóudǐng	the roof of a building	189
流传千古	phr.	liúchuán qiāngǔ	pass down through the ages	147
流动	n.	liúdòng	(of people) flow	35
流浪汉	phr.	liúlàng hàn	homeless people	237
留守儿童	phr.	liúshǒu értóng	left-behind children (children in foster care of grandparents or other relatives while their parents work in other cities)	119
留学	v.	liúxué	study abroad	89
留学潮	n.	liúxué cháo	(a term used to describe the period beginning in late Qing Qynasty, when many young people went abroad to study)	96
卢浮宫	p.n.	Lú Fú Gōng	the Louvre Museum	103
陆地	n.	lùdì	land	15
路线	n.	lùxiàn	route	129
轮子	n.	lúnzi	tire	45
论坛	n.	lùntán	forum	123
洛杉矶	p.n.	Luòshānjī	Los Angeles	101
旅馆	n.	lǚguǎn	hotel	174
率	n.	lǜ	rate, ratio	117

M

Chinese	Type	Pinyin	Definition	Page
麻州	p.n.	Má Zhōu	Massachusetts	89
马尔代夫	p.n.	Mǎ'ěrdàifū	Maldives (a tropical nation in the Indian Ocean)	183
蚂蚁金服	p.n.	Mǎyǐ Jīnfú	Ant Financial (a fintech company which is affiliated to Alibaba)	246
麦当劳	p.n.	Màidāngláo	McDonald's	245
满足	v.	mǎnzú	satisfy	248
曼哈顿	p.n.	Mànhādùn	Manhattan	123
牦牛	n.	máoniú	yak	5
梅里雪山	p.n.	Méilǐ Xuěshān	Meili Snow Mountains (a mountain range in Yunnan Province, China)	174
媒体	n.	méitǐ	media	156
煤炭	n.	méitàn	coal	188
梅西	p.n.	Méixī	Macy's	242
美籍	n.	Měijí	American	102
美元	n.	měiyuán	U.S. dollar	69
美洲	p.n.	Měizhōu	the Americas	9
谜底	n.	mídǐ	answer to a riddle	103
麋鹿	n.	mílù	Père David's deer	176
米其林星级	phr.	Mǐqílín xīngjí	Michelin-starred	237
秘诀	n.	mìjué	secret (of success)	102
密码	n.	mìmǎ	secret code	103
密密麻麻	adj.	mìmimámá	numerous and close together	128
密切	adj.	mìqiè	close	124
面积	n.	miànjī	area	68
描述	v.	miáoshù	describe	68
描写	v.	miáoxiě	depict, portray	147
灭绝	v.	mièjué	die out	183
民生疾苦	phr.	mínshēng jíkǔ	sufferings of the people	147
民主	n.	mínzhǔ	democracy	96
民族英雄	phr.	mínzú yīngxióng	national hero	156
明代	p.n.	Míngdài	Ming Dynasty (1368-1644)	9
明亮	adj.	míngliàng	bright	118
名山大川	phr.	míng shān dà chuān	famous mountains and rivers	146
明显	adj.	míngxiǎn	obvious	188
明治维新	p.n.	Míngzhì Wéixīn	Meiji Reformation	94
摸	v.	mō	feel, touch	236
摸索	v.	mōsuǒ	try to find out	236
模仿	v.	mófǎng	imitate	158
模拟	v.	mónǐ	simulate	175
模式	n.	móshì	mode, model	45
摩天	v.	mótiān	skyscraping	123
摩托罗拉	p.n.	Mótuōluólā	Motorala	245
莫奈	p.n.	Mònài	Claude Monet (1840-1926) (a French painter and founder of French Impressionist painting)	152
末年	n.	mònián	last years of a dynasty or reign	96
末日	n.	mòrì	doomsday	184
陌生	adj.	mòshēng	unfamiliar	148
幕	m.w.	mù	scene	103
募捐	v.	mùjuān	raise donations	118
敏锐	adj.	mǐnruì	sharp	248

N

Chinese	Type	Pinyin	Definition	Page
耐人寻味	phr.	nài rén xún wèi	provide food for thought	158

难得	adj.	nándé	rare, hard to come by	188
能源	n.	néngyuán	energy	16
溺爱	v.	nì'ài	spoil (a child)	64
逆向	v.	nìxiàng	reverse	129
年代	n.	niándài	decade, era	45
纽约	p.n.	Niǔyuē	New York	123
纽约时报	p.n.	Niǔyuē Shíbào	New York Times	123
农村	n.	nóngcūn	village	63
农村教育行动计划	phr.	Nóngcūn Jiàoyù Xíngdòng Jìhuà	Rural Education Action Program (REAP)	117
浓度	n.	nóngdù	concentration	188
农民工	n.	nóngmín gōng	migrant worker	119
诺贝尔物理奖	p.n.	Nuòbèi'ěr Wùlǐ Jiǎng	Nobel Prize in Physics	103
女扮男装	phr.	nǚ bàn nán zhuāng	a female impersonating as a male	156

O

欧洲	p.n.	Ōuzhōu	Europe	4

P

拍摄	v.	pāishè	film (a movie)	156
排队	v.	páiduì	queue, line up	217
排放物	n.	páifàngwù	emission	189
排球	n.	páiqiú	volleyball	68
派发	v.	pàifā	distribute	118
攀爬	v.	pānpá	climb	175
庞大	adj.	pángdà	huge	211
彷徨	adj.	pánghuáng	hesitant, not knowing where to go in life	74
配戴	v.	pèi dài	wear	118
配合	v.	pèihé	match	247
配种	v.	pèizhǒng	breed	176
皮革	n.	pígé	leather	5
票房	n.	piàofáng	box office (earnings from a movie)	156
拼搏	v.	pīnbó	go all out in work	69
频繁	adj.	pínfán	frequent	35
贫穷	adj.	pínqióng	poor	236
品牌	n.	pǐnpái	brand	245
聘请	v.	pìnqǐng	hire, employ	247
凭	v.	píng	rely on	248
平等	adj.	píngděng	equal, fair	219
平米	m.w.	píngmǐ	square meter	69
破案	v.	pò'àn	crack a criminal case	102
破坏	n.	pòhuài	damage	183
迫切	adj.	pòqiè	urgent	218
普遍	adj.	pǔbiàn	common	69
普及	v.	pǔjí	popularize	96

Q

沏茶	v.o.	qī chá	make tea	157
期待	n.	qīdài	expectation	74
欺负	v.	qīfu	bully	90
期间	n.	qījiān	period	128
起点	n.	qǐdiǎn	starting point	4
企鹅	n.	qǐ'é	penguin	177
气候	n.	qìhòu	climate	182
气象	n.	qìxiàng	scene, atmosphere	247
迁出	v.	qiānchū	move out	129
迁入	v.	qiānrù	move in	129
签署	v.	qiānshǔ	sign (an agreement)	183
迁徙	v.	qiānxǐ	move, migrate	128
千禧一代	phr.	qiānxǐ yí dài	millennials	62
前进	v.	qiánjìn	go forward	219
潜能	n.	qiánnéng	potential	247
前所未有	adj.	qián suǒ wèi yǒu	unprecedented	129
前卫	adj.	qiánwèi	fashionable, modern	123
浅易	adj.	qiǎnyì	simple and easy	96
浅	adj.	qiǎn	shallow	148
强大	adj.	qiángdà	powerful	210
强调	v.	qiángdiào	emphasize	184
强劲	adj.	qiángjìn	strong, powerful	241
抢劫	v.	qiǎngjié	rob	207
桥梁	n.	qiáoliáng	bridge	16
巧妙	adj.	qiǎomiào	ingenious, clever	157
清朝	p.n.	Qīng Cháo	Qing Dynasty (1644-1912)	89
轻轨	n.	qīngguǐ	light rail	34
清华大学	p.n.	Qīnghuá Dàxué	Tsinghua University	90
青睐	n.	qīnglài	favor	242
清晰	adj.	qīngxī	distinct, clear	118
清真寺	n.	qīngzhēnsì	mosque	5
情怀	n.	qínghuái	emotion, sentiment	148
情节	n.	qíngjié	plot, story	102
情谊	n.	qíngyì	friendship	90
求职	v.o.	qiúzhí	apply for a job	72
区别	n.	qūbié	difference	15
趋势	n.	qūshì	trend	241
区域	n.	qūyù	area	123
渠道	n.	qúdào	channel	242
取代	v.	qǔdài	replace	96
取名	v.o.	qǔmíng	give a name to, be named as	44
取暖	v.	qǔnuǎn	warm oneself	188
全面	adj.	quánmiàn	entire, total	216
全球化	n.	quánqiúhuà	globalization	5
全球视野	phr.	quánqiú shìyě	global perspective	159
权威	adj.	quánwēi	authoritative	95
券	n.	quàn	voucher	118
缺乏	v.	quēfá	lack	119
雀巢	p.n.	Quècháo	Nestle	245
确立	v.	quèlì	establish	183
群众	n.	qúnzhòng	the masses	156

R

燃烧	v.	ránshāo	burn	189
燃油车	n.	rányóu chē	vehicle that runs on gasoline or diesel	39
热潮	n.	rècháo	fervor	241

热点	adj.	rèdiǎn	hot (topics)	68
热浪	n.	rèlàng	heat wave	184
热门地段	phr.	rèmén dìduàn	popular sites	72
热议	n.	rèyì	spirited discussion	156
仁爱	n.	rén'ài	benevolence	147
人潮	n.	réncháo	crowd	45
人次	m.w.	réncì	person (referring to passenger traffic volume)	211
人工智能	phr.	réngōng zhìnéng	artificial intelligence	210
人口	n.	rénkǒu	population	35
人类	n.	rénlèi	mankind	96
人民币	n.	rénmínbì	Chinese yuan	69
人山人海	phr.	rén shān rén hǎi	full of people	235
人造	adj.	rénzào	man-made, artificial	210
任何	pron.	rènhé	any	157
仍然	adv.	réngrán	still	39
日趋	adv.	rìqū	increasingly, day by day	45
融合	v.	rónghé	integrate	5
容闳	p.n.	Róng Hóng	Yung Wing (1828-1912) (the first Chinese to graduate from an American college)	89
融资	v.	róngzī	raise funds	45
儒家	p.n.	Rújiā	Confucianism	147
瑞幸咖啡	p.n.	Ruìxìng Kāfēi	Luckin Coffee (a Beijing-based start-up that has hundreds of outlets across China's major cities)	247

S

三藩市	p.n.	Sānfānshì	San Francisco	40
三里屯	p.n.	Sānlǐtún	Sanlitun (a popular destination for shopping, dining and entertainment in Beijing, China)	235
三五成群	phr.	sān-wǔ chéngqún	in groups of three or four	175
三峡	p.n.	Sānxiá	Three Gorges	146
扫	v.	sǎo	scan	44
森林野火	phr.	sēnlín yěhuǒ	forest fire	184
陕西	p.n.	Shǎnxī	Shaanxi (a province in Northwest China)	236
善于	v.	shànyú	be good at	248
商品房	n.	shāngpǐnfáng	commercial housing	72
商业	n.	shāngyè	business	242
上市	v.	shàngshì	become a publicly owned company	246
奢侈品	phr.	shēchǐ pǐn	luxury goods	241
设备	n.	shèbèi	equipment	94
社会主义	n.	shèhuì zhǔyì	socialism	236
社团	n.	shètuán	club, association	89
申奥	v.o.	shēn Ào	bid to host an Olympic Games	35
深度学习	phr.	shēndù xuéxí	deep learning	212
深厚	adj.	shēnhòu	deep, solid	90
深入浅出	phr.	shēnrù qiǎnchū	explain complex matters in simple terms	102
深圳	p.n.	Shēnzhèn	Shenzhen (a city in Guangdong Province)	69
神探	n.	shéntàn	a great detective	102
渗透	v.	shèntòu	pervade	216
生产	n.	shēngchǎn	production	212
生存	v.	shēngcún	survive	119
生态学	n.	shēngtàixué	ecology	175
生育	v.	shēngyù	give birth to	62
省	n.	shěng	province	35
盛	adj.	shèng	prosperous	10
盛名	n.	shèngmíng	great reputation	148
师傅	n.	shīfu	master, teacher	159
失衡	v.	shīhéng	lose balance	64
失落	adj.	shīluò	lost	74
诗圣	p.n.	Shīshèng	Poet-Sage	146
诗仙	p.n.	Shīxiān	Poet Immortal	146
师兄师姐	phr.	shīxiōng shījiě	senior fellow apprentices	158
师资	n.	shīzī	teachers	119
时代广场	p.n.	Shídài Guǎngchǎng	Times Square	123
时代周刊	p.n.	Shídài Zhōukān	Time Magazine	40
时期	n.	shíqī	a particular period	10
实时	n.	shíshí	real-time	129
实施	v.	shíshī	implement	39
实体店	n.	shítǐdiàn	physical store	241
实习	v.	shíxí	work as an intern	69
实验室	n.	shíyànshì	laboratory	175
实用主义	n.	shíyòng zhǔyì	pragmatism	236
石油	n.	shíyóu	petroleum, oil	177
使	v.	shǐ	cause	35
市场份额	phr.	shìchǎng fèn'é	market share	241
市场经济	phr.	shìchǎng jīngjì	market economy	236
市场推广	n.	shìchǎng tuīguǎng	marketing	74
事迹	n.	shìjì	deed, achievement	10
世纪	n.	shìjì	century	15
世界银行	p.n.	Shìjiè Yínháng	World Bank (an international financial institution)	189
视力	n.	shìlì	vision, eyesight	118
市民	n.	shìmín	city residents	124
拭目以待	phr.	shì mù yǐ dài	wait expectantly	242
试图	v.	shìtú	attempt to	247
视野	n.	shìyě	vision, horizon	69
适应	v.	shìyìng	adapt to	90
誓约	n.	shìyuē	pledge, promise	190
市值	n.	shìzhí	market capitalization	246
收藏	v.	shōucáng	collect and keep	151
收费	n.	shōufèi	fee	44
收购	v.	shōugòu	acquire	40
收集	v.	shōují	collect, gather	152
收入	n.	shōurù	income	240
首都	n.	shǒudū	capital city	4
首席运营官	n.	shǒuxí yùnyíng guān	chief operating officer	40
受孕	v.	shòuyùn	become pregnant	175
兽医学	n.	shòuyīxué	veterinary science	175
输出	v.	shūchū	export	5
输入	v.	shūrù	import	5
舒心	adj.	shūxīn	relaxed	69

熟悉	v.	shúxī	be familiar with	245
束缚	n.	shùfù	fetters	157
数据	n.	shùjù	data	118
双独二孩	phr.	shuāng dú èr hái	(a term that refers to the condition in China's two-child policy, where a couple is allowed to have a second child if they are both an only child)	63
双十一光棍节	p.n.	Shuāngshíyī Guānggùnjié	Singles' Day (November 11th)	241
水力发电	phr.	shuǐlì fādiàn	hydroelectricity	189
水墨画	n.	shuǐmòhuà	ink wash painting	151
水师	n.	shuǐshī	navy (a term used in ancient times)	90
水灾	n.	shuǐzāi	flood	184
顺风车	n.	shùnfēngchē	hitch ride (a Didi service)	40
瞬息万变	adj.	shùnxī wàn biàn	fast changing	242
丝绸之路	p.n.	Sīchóu zhī Lù	the Silk Road	4
思考	v.	sīkǎo	think deeply, ponder over	237
思索	v.	sīsuǒ	think deeply, ponder	157
斯坦福大学	p.n.	Sītǎnfú Dàxué	Stanford University	117
思维	n.	sīwéi	thinking	248
思乡	v.	sīxiāng	miss one's hometown	148
四通八达	adj.	sì tōng bā dá	(of road networks) extensive and convenient	34
宋词	p.n.	Sòng Cí	classical Chinese poetry of the Song Dynasty	148
艘	m.w.	sōu	(measure word for ship)	10
苏州博物馆	p.n.	Sūzhōu Bówùguǎn	Suzhou Museum	103
塑造	v.	sùzào	portray	157
随时	adv.	suíshí	at any time	63
随时随地	phr.	suíshí suídì	anytime and anywhere	242
孙中山	p.n.	Sūn Zhōngshān	Sun Yat-sen (1866-1925) (the first president and founding father of the Republic of China)	95
缩影	n.	suōyǐng	epitome, microcosm	119
所谓	v.	suǒwèi	what is called	69

T

台北	p.n.	Táiběi	Taipei	34
台湾桃园机场	p.n.	Táiwān Táoyuán Jīchǎng	Taiwan Taoyuan Airport	34
太极	p.n.	Tàijí	Tai chi (a type of Chinese martial art)	158
太平洋	p.n.	Tàipíngyáng	Pacific Ocean	183
太阳能	n.	tàiyángnéng	solar energy	189
太阳能板	phr.	tàiyángnéng bǎn	solar panel	190
贪污	v.	tānwū	embezzle	207
碳	n.	tàn	carbon	184
探索精神	phr.	tànsuǒ jīngshén	exploratory spirit	236
探险家	n.	tànxiǎnjiā	explorer	4
唐国安	p.n.	Táng Guó'ān	Tong Kwo On (1858-1913) (the founding president of Tsinghua University)	90
螳螂	n.	tángláng	mantis	158
唐山大兄	p.n.	Tángshān Dàxiōng	The Big Boss (Hong Kong martial arts film starring Bruce Lee)	101
唐绍仪	p.n.	Táng Shàoyí	Tang Shaoyi (1862-1938) (the first premier of the Republic of China who took office in 1912)	90
逃离	v.	táolí	get away from	72
套	m.w.	tào	suite (measure word for houses)	68
特产	n.	tèchǎn	local specialty	10
特殊	adj.	tèshū	special	151
特斯拉	p.n.	Tèsīlā	Tesla	235
腾讯	p.n.	Téngxùn	Tencent (a Chinese multinational investment holding conglomerate specializing in Internet-related services and products, entertainment, AI, and technology)	245
提倡	v.	tíchàng	advocate	62
提前	v.	tíqián	move to an earlier date	128
提早	v.	tízǎo	be sooner than planned	190
体力	n.	tǐlì	physical strength	211
体验	v.	tǐyàn	experience	4
替	prep.	tì	on behalf of	217
天际线	n.	tiānjìxiàn	skyline	123
天津	p.n.	Tiānjīn	Tianjin (a municipality of China)	39
天人合一	phr.	tiān rén hé yī	harmony between heaven and man	158
天演论	p.n.	Tiānyǎnlùn	Evolution and Ethics (Chinese translated work of Yan Fu, originally written by Thomas Henry Huxley)	95
铁路	n.	tiělù	railway	90
贴切	adj.	tiēqiè	apt	34
停顿	v.	tíngdùn	halt	216
停放	v.	tíngfàng	park (a vehicle)	44
通道	n.	tōngdào	pathway	5
通讯	n.	tōngxùn	communications	16
同盟会	p.n.	Tóngménghuì	Tung Meng Hui, Chinese Revolutionary League (founded in 1905)	95
统计	n.	tǒngjì	statistics	218
痛点	n.	tòngdiǎn	pain point (a specific problem that prospective customers of a business are experiencing)	248
偷窃	v.	tōuqiè	steal	207
投票	v.	tóupiào	cast a vote	218
徒弟	n.	túdì	protege	159
图片	n.	túpiàn	image	217
团队	n.	tuánduì	team	175
推出	v.	tuīchū	roll out, launch	40
推翻	v.	tuīfān	overthrow	95
推广	v.	tuīguǎng	promote, spread	45
推行	v.	tuīxíng	promote, advocate	207
推销	v.	tuīxiāo	promote	241
脱口秀节目	phr.	tuōkǒuxiù jiémù	talk show	69
脱离	v.	tuōlí	separate oneself from	124
拓展	v.	tuòzhǎn	expand	35

W

外观	n.	wàiguān	exterior appearance	35
外交家	n.	wàijiāojiā	diplomat	5

弯道超车	phr.	wāndào chāochē	overtaking at a turn	236
挽救	v.	wǎnjiù	save	184
网购狂欢节	p.n.	Wǎnggòu Kuánghuānjié	Online Shopping Carnival	241
往来	v.	wǎnglái	come and go	5
网络	n.	wǎngluò	network	216
网络星期一	p.n.	Wǎngluò Xīngqīyī	Cyber Monday	241
网民	n.	wǎngmín	web user, netizen	219
望京SOHO	p.n.	Wàngjīng SOHO	Wangjing SOHO (a landmark in Beijing, China)	123
微软	p.n.	Wēiruǎn	Microsoft	190
威望	n.	wēiwàng	prestige	158
危险	adj.	wēixiǎn	dangerous	176
威胁	n.	wēixié	threat	177
微信钱包	p.n.	Wēixìn Qiánbāo	WeChat Wallet	236
微信支付	p.n.	Wēixìn Zhīfù	WeChat Pay (a mobile payment platform)	206
维西傈僳族自治县	p.n.	Wéixī Lìsùzú Zìzhìxiàn	Weixi Lisu Autonomous County (an autonomous county in Diqing Prefecture, Yunnan Province, China)	174
唯一	adj.	wéiyī	only	184
温度	n.	wēndù	temperature	182
温室气体	phr.	wēnshì qìtǐ	greenhouse gas	182
温室效应	phr.	wēnshì xiàoyìng	greenhouse effect	182
味道	n.	wèidào	taste	5
未来性	adj.	wèilái xìng	futuristic	123
文化背景	phr.	wénhuà bèijǐng	cultural background	218
文化遗产	phr.	wénhuà yíchǎn	cultural heritage	148
文明	n.	wénmíng	civilization	96
文言文	n.	wényánwén	classical Chinese	96
文字	n.	wénzì	writing	217
稳定	v.	wěndìng	stabilize	129
蜗居	p.n.	Wōjū	Dwelling Narrowness (name of a Chinese TV series)	68
沃尔玛	p.n.	Wò'ěrmǎ	Walmart	190
无人机	n.	wúrénjī	drone	248
无现金	adj.	wú xiànjīn	cashless	205
五道口	p.n.	Wǔdàokǒu	Wudaokou (a neighborhood in Beijing)	206
吴冠中	p.n.	Wú Guànzhōng	Wu Guanzhong (1919-2010) (a renowned painter in contemporary China)	151
五环	p.n.	Wǔhuán	5th Ring Road (a major expressway in Beijing)	69
五禽戏	p.n.	Wǔqínxì	Five Animals Mimic Boxing (a kind of training which imitates the movements of the tiger, deer, bear, ape, and bird)	158
五四运动	p.n.	Wǔ-Sì Yùndòng	the May 4th Movement (1919) (an anti-imperialist, anti-feudal, political and cultural movement influenced by the October Revolution and led by intellectuals having the rudiments of Communist ideology)	96
舞台	n.	wǔtái	stage	68
武侠	n.	wǔxiá	a martial artist with chivalrous conduct	157
物流	n.	wùliú	logistics	240
物由心生	phr.	wù yóu xīn shēng	appearance stems from the mind	152
物种	n.	wùzhǒng	species	177

X

稀	adj.	xī	rare	62
稀少	adj.	xīshǎo	few, rare	175
牺牲	v.	xīshēng	sacrifice	207
吸收	n.	xīshōu	absorption	184
悉心	adv.	xīxīn	devote all attention to	159
西洋	p.n.	Xīyáng	seas to the west of China	9
西亚	p.n.	Xīyà	West Asia	5
稀有动物	phr.	xīyǒu dòngwù	rare animal	174
喜悦	adj.	xǐyuè	happy	148
戏剧	n.	xìjù	drama, play	68
系统	n.	xìtǒng	system	16
下单	v.	xiàdān	place an order	39
夏令营	n.	xiàlìngyíng	summer camp	4
仙鹤	n.	xiānhè	fairy crane	158
先进	adj.	xiānjìn	advanced	10
鲜艳夺目	adj.	xiānyàn duómù	bright and eye-catching	44
闲置	v.	xiánzhì	leave unused	45
现代感	n.	xiàndàigǎn	modern sense	102
现代化	n.	xiàndàihuà	modernization	235
限购	v.	xiàngòu	limit one's purchase	39
现金	n.	xiànjīn	cash	205
线路	n.	xiànlù	route	35
羡慕	v.	xiànmù	envy	174
现实主义	n.	xiànshí zhǔyì	realism	147
现象	n.	xiànxiàng	phenomenon	69
乡愁	n.	xiāngchóu	yearning for home	148
香格里拉	p.n.	Xiāng Gé Lǐ Lā	Shangri-La (a county-level city in Yunnan Province, China)	174
香料	n.	xiāngliào	spices	5
相似	adj.	xiāngsì	similar	74
乡镇	n.	xiāngzhèn	villages and towns	118
想象	v.	xiǎngxiàng	imagine	216
想象力	n.	xiǎngxiànglì	imagination	148
项目	n.	xiàngmù	project	4
消费者	n.	xiāofèizhě	consumer	240
潇洒自如	phr.	xiāosǎ zìrú	natural and unrestrained	148
小皇帝	n.	xiǎohuángdì	(lit.) little emperor (a term used to describe an only child who gains excessive amounts of attention from his/her parents and grandparents)	64
小麦	n.	xiǎomài	wheat	5
小米	p.n.	Xiǎomǐ	Xiaomi (a Chinese electronics company)	245
小说	n.	xiǎoshuō	novel	68
孝	n.	xiào	filial piety	157
协议	n.	xiéyì	agreement	183
新宠	n.	xīnchǒng	new favorite	235

薪酬	n.	xīnchóu	salary	45
新高	n.	xīngāo	new high	68
辛亥革命	p.n.	Xīnhài Gémìng	the Revolution of 1911 (the Chinese bourgeois democratic revolution led by Dr. Sun Yat-sen which overthrew the Qing Dynasty)	95
新疆	p.n.	Xīnjiāng	Xinjiang (a province in Northwest China)	5
新文化运动	p.n.	Xīn Wénhuà Yùndòng	the New Culture Movement (around the time of the May 4th Movement in 1919)	96
新兴市场	phr.	xīnxīng shìchǎng	new and developing market	159
星巴克	p.n.	Xīngbākè	Starbucks	190
形成	v.	xíngchéng	form	103
形容	v.	xíngróng	describe	128
行驶	v.	xíngshǐ	drive	39
形式	n.	xíngshì	format, pattern	158
刑事鉴识学	phr.	xíngshì jiànshíxué	criminal forensics	102
形象	adj.	xíngxiàng	vivid	148
形象化	adj.	xíngxiànghuà	visual	45
行云流水	phr.	xíngyún liúshuǐ	natural and spontaneous	148
幸好	adv.	xìnghǎo	fortunately	188
性价比	n.	xìngjiàbǐ	price-performance ratio	242
性骚扰	n.	xìngsāorǎo	sexual harassment	219
熊猫基地	phr.	xióngmāo jīdì	panda base	175
雄心	n.	xióngxīn	great ambitions	123
休斯顿	p.n.	Xiūsīdùn	Houston	68
修筑	v.	xiūzhù	build, construct	90
需求	n.	xūqiú	demand	35
许可	n.	xǔkě	permit, license	39
寻求	v.	xúnqiú	seek	183
迅猛	adj.	xùnměng	swift and strong	245
宣传片	phr.	xuānchuán piàn	promotional film	242
学期	n.	xuéqī	semester	4

Y

押金	n.	yājīn	deposit	44
鸦片战争	p.n.	Yāpiàn Zhànzhēng	Opium Wars (1840-1842; 1856-1860)	90
亚当·斯密	p.n.	Yàdāng Sīmì	Adam Smith (1723-1790) (Scottish economist, philosopher and author)	95
亚马逊	p.n.	Yàmǎxùn	Amazon	211
亚洲	p.n.	Yàzhōu	Asia	4
淹没	v.	yānmò	flood, submerge	183
研发	v.	yánfā	develop	212
严复	p.n.	Yán Fù	Yan Fu (1854-1921) (Chinese scholar and translator, President of Fudan University)	95
沿海	n.	yánhǎi	along the coast	130
研究员	n.	yánjiūyuán	researcher	174
严峻	adj.	yánjùn	severe	64
严肃	adj.	yánsù	serious, solemn	102
演变	v.	yǎnbiàn	evolve	241
演技	n.	yǎnjì	acting skills	102
眼神	n.	yǎnshén	the expression in one's eyes	74
验票口	n.	yàn piào kǒu	fare gate, ticket barrier	206
央视	p.n.	Yāngshì	China Central Television (abbreviation of 中央电视)	128
洋务运动	p.n.	Yángwù Yùndòng	Self-Strengthening Movement (1861-1895) (a drive to learn Western concepts of modernization)	90
杨振宁	p.n.	Yáng Zhènníng	Chen-Ning Frank Yang (a Chinese physicist)	103
摇号	n.	yáohào	lottery system	39
药材	n.	yàocái	medicinal materials, herbs	10
耶鲁大学	p.n.	Yēlǔ Dàxué	Yale University	89
耶鲁大学美术馆	p.n.	Yēlǔ Dàxué Měishùguǎn	Yale University Art Gallery	151
叶	n.	yè	a time period	184
一线	adj.	yī xiàn	first-tier	69
医疗	n.	yīliáo	medical treatment	212
遗传学	n.	yíchuánxué	genetics	175
一带一路	p.n.	Yí Dài Yí Lù	the Belt and Road Initiative	15
一旦	conj.	yídàn	once	217
移动	adj.	yídòng	mobile	241
移动支付	phr.	yídòng zhīfù	mobile payment	205
疑惑	n.	yíhuò	doubt	236
宜家	p.n.	Yíjiā	IKEA	190
一阵子	n.	yízhènzi	a period of time	69
亿	num.	yì	hundred million	211
一举多得	phr.	yì jǔ duō dé	achieve several aims with one action	40
一言为定	phr.	yì yán wéi dìng	that is settled then	124
一卡通	p.n.	Yìkǎtōng	iPASS (a card used for traveling on public transporation in Taiwan)	35
一流	adj.	yìliú	first class	35
意识	n.	yìshí	awareness	177
一胎化政策	phr.	yìtāihuà zhèngcè	one-child policy	62
易通行	p.n.	Yìtōngxíng	Yitongxing (an app for payment)	206
意味	v.	yìwèi	imply, mean	64
义务	n.	yìwù	duty	184
义务教育	phr.	yìwù jiàoyù	compulsory education	117
意想不到	phr.	yìxiǎng búdào	unexpected	245
音箱	n.	yīnxiāng	speaker	248
阴阳	n.	yīnyáng	yin and yang (complementary forces in Chinese philosophy)	158
银河 SOHO	p.n.	Yínhé SOHO	Galaxy SOHO (a landmark in Beijing, China)	123
引导	v.	yǐndǎo	guide	159
引发	v.	yǐnfā	cause, lead to	237
引进	v.	yǐnjìn	introduce	241
引起	v.	yǐnqǐ	give rise to	210
隐私	n.	yǐnsī	privacy	207
印	v.	yìn	print	207
印度洋	p.n.	Yìndùyáng	Indian Ocean	9
婴	n.	yīng	infant	64
英勇善战	phr.	yīngyǒng shànzhàn	brave and good at fighting	156

赢	v.	yíng	win	156
迎合	v.	yínghé	cater to	159
迎接	v.	yíngjiē	meet, welcome	153
应用	n.	yìngyòng	app	40
应用	v.	yìngyòng	apply	212
应用程序	n.	yìngyòng chéngxù	application	217
应运而生	phr.	yìngyùn ér shēng	emerge as the times demand	218
勇气	n.	yǒngqì	courage	74
永寿县	p.n.	Yǒngshòu Xiàn	Yongshou County (a county in Shaanxi Province, China)	117
用户	n.	yònghù	user	128
优步	p.n.	Yōubù	Uber	40
忧国忧民	phr.	yōu guó yōu mín	concerned about one's country and people	147
优化	v.	yōuhuà	optimize	210
悠久	adj.	yōujiǔ	long, age-old	89
优酷	p.n.	Yōukù	Youku (a video hosting service based in Beijing, China)	217
优秀	adj.	yōuxiù	outstanding, excellent	95
优异	adj.	yōuyì	excellent, outstanding	90
油画	n.	yóuhuà	oil painting	151
邮件	n.	yóujiàn	mail	216
油气管道	phr.	yóuqì guǎndào	oil and gas pipelines	16
邮政	n.	yóuzhèng	postal	16
游子	n.	yóuzǐ	a person traveling or residing in a place far away from home	148
有待	v.	yǒudài	await	237
有限	adj.	yǒuxiàn	limited	211
友谊	n.	yǒuyì	friendship	10
幼童	n.	yòutóng	young child	90
幼仔	n.	yòuzǎi	young animal	175
余光中	p.n.	Yú Guāngzhōng	Yu Kwang-Chung (1928-2017) (a famous Taiwanese writer, poet, educator, and critic)	148
于是	conj.	yúshì	hence	94
与其	conj.	yǔqí	rather than	146
语音	n.	yǔyīn	voice (message)	212
语言	n.	yǔyán	language	96
预购	v.	yùgòu	purchase in advance	128
预约	v.	yùyuē	make a reservation or booking	40
原富	p.n.	Yuán Fù	The Wealth of Nations (Chinese translated work of Yan Fu, originally written by Adam Smith)	95
元曲	p.n.	Yuán Qǔ	Qu, a form of poetry from the Yuan Dynasty	148
元年	n.	yuánnián	first year	213
源自	v.	yuánzì	originate from	184
岳	n.	Yuè	Yue (Chinese surname)	205
阅读	v.	yuèdú	read	216
云端储存	phr.	yúnduān chǔcún	cloud storage	246
云计算	n.	yún jìsuàn	cloud computing	211
云南	p.n.	Yúnnán	Yunnan (a province in Southern China)	9
蕴藏	v.	yùncáng	contain	158
运输	v.	yùnshū	transport	128
运算	v.	yùnsuàn	carry out an (mathematical) operation	210
运营	v.	yùnyíng	operate	34
运作	v.	yùnzuò	operate	123

Z

再度	adv.	zàidù	once again	210
灾害	n.	zāihài	disaster	184
在线	adj.	zàixiàn	online	247
暂时	adv.	zànshí	temporarily	39
藏羚羊	n.	Zànglíngyáng	Tibetan antelope	176
藏族	p.n.	Zàngzú	Tibetan Ethnic Minority	174
遭到	v.	zāodào	suffer, encounter	183
赠送	v.	zèngsòng	give us a present	176
增长	v.	zēngzhǎng	increase, grow	211
扎根	v.	zhāgēn	take root, settle down in a place	73
窄	adj.	zhǎi	narrow	148
詹天佑	p.n.	Zhān Tiānyòu	Jeme Tien Yow (1861-1919) (a pioneering Chinese railroad engineer)	90
占	v.	zhàn	constitute	64
战斗	n.	zhàndòu	battle, fight	40
战胜	v.	zhànshèng	defeat, triumph over	157
张骞	p.n.	Zhāng Qiān	Zhang Qian (an ancient diplomat)	5
涨	v.	zhǎng	rise	72
障碍	n.	zhàng'ài	obstacle, barrier	90
账户	n.	zhànghù	account	205
账目	n.	zhàngmù	accounts	45
召开	v.	zhàokāi	convene	183
照明	n.	zhàomíng	lighting	189
哲理	n.	zhélǐ	philosophy	158
针对	v.	zhēnduì	direct at	39
真实	adj.	zhēnshí	real	157
震惊	adj.	zhènjīng	amazed, shocked	123
争夺	v.	zhēngduó	vie	40
争取	v.	zhēngqǔ	strive for	183
挣扎	v.	zhēngzhá	struggle	119
拯救	adj.	zhěngjiù	save	159
正常	adj.	zhèngcháng	normal	64
政府	n.	zhèngfǔ	government	39
正好	adv.	zhènghǎo	happen to	89
郑和	p.n.	Zhèng Hé	Zheng He (a famous navigator of China)	9
政治	n.	zhèngzhì	politics	16
郑州	p.n.	Zhèngzhōu	Zhengzhou (the capital city of Henan Province, China)	130
脂肪层	n.	zhīfángcéng	fat layer	176
支付	v.	zhīfù	pay	45
支付宝	p.n.	Zhīfù Bǎo	Alipay (a mobile and online payment platform)	206
芝加哥	p.n.	Zhījiāgē	Chicago	101
知识分子	n.	zhīshi fènzǐ	intellectuals	94

职场	n.	zhíchǎng	workplace	248
值得	v.	zhídé	be worthy of	35
直接	adj.	zhíjiē	direct	39
指日可待	phr.	zhǐrì kědài	just around the corner	190
智慧	n.	zhìhuì	intelligence, wisdom	210
治理	v.	zhìlǐ	control	188
质量	n.	zhìliàng	quality	119
秩序	n.	zhìxù	order	236
至于	prep.	zhìyú	as for	102
忠	n.	zhōng	loyalty	157
中东	p.n.	Zhōngdōng	the Middle East	15
中国城	n.	Zhōngguó Chéng	Chinatown	101
中国银行大厦	p.n.	Zhōngguó Yínháng Dàshà	Bank of China Tower	103
中华民国	p.n.	Zhōnghuá Mínguó	the Republic of China	90
终年	n.	zhōngnián	throughout the year	174
中亚	p.n.	Zhōngyà	Central Asia	5
中央电视台	p.n.	Zhōngyāng Diànshìtái	China Central Television	90
中央美术学院	p.n.	Zhōngyāng Měishù Xuéyuàn	Central Academy of Fine Arts	153
终于	adv.	zhōngyú	finally	40
种族	n.	zhǒngzú	race	218
重大	adj.	zhòngdà	major	35
众多	adj.	zhòngduō	numerous	35
重任	n.	zhòngrèn	important task	159
众所周知	phr.	zhòng suǒ zhōu zhī	as everyone knows	176
周恩来	p.n.	Zhōu Ēnlái	Zhou Enlai (1898-1976) *(the first premier of the People's Republic of China who took office in 1949)*	96
珠宝	n.	zhūbǎo	pearls and jewels	10
珠江三角洲	p.n.	Zhūjiāng Sānjiǎo Zhōu	Pearl River Delta *(a metropolitan region)*	124
主导	v.	zhǔdǎo	leading	189
准确	adj.	zhǔnquè	accurate	212
主任	n.	zhǔrèn	director, head	119
主题	n.	zhǔtí	theme	159
住房	n.	zhùfáng	housing, lodging	68
著作	n.	zhùzuò	book	95
专车	n.	zhuānchē	an exclusive ride *(a Didi service)*	40
转发	v.	zhuǎnfā	forward	123
赚钱	v.o	zhuànqián	make money	207
庄子	p.n.	Zhuāngzǐ	Zhuangzi (369-286 BC) *(an influential Chinese philosopher of the Warring States period)*	158
追逐	v.	zhuīzhú	pursue	124
追逐	v.	zhuīzhú	chase	175
资本主义	n.	zīběn zhǔyì	capitalism	236
资讯	n.	zīxùn	information	218
滋养	v.	zīyǎng	nurture	159
自产量	phr.	zìchǎnliàng	volume of self-production	190
自动	adj.	zìdòng	automatic	206
自然保护区	phr.	zìrán bǎohùqū	nature reserve	174
自然风光	phr.	zìrán fēngguāng	natural scenery	148
自我价值	phr.	zìwǒ jiàzhí	value of self	157
自信	v.	zìxìn	have confidence in oneself	118
自由	adj.	zìyóu	free (to do something)	39
自主	v.	zìzhǔ	act on one's own	90
总理	n.	zǒnglǐ	premier	90
总里程	n.	zǒnglǐchéng	total mileage	35
纵横交错	phr.	zònghéng jiāocuò	crisscross	35
租	v.	zū	rent	45
租金	n.	zūjīn	rental	74
足迹	n.	zújì	footprint	146
族群	n.	zúqún	ethnic group	103
祖国	n.	zǔguó	home country	147
做生意	v.o.	zuò shēngyi	do business	16
作用	n.	zuòyòng	effect	96

ABBREVIATIONS FOR GRAMMATICAL TERMS

n.	noun	m.w.	measure word	num.	numeral
v.	verb	pron.	pronoun	aux.v.	auxiliary verb
adj.	adjective	prep.	preposition	phr.	phrase
adv.	adverb	conj.	conjunction	v.o.	verb-object construction

2. 生词索引（英汉）VOCABULARY INDEX (ENGLISH TO CHINESE)

A

(a term describing people working in Beijing who are not registered residents there)	北漂一族	phr.	běi piāo yì zú	72
(a term that refers to the condition in China's two-child policy, where a couple is allowed to have a second child if either of them is an only child)	单独二孩	phr.	dān dú èr hái	63
(a term that refers to the condition in China's two-child policy, where a couple is allowed to have a second child if they are both an only child)	双独二孩	phr.	shuāng dú èr hái	63
(a term used to describe the period beginning in late Qing Qynasty, when many young people went abroad to study)	留学潮	n.	liúxué cháo	96
a stream of	股	m.w.	gǔ	219
abbreviated form of a name	简称	n.	jiǎnchēng	69
abnormal	反常	adj.	fǎncháng	184
absolutely	绝对	adv.	juéduì	148
absorption	吸收	n.	xīshōu	184
abstract	抽象	adj.	chōuxiàng	148
abundant	充沛	adj.	chōngpèi	248
account	账户	n.	zhànghù	205
accounts	账目	n.	zhàngmù	45
accurate	准确	adj.	zhǔnquè	212
achieve several aims with one action	一举多得	phr.	yì jǔ duō dé	40
achieve, accomplish	成就	v.	chéngjiù	159
acquire	收购	v.	shōugòu	40
act on one's own	自主	v.	zìzhǔ	90
acting skills	演技	n.	yǎnjì	102
active	活跃	adj.	huóyuè	240
Adam Smith (1723-1790) (Scottish economist, philosopher and author)	亚当·斯密	p.n.	Yàdāng Sīmì	95
adapt from	改编	v.	gǎibiān	68
adapt to	适应	v.	shìyìng	90
admittedly, it is true that	固然	adv.	gùrán	119
advanced	先进	adj.	xiānjìn	10
advantage	利	n.	lì	207
advocate	提倡, 倡导	v.	tíchàng, chàngdǎo	62, 189
Africa	非洲	p.n.	Fēizhōu	4
again	重新	adv.	chóngxīn	45
agile	灵活	adj.	línghuó	175
aging	老龄化	n.	lǎolínghuà	64
agreement	协议	n.	xiéyì	183
Airbnb	爱彼迎	p.n.	Àibǐyíng	45
alarmingly dangerous	惊险	adj.	jīngxiǎn	174
Alibaba (a Chinese multinational e-commerce, retail, Internet, AI and technology conglomerate)	阿里巴巴	p.n.	Ālǐbābā	245
Alipay (a mobile and online payment platform)	支付宝	p.n.	Zhīfù Bǎo	206
all the rage	风靡一时	phr.	fēngmí yì shí	44
all the same, in any case	反正	adv.	fǎnzhèng	69
along the coast	沿海	n.	yánhǎi	130
AlphaGo (a computer program that plays the board game Go)	阿尔法围棋	p.n.	Ā'ěrfǎ Wéiqí	210
amazed, shocked	震惊	adj.	zhènjīng	123
Amazon	亚马逊	p.n.	Yàmǎxùn	211
ambassador	大使	n.	dàshǐ	10
American	美籍	n.	Měijí	102
Americas	美洲	p.n.	Měizhōu	9
analyze	分析	v.	fēnxī	211
analyze, interpret	解读	v.	jiědú	129
ancient time	古代	n.	gǔdài	9
angle, perspective	角度	n.	jiǎodù	16
animation movie	动画片	n.	dònghuàpiàn	156
answer to a riddle	谜底	n.	mídǐ	103
Ant Financial (a fintech company which is affiliated to Alibaba)	蚂蚁金服	p.n.	Mǎyǐ Jīnfú	246
any	任何	pron.	rènhé	157
anytime and anywhere	随时随地	phr.	suíshí suídì	242
apartment	公寓	n.	gōngyù	45
app	应用	n.	yìngyòng	40
appearance stems from the mind	物由心生	phr.	wù yóu xīn shēng	152
application	应用程序	n.	yìngyòng chéngxù	217
apply	应用	v.	yìngyòng	212
apply for a job	求职	v.o.	qiúzhí	72
approximately	大约	adv.	dàyuē	103
apt	贴切	adj.	tiēqiè	34
area	面积, 区域	n.	miànjī, qūyù	68, 123
area, district	地区	n.	dìqū	117
area, field	领域	n.	lǐngyù	151
artificial intelligence	人工智能	phr.	réngōng zhìnéng	210

English	Chinese	POS	Pinyin	Page
as everyone knows	众所周知	phr.	zhòng suǒ zhōu zhī	176
as for	至于	prep.	zhìyú	102
as fully as possible	充分	adv.	chōngfèn	147
Asia	亚洲	p.n.	Yàzhōu	4
associate with	联想	v.	liánxiǎng	45
at any time	随时	adv.	suíshí	63
at one's leisure	茶余饭后	phr.	chá yú fàn hòu	44
at regular intervals	定期	adv.	dìngqī	118
at that time	当时	adv.	dāngshí	10
atmosphere	大气层	n.	dàqìcéng	182
attempt to	试图	v.	shìtú	247
authoritative	权威	adj.	quánwēi	95
automatic	自动	adj.	zìdòng	206
aviation	航空	n.	hángkōng	211
await	有待	v.	yǒudài	237
award	奖项	n.	jiǎngxiàng	89
awareness	意识	n.	yìshí	177

B

English	Chinese	POS	Pinyin	Page
background	背景	n.	bèijǐng	147
Baidi City (an ancient temple complex in Chongqing, China)	白帝城	p.n.	Báidìchéng	146
Baidu (a Chinese multinational technology company)	百度	p.n.	Bǎidù	128
bank note	钞票	n.	chāopiào	207
Bank of China Tower	中国银行大厦	p.n.	Zhōngguó Yínháng Dàshà	103
battle, fight	战斗	n.	zhàndòu	40
be a foil to	衬托	v.	chèntuō	147
bear	承担	v.	chéngdān	64
become a publicly owned company	上市	v.	shàngshì	246
become extinct, die out	绝种	v.	juézhǒng	174
become pregnant	受孕	v.	shòuyùn	175
becoming extreme	极端化	n.	jíduānhuà	183
Belt and Road Initiative	一带一路	p.n.	Yí Dài Yí Lù	15
benevolence	仁爱	n.	rén'ài	147
best, top	顶尖	adj.	dǐngjiān	237
bewildered	困惑	adj.	kùnhuò	74
bicycle sharing	共享单车	phr.	gòngxiǎng dānchē	44
bid to host an Olympic Games	申奥	v.o.	shēn Ào	35
big data	大数据	n.	dà shùjù	207
big scale	大规模	n.	dà guīmó	128
Black Friday	黑色星期五	p.n.	Hēisè Xīngqīwǔ	241
Boeing Company	波音公司	p.n.	Bōyīn Gōngsī	241
book	著作	n.	zhùzuò	95
book tickets	订票	v.o.	dìng piào	211
Boston	波士顿	p.n.	Bōshìdùn	89
box office (earnings from a movie)	票房	n.	piàofáng	156
Boxer Rebellion Indemnity (1900)	庚子赔款	p.n.	Gēngzǐ Péikuǎn	95
brand	品牌	n.	pǐnpái	245
brave and good at fighting	英勇善战	phr.	yīngyǒng shànzhàn	156
break	打破	v.	dǎpò	213
breed	繁育, 配种	v.	fányù, pèizhǒng	175, 176
bridge	桥梁	n.	qiáoliáng	16
bright	明亮	adj.	míngliàng	118
bright and eye-catching	鲜艳夺目	adj.	xiānyàn duómù	44
bring	带来	v.	dàilái	45
bring glory to one's ancestors	光宗耀祖	phr.	guāngzōng yàozǔ	157
bring into play, give free rein to	发挥	v.	fāhuī	159
broad	广阔	adj.	guǎngkuò	69
brought into	传入	v.	chuánrù	5
Bruce Lee (1940-1973) (a martial arts actor and martial artist)	李小龙	p.n.	Lǐ Xiǎolóng	101
Buddhism	佛教	p.n.	Fójiào	5
build	建立, 搭建	v.	jiànlì, dājiàn	10, 207
build, construct	修筑, 构建	v.	xiūzhù, gòujiàn	90, 236
bully	欺负	v.	qīfu	90
burn	燃烧	v.	ránshāo	189
business	商业	n.	shāngyè	242

C

English	Chinese	POS	Pinyin	Page
call, appeal	号召	v.	hàozhào	190
Cantonese	广东人	n.	Guǎngdōngrén	89
capacity	量	n.	liàng	130
capital	京城	n.	jīngchéng	147
capital city	首都	n.	shǒudū	4
capitalism	资本主义	n.	zīběn zhǔyì	236
capture	捕捉	v.	bǔzhuō	248
car show	车展	n.	chēzhǎn	235
carbon	碳	n.	tàn	184
care for	关怀	v.	guānhuái	147
carrot	胡萝卜	n.	húluóbo	5
carry on	继承	v.	jìchéng	152
carry out an (mathematical) operation	运算	v.	yùnsuàn	210
case	案件	n.	ànjiàn	102
case (example)	案例	n.	ànlì	247

English	Chinese	Part	Pinyin	Page
cash	现金	n.	xiànjīn	205
cashless	无现金	adj.	wú xiànjīn	205
cast a vote	投票	v.	tóupiào	218
casually, carelessly	胡乱	adv.	húluàn	45
catalyst	催化剂	n.	cuīhuàjì	211
cater to	迎合	v.	yínghé	159
cause	使	v.	shǐ	35
cause, lead to	引发	v.	yǐnfā	237
Central Academy of Fine Arts	中央美术学院	p.n.	Zhōngyāng Měishù Xuéyuàn	153
Central Asia	中亚	p.n.	Zhōngyà	5
century	世纪	n.	shìjì	15
chain reaction	连锁反应	phr.	liánsuǒ fǎnyìng	183
champion	冠军	n.	guànjūn	210
change	变化	n.	biànhuà	35
channel	渠道	n.	qúdào	242
chase	追逐	v.	zhuīzhú	175
cheap	廉价	adj.	liánjià	245
Cheng Yu (a metropolitan region)	成渝	p.n.	Chéngyú	124
Chengdu (the capital city of Sichuan Province, China)	成都	p.n.	Chéngdū	39
Chen-Ning Frank Yang (a Chinese physicist)	杨振宁	p.n.	Yáng Zhènníng	103
Chicago	芝加哥	p.n.	Zhījiāgē	101
chief operating officer	首席运营官	n.	shǒuxí yùnyíng guān	40
children of migrant workers	打工子弟	phr.	dǎgōng zǐdì	119
China Central Television	中央电视台	p.n.	Zhōngyāng Diànshìtái	90
China Central Television (abbreviation of 中央电视)	央视	p.n.	Yāngshì	128
Chinatown	中国城	n.	Zhōngguó Chéng	101
Chinese characters	汉字	n.	hànzì	217
Chinese economic reform	改革开放	phr.	gǎigé kāifàng	124
Chinese yuan	人民币	n.	rénmínbì	69
Chongqing (a city in Southwest China)	重庆	p.n.	Chóngqìng	130
Christianity	基督教	p.n.	Jīdūjiào	5
Christopher Columbus	哥伦布	p.n.	Gēlúnbù	9
city cluster	城市群	n.	chéngshì qún	123
city residents	市民	n.	shìmín	124
city-state	城邦	n.	chéngbāng	124
civilization	文明	n.	wénmíng	96
clan, family	家族	n.	jiāzú	157
classical Chinese	文言文	n.	wényánwén	96
classical Chinese poetry of the Song Dynasty	宋词	p.n.	Sòng Cí	148
Claude Monet (1840-1926) (a French painter and founder of French Impressionist painting)	莫奈	p.n.	Mònài	152
climate	气候	n.	qìhòu	182
climb	攀爬	v.	pānpá	175
close	密切	adj.	mìqiè	124
close down	倒闭	v.	dǎobì	242
close range	近距离	adj.	jìnjùlí	175
cloud computing	云计算	n.	yún jìsuàn	211
cloud storage	云端储存	phr.	yúnduān chǔcún	246
club, association	社团	n.	shètuán	89
coal	煤炭	n.	méitàn	188
Coca Cola	可口可乐	p.n.	Kěkǒu Kělè	245
code	代码	n.	dàimǎ	74
co-exist peacefully	和平共处	phr.	hépíng gòngchǔ	10
collaborate	合作	v.	hézuò	16
collect and keep	收藏	v.	shōucáng	151
collect, gather	收集	v.	shōují	152
color	彩色	n.	cǎisè	240
come and go	往来	v.	wǎnglái	5
commercial housing	商品房	n.	shāngpǐnfáng	72
commit a crime	犯罪	v.	fànzuì	207
common	普遍	adj.	pǔbiàn	69
communications	通讯	n.	tōngxùn	16
complement one another	互补	v.	hùbǔ	16
compulsory education	义务教育	phr.	yìwù jiàoyù	117
concentrate	集中	v.	jízhōng	129
concentration	浓度	n.	nóngdù	188
concern, have a bearing on	关系	v.	guānxì	157
concerned about one's country and people	忧国忧民	phr.	yōu guó yōu mín	147
conclusion	结论	n.	jiélùn	184
conference	会议	n.	huìyì	184
Confucianism	儒家	p.n.	Rújiā	147
Connecticut	康州	p.n.	Kāng Zhōu	89
consensus, agreement	共识	n.	gòngshí	183
conservative	保守	adj.	bǎoshǒu	63
constitute	占	v.	zhàn	64
construction	建设	n.	jiànshè	35
consumer	消费者	n.	xiāofèizhě	240
contain	蕴藏	v.	yùncáng	158
continuously	不断	adv.	búduàn	45
contribution	贡献	n.	gòngxiàn	10
control	治理	v.	zhìlǐ	188

English	Chinese	Part	Pinyin	Page
convene	召开	v.	zhàokāi	183
convenient	便捷	adj.	biànjié	35
copy, imitate	仿造	v.	fǎngzào	245
cost	成本	n.	chéngběn	45
counterfeit goods	假货	n.	jiǎhuò	245
courage	勇气	n.	yǒngqì	74
cover	覆盖	v.	fùgài	35
crack a criminal case	破案	v.	pò'àn	102
Crazy Rich Asians (a Hollywood movie)	疯狂的亚洲富豪	p.n.	Fēngkuáng de Yàzhōu Fùháo	156
create	创造	v.	chuàngzào	217
criminal forensics	刑事鉴识学	phr.	xíngshì jiànshíxué	102
crisscross	纵横交错	phr.	zònghéng jiāocuò	35
cross-border	跨境	phr.	kuàjìng	241
cross-cultural	跨文化	v.o.	kuà wénhuà	159
crowd	人潮	n.	réncháo	45
crystal clear	晶莹剔透	adj.	jīngyíng tītòu	103
cultural background	文化背景	phr.	wénhuà bèijīng	218
cultural heritage	文化遗产	phr.	wénhuà yíchǎn	148
customer	顾客	n.	gùkè	207
customer, client	客户	n.	kèhù	242
Cyber Monday	网络星期一	p.n.	Wǎngluò Xīngqīyī	241

D

English	Chinese	Part	Pinyin	Page
Dà-Jiāng Innovations (DJI) (a Chinese technology company)	大疆	p.n.	Dàjiāng	248
Da Vinci Code	达·芬奇的密码	p.n.	Dá Fēnqí de Mìmǎ	103
damage	破坏	n.	pòhuài	183
dangerous	危险	adj.	wēixiǎn	176
Daoism	道教	p.n.	Dàojiào	148
data	数据	n.	shùjù	118
decade, era	年代	n.	niándài	45
deed, achievement	事迹	n.	shìjì	10
deep learning	深度学习	phr.	shēndù xuéxí	212
deep, solid	深厚	adj.	shēnhòu	90
deepen	加深	v.	jiāshēn	90
defeat	打败	v.	dǎbài	94
defeat, triumph over	战胜	v.	zhànshèng	157
definitely	肯定	adv.	kěndìng	129
definition	定义	n.	dìngyì	218
demand	需求	n.	xūqiú	35
democracy	民主	n.	mínzhǔ	96
Deng Xiaoping (1904-1997) (former leader of the People's Republic of China who is widely credited with the economic reforms of the 1980s which propelled China to the economic powerhouse it is today)	邓小平	p.n.	Dèng Xiǎopíng	96
depict, portray	描写	v.	miáoxiě	147
deposit	押金	n.	yājīn	44
describe	描述	v.	miáoshù	68
describe	形容	v.	xíngróng	128
designated driver service (a Didi service)	代驾	n.	dàijià	40
destructive	毁灭性	adj.	huǐmièxìng	184
develop	研发	v.	yánfā	212
developed	发达	adj.	fādá	124
developing country	发展中国家	phr.	fāzhǎn zhōng guójiā	235
devote all attention to	悉心	adv.	xīxīn	159
Dhaka (the capital of Bangladesh)	达卡	p.n.	Dákǎ	183
dialog	对话	n.	duìhuà	4
Didi (a Chinese ride-sharing company)	滴滴	p.n.	Dīdī	40
die out	灭绝	v.	mièjué	183
difference	区别, 差别	n.	qūbié, chābié	15, 205
diplomat	外交家	n.	wàijiāojiā	5
direct	直接	adj.	zhíjiē	39
direct at	针对	v.	zhēnduì	39
director, head	主任	n.	zhǔrèn	119
disadvantage	弊	n.	bì	207
disaster	灾害	n.	zāihài	184
distinct, clear	清晰	adj.	qīngxī	118
distribute	派发	v.	pàifā	118
distribution	分销	n.	fēnxiāo	240
district	街区	n.	jiēqū	237
diversity	多样性	n.	duōyàngxìng	177
division	分化	n.	fēnhuà	237
do business	做生意	v.o.	zuò shēngyi	16
do one's utmost	极力	adv.	jílì	183
documentary	纪录片	n.	jìlùpiàn	184
Dongzhimen (a subway station in Beijing, China)	东直门	p.n.	Dōngzhímén	206
doomsday	末日	n.	mòrì	184
doubt	疑惑	n.	yíhuò	236
drama, play	戏剧	n.	xìjù	68
drift ice	浮冰	n.	fúbīng	176
drive	行驶	v.	xíngshǐ	39
drive (a vehicle)	驾驶	v.	jiàshǐ	213
drone	无人机	n.	wúrénjī	248

English	Chinese	Part	Pinyin	Page
drop out of school	辍学	v.	chuòxué	117
drought	干旱	n.	gānhàn	184
Du Fu (712-770) (a prominent Chinese poet of the Tang Dynasty)	杜甫	p.n.	Dù Fǔ	146
duty	义务	n.	yìwù	184
Dwelling Narrowness (name of a Chinese TV series)	蜗居	p.n.	Wōjū	68
dynasty	朝代	n.	cháodài	4

E

English	Chinese	Part	Pinyin	Page
earth	地球	n.	dìqiú	177
ecology	生态学	n.	shēngtàixué	175
economic zone	经济带	phr.	jīngjì dài	15
economy	经济体	n.	jīngjìtǐ	235
Education in Sight (an NGO in China that seeks to improve the eyesight of children in rural areas)	点亮眼睛	p.n.	Diǎnliàng Yǎnjing	118
effect	作用	n.	zuòyòng	96
efficient	高效	adj.	gāoxiào	218
electric car	电动车	n.	diàndòng chē	39
elegant	典雅	adj.	diǎnyǎ	147
embezzle	贪污	v.	tānwū	207
emerge as the times demand	应运而生	phr.	yìngyùn ér shēng	218
emission	排放物	n.	páifàngwù	189
emotion, sentiment	情怀	n.	qínghuái	148
emphasize	强调	v.	qiángdiào	184
encouraging	鼓舞	adj.	gǔwǔ	190
end	结束	v.	jiéshù	241
enemy	敌人	n.	dírén	159
energy	能源	n.	néngyuán	16
entire, total	全面	adj.	quánmiàn	216
envy	羡慕	v.	xiànmù	174
epitome, microcosm	缩影	n.	suōyǐng	119
epoch-making	划时代	adj.	huàshídài	96
equal, fair	平等	adj.	píngděng	219
equipment	设备	n.	shèbèi	94
establish	成立, 确立	v.	chénglì, quèlì	95, 183
estimate	估计	v.	gūjì	64
ethnic group	族群	n.	zúqún	103
Europe	欧洲	p.n.	Ōuzhōu	4
everything	凡事	n.	fánshì	207
Evolution and Ethics (Chinese translated work of Yan Fu, originally written by Thomas Henry Huxley)	天演论	p.n.	Tiānyǎnlùn	95
evolve	演变	v.	yǎnbiàn	241
exactly	究竟	adv.	jiūjìng	182
excellent, outstanding	优异	adj.	yōuyì	90
exchange	交换	v.	jiāohuàn	10
exchange something for	换取	v.	huànqǔ	118
exclusive ride (a Didi service)	专车	n.	zhuānchē	40
executive	高管	n.	gāoguǎn	190
exist	存在	v.	cúnzài	64
expand	拓展	v.	tuòzhǎn	35
expectation	期待	n.	qīdài	74
expenses	开支	n.	kāizhī	189
experience	体验	v.	tǐyàn	4
experience	经验	n.	jīngyàn	123
explain	解释, 解说	v.	jiěshì, jiěshuō	15, 102
explain complex matters in simple terms	深入浅出	phr.	shēnrù qiǎnchū	102
exploit	开发	v.	kāifā	189
exploratory spirit	探索精神	phr.	tànsuǒ jīngshén	236
explorer	探险家	n.	tànxiǎnjiā	4
export	输出	v.	shūchū	5
express, say	表示	v.	biǎoshì	118
express ride (a Didi service)	快车	n.	kuàichē	40
expression in one's eyes	眼神	n.	yǎnshén	74
extensive	广泛	adj.	guǎngfàn	212
(of road networks) extensive and convenient	四通八达	adj.	sì tōng bā dá	34
extent of a country	幅员	n.	fúyuán	35
extent, degree	程度	n.	chéngdù	39
exterior appearance	外观	n.	wàiguān	35
extract	开采	v.	kāicǎi	177

F

English	Chinese	Part	Pinyin	Page
fairy crane	仙鹤	n.	xiānhè	158
familiar with	熟悉	v.	shúxī	245
famous mountains and rivers	名山大川	phr.	míng shān dà chuān	146
fare gate, ticket barrier	验票口	n.	yàn piào kǒu	206
fashionable, modern	前卫	adj.	qiánwèi	123
fast changing	瞬息万变	adj.	shùnxī wàn biàn	242
fat layer	脂肪层	n.	zhīfángcéng	176
favor	青睐	n.	qīnglài	242
fee	收费	n.	shōufèi	44
feel, touch	摸	v.	mō	236
female impersonating as a male	女扮男装	phr.	nǚ bàn nán zhuāng	156
fennel	茴香	n.	huíxiāng	5
fervor	热潮	n.	rècháo	241
fetters	束缚	n.	shùfù	157
feudalistic	封建	adj.	fēngjiàn	95
few, rare	稀少	adj.	xīshǎo	175

English	Chinese	Part	Pinyin	Page
Fifth Avenue	第五大道	p.n.	Dì Wǔ Dàdào	123
5th Ring Road (a major expressway in Beijing)	五环	p.n.	Wǔhuán	69
fight a battle	打仗	v.	dǎzhàng	156
filial piety	孝	n.	xiào	157
film (a movie)	拍摄	v.	pāishè	156
film director	导演	n.	dǎoyǎn	156
finally	终于	adv.	zhōngyú	40
first class	一流	adj.	yìliú	35
First Sino-Japanese War (1894-1895) (launched by Japanese imperialism to annex Korea and invade China)	甲午战争	p.n.	Jiǎwǔ Zhànzhēng	94
first year	元年	n.	yuánnián	213
first-tier	一线	adj.	yī xiàn	69
Fist of Fury (Hong Kong martial arts film starring Bruce Lee)	精武门	p.n.	Jīngwǔmén	101
fit	符合	v.	fúhé	217
Five Animals Mimic Boxing (a kind of training which imitates the movements of the tiger, deer, bear, ape, and bird)	五禽戏	p.n.	Wǔqínxì	158
fleet	船队	n.	chuánduì	9
flood	水灾	n.	shuǐzāi	184
flood, submerge	淹没	v.	yānmò	183
(of people) flow	流动	n.	liúdòng	35
focus perspective (an art technique)	焦点透视法	phr.	jiāodiǎn tòushì fǎ	152
food and beverage	餐饮	n.	cānyǐn	242
footprint	足迹	n.	zújì	146
for example	比方	v.	bǐfang	44
foreign citizen of Chinese origin	华裔	n.	huáyì	103
forest fire	森林野火	phr.	sēnlín yěhuǒ	184
form	形成	v.	xíngchéng	103
format, pattern	形式	n.	xíngshì	158
fortunately	幸好	adv.	xìnghǎo	188
forum	论坛	n.	lùntán	123
forward	转发	v.	zhuǎnfā	123
fossil fuel	化石燃料	phr.	huàshí ránliào	189
found	创立	v.	chuànglì	40
foundation	基金会	n.	jījīn huì	118
founder	创始人	n.	chuàngshǐrén	45
free (to do something)	自由	adj.	zìyóu	39
frequent	频繁	adj.	pínfán	35
friendship	友谊, 情谊	n.	yǒuyì, qíngyì	10, 90
full of people	人山人海	phr.	rén shān rén hǎi	235
futuristic	未来性	adj.	wèilái xìng	123

G

English	Chinese	Part	Pinyin	Page
Galaxy SOHO (a landmark in Beijing, China)	银河SOHO	p.n.	Yínhé SOHO	123
Gansu (a province in Northwest China)	甘肃	p.n.	Gānsù	5
genetics	遗传学	n.	yíchuánxué	175
geographer	地理学家	n.	dìlǐ xuéjiā	5
get around	出行	v.	chūxíng	34
get away from	逃离	v.	táolí	72
give a name to, be named as	取名	v.o.	qǔmíng	44
give birth to	生育	v.	shēngyù	62
give expression to one's feelings	寄情	v.	jìqíng	148
give rise to	引起	v.	yǐnqǐ	210
give the credit to	归功	v.	guīgōng	205
give us a present	赠送	v.	zèngsòng	176
glass ceiling	玻璃天花板	phr.	bōli tiānhuābǎn	248
global perspective	全球视野	phr.	quánqiú shìyě	159
globalization	全球化	n.	quánqiúhuà	5
glory	光荣	n.	guāngróng	157
go against	背道而驰	phr.	bèi dào ér chí	63
go all out in work	拼搏	v.	pīnbó	69
go forward	前进	v.	qiánjìn	219
gold	黄金	n.	huángjīn	147
good at	善于	v.	shànyú	248
good fortune	福气	n.	fúqì	63
Google	谷歌	p.n.	Gǔgē	74
government	政府	n.	zhèngfǔ	39
great ambitions	雄心	n.	xióngxīn	123
great detective	神探	n.	shéntàn	102
great reputation	盛名	n.	shèngmíng	148
greenhouse effect	温室效应	phr.	wēnshì xiàoyìng	182
greenhouse gas	温室气体	phr.	wēnshì qìtǐ	182
grill meat, barbecue	烤肉	v.o.	kǎoròu	68
Guangzhou (a city in Guangdong Province, China)	广州	p.n.	Guǎngzhōu	69
guide	引导	v.	yǐndǎo	159

H

English	Chinese	Part	Pinyin	Page
Haidian District (a district in Beijing)	海淀区	p.n.	Hǎidiànqū	68
Hai'er (a Chinese collective multinational consumer electronics and home appliances company)	海尔	p.n.	Hǎi'ěr	245
Haitao (a cross-border e-commerce platform by Alibaba)	海淘	p.n.	Hǎitáo	241

English	Chinese	Part	Pinyin	Page
halt	停顿	v.	tíngdùn	216
Han Dynasty (202 B.C. - 220 A.D.)	汉代	p.n.	Hàndài	5
Hangzhou (the capital city of Zhejiang Province, China)	杭州	p.n.	Hángzhōu	39
happen to	正好	adv.	zhènghǎo	89
happy	喜悦	adj.	xǐyuè	148
harmony	和谐	n.	héxié	158
harmony between heaven and man	天人合一	phr.	tiān rén hé yī	158
hashtag	标签	n.	biāoqiān	219
have an interval	间隔	v.	jiàngé	63
have confidence in oneself	自信	v.	zìxìn	118
having a keen insight into nature's mysteries	洞识天机	phr.	dòngshí tiānjī	158
headline	标题	n.	biāotí	123
heat wave	热浪	n.	rèlàng	184
heavy	沉重	adj.	chénzhòng	63
Hebei (a province in Northern China)	河北	p.n.	Héběi	124
Hefei (capital city of Anhui Province)	合肥	p.n.	Héféi	72
help the poor	扶贫	v.	fúpín	237
Hema Xiansheng (a supermarket chain by Alibaba that integrates physical retail and e-commerce)	盒马鲜生	p.n.	Hémǎ Xiānshēng	242
hence	于是	conj.	yúshì	94
Henry Chang-Yu Lee (a Chinese American forensic scientist)	李昌钰	p.n.	Lǐ Chāngyù	102
heroine	巾帼	n.	jīnguó	157
hesitant, not knowing where to go in life	彷徨	adj.	pánghuáng	74
hide	藏	v.	cáng	103
high technology	高科技	n.	gāo kējì	44
high-speed rail	高铁	n.	gāotiě	35
highway	公路	n.	gōnglù	211
hire, employ	聘请	v.	pìnqǐng	247
history	历史	n.	lìshǐ	4
hitch ride (a Didi service)	顺风车	n.	shùnfēngchē	40
hitch-riding service by Didi	滴滴顺风车	phr.	Dīdī shùnfēngchē	130
hold a post	担任	v.	dānrèn	74
home	家乡	n.	jiāxiāng	148
home country	祖国	n.	zǔguó	147
homeless people	流浪汉	phr.	liúlàng hàn	237
hot (topics)	热点	adj.	rèdiǎn	68
hotel	旅馆	n.	lǚguǎn	174
household registration	户籍	n.	hùjí	119
housing, lodging	住房	n.	zhùfáng	68
Houston	休斯顿	p.n.	Xiūsīdùn	68
Hu Shi (1891-1962) (a scholar widely credited with language reform by advocating the use of written vernacular Chinese)	胡适	p.n.	Hú Shì	95
Hua Tuo (140-208) (a famous Chinese physician of the late Eastern Han Dynasty)	华佗	p.n.	Huà Tuó	158
Huawei (a Chinese multinational networking, telecommunications equipment, and services company)	华为	p.n.	Huáwéi	245
huge	巨大	adj.	jùdà	211
huge	庞大	adj.	pángdà	211
hundred million	亿	num.	yì	211
hunt for food	猎食	v.	lièshí	176
hurricane	飓风	n.	jùfēng	184
husband and wife	夫妻	n.	fūqī	68
hutong (a type of narrow street or alley in northern Chinese cities)	胡同	n.	hútòng	124
hydroelectricity	水力发电	phr.	shuǐlì fādiàn	189

I

English	Chinese	Part	Pinyin	Page
ice field	冰原	n.	bīngyuán	183
idea	观念, 理念	n.	guānniàn, lǐniàn	63, 96
Ieoh Ming Pei (a Chinese American architect)	贝聿铭	p.n.	Bèi Yùmíng	102
IKEA	宜家	p.n.	Yíjiā	190
image	图片	n.	túpiàn	217
imagination	想象力	n.	xiǎngxiànglì	148
imagine	想象	v.	xiǎngxiàng	216
imitate	模仿	v.	mófǎng	158
impact	冲击	n.	chōngjī	153
implement	实施	v.	shíshī	39
imply, mean	意味	v.	yìwèi	64
import	输入	v.	shūrù	5
important task	重任	n.	zhòngrèn	159
impose a fine on	罚款	v.	fákuǎn	39
improve	改良	v.	gǎiliáng	94
in groups of three or four	三五成群	phr.	sān-wǔ chéngqún	175
include	包括	v.	bāokuò	189
income	收入	n.	shōurù	240
increase, grow	增长	v.	zēngzhǎng	211
increasingly, day by day	日趋	adv.	rìqū	45
independence	独立	n.	dúlì	157
Indian Ocean	印度洋	p.n.	Yìndùyáng	9
Industrial Revolution	工业革命	phr.	Gōngyè Gémìng	213
industry	产业	n.	chǎnyè	90

English	Chinese	POS	Pinyin	Page
industry chain	产业链	phr.	chǎnyè liàn	245
inevitable	必然	adj.	bìrán	237
infant	婴	n.	yīng	64
information	资讯	n.	zīxùn	218
infrastructure	基础建设	phr.	jīchǔ jiànshè	16
ingenious, clever	巧妙	adj.	qiǎomiào	157
initially	初步	adv.	chūbù	63
initiate	发起	v.	fāqǐ	190
ink wash painting	水墨画	n.	shuǐmòhuà	151
innovate	创新	v.	chuàngxīn	45
innovative	革新性	adj.	géxīnxìng	216
inspection	检查	n.	jiǎnchá	118
inspiration	灵感	n.	línggǎn	158
instructor, coach	教练	n.	jiàoliàn	207
integrate	融合	v.	rónghé	5
intellectuals	知识分子	n.	zhīshi fènzǐ	94
intelligence, wisdom	智慧	n.	zhìhuì	210
interview	访问	v.	fǎngwèn	90
introduce	引进	v.	yǐnjìn	241
investigate	调查	v.	diàochá	102
iPASS (a card used for traveling on public transporation in Taiwan)	一卡通	p.n.	Yīkǎtōng	35
is not	并非	adv.	bìngfēi	129
Islam	回教	p.n.	Huíjiào	5
island	岛屿	n.	dǎoyǔ	183
it can be said that …	可谓	v.	kěwèi	35
it is obvious that	可想而知	phr.	kě xiǎng ér zhī	216

J

English	Chinese	POS	Pinyin	Page
Jeme Tien Yow (1861-1919) (a pioneering Chinese railroad engineer)	詹天佑	p.n.	Zhān Tiānyòu	90
Jiangsu (a province in Eastern China)	江苏	p.n.	Jiāngsū	151
Jingjinji (a metropolitan region)	京津冀	p.n.	Jīngjīnjì	123
just around the corner	指日可待	phr.	zhǐrì kědài	190

K

English	Chinese	POS	Pinyin	Page
Kentucky Fried Chicken	肯德基	p.n.	Kěndéjī	245
Kenya	肯尼亚	p.n.	Kěnníyà	9
Kolkata (the capital city of the state of West Bengal, India)	加尔各答	p.n.	Jiā'ěrgèdá	183
Kungfu Panda (a Hollywood movie)	功夫熊猫	p.n.	Gōngfu Xióngmāo	156
Kunming (capital city of Yunnan Province)	昆明	p.n.	Kūnmíng	74
Kyoto (the capital city of Kyoto Prefecture, Japan)	京都	p.n.	Jīngdū	183

L

English	Chinese	POS	Pinyin	Page
labor force	劳动力	n.	láodònglì	63
laboratory	实验室	n.	shíyànshì	175
lack	缺乏	v.	quēfá	119
lake	湖泊	n.	húpō	175
land	陆地	n.	lùdì	15
lanes and alleys in Shanghai	里弄	n.	lǐlòng	68
language	语言	n.	yǔyán	96
last years of a dynasty or reign	末年	n.	mònián	96
later generations	后人	n.	hòurén	90
Latin	拉丁文	n.	Lādīngwén	124
lead	带领	v.	dàilǐng	102
leader	领导人	n.	lǐngdǎorén	96
leading	领军	adj.	lǐngjūn	90
leading	主导	v.	zhǔdǎo	189
leapfrog development	跨越式发展	phr.	kuàyuè shì fāzhǎn	236
leather	皮革	n.	pígé	5
leave unused	闲置	v.	xiánzhì	45
lecture	讲座	n.	jiǎngzuò	123
left-behind children (children in foster care of grandparents or other relatives while their parents work in other cities)	留守儿童	phr.	liúshǒu értóng	119
Lenovo (a Chinese multinational technology company)	联想	p.n.	Liánxiǎng	245
level	层面	n.	céngmiàn	216
Li Bai (701-762) (a prominent Chinese poet of the Tang Dynasty)	李白	p.n.	Lǐ Bái	146
lift a ban or restriction	开放	v.	kāifàng	62
light rail	轻轨	n.	qīngguǐ	34
lighting	照明	n.	zhàomíng	189
limit	局限	v.	júxiàn	241
limit one's purchase	限购	v.	xiàngòu	39
limited	有限	adj.	yǒuxiàn	211
link	连接, 邦定	v.	liánjiē, bāngdìng	4, 206
(lit.) little emperor (a term used to describe an only child who gains excessive amounts of attention from his/her parents and grandparents)	小皇帝	n.	xiǎohuángdì	64
local flavor	风味	n.	fēngwèi	124
local specialty	特产	n.	tèchǎn	10
location	定位	n.	dìngwèi	128
log in	登录	v.	dēnglù	44
logistics	物流	n.	wùliú	240
long, age-old	悠久	adj.	yōujiǔ	89
long-distance	长途	adj.	chángtú	130
Los Angeles	洛杉矶	p.n.	Luòshānjī	101

English	Chinese	Part	Pinyin	Page
lose balance	失衡	v.	shīhéng	64
lost	失落	adj.	shīluò	74
lottery system	摇号	n.	yáohào	39
Louvre Museum	卢浮宫	p.n.	Lú Fú Gōng	103
Louvre Pyramid	玻璃金字塔	p.n.	Bōli Jīnzìtǎ	103
loyalty	忠	n.	zhōng	157
Luckin Coffee (a Beijing-based start-up that has hundreds of outlets across China's major cities)	瑞幸咖啡	p.n.	Ruìxìng Kāfēi	247
luxury goods	奢侈品	phr.	shēchǐ pǐn	241

M

English	Chinese	Part	Pinyin	Page
machine	机器	n.	jīqì	210
Macy's	梅西	p.n.	Méixī	242
magnate	巨头	n.	jùtóu	245
mail	邮件	n.	yóujiàn	216
major	重大	adj.	zhòngdà	35
make a reservation or booking	预约	v.	yùyuē	40
make laws, legislate	立法	v.	lìfǎ	207
make money	赚钱	v.o.	zhuànqián	207
make tea	沏茶	v.o.	qī chá	157
make, create	打造	v.	dǎzào	123
Maldives (a tropical nation in the Indian Ocean)	马尔代夫	p.n.	Mǎ'ěrdàifū	183
Manhattan	曼哈顿	p.n.	Mànhādùn	123
mankind	人类	n.	rénlèi	96
man-made, artificial	人造	adj.	rénzào	210
mantis	螳螂	n.	tángláng	158
manufacture of machinery	机械制造	phr.	jīxiè zhìzào	90
Maritime Silk Road	海上丝绸之路	p.n.	Hǎishang Sīchóu zhī Lù	9
mark, imprint	烙印	n.	làoyìn	148
market capitalization	市值	n.	shìzhí	246
market economy	市场经济	phr.	shìchǎng jīngjì	236
market share	市场份额	phr.	shìchǎng fèn'é	241
marketing	市场推广	n.	shìchǎng tuīguǎng	74
martial artist with chivalrous conduct	武侠	n.	wǔxiá	157
mass rapid transit system	大众捷运系统	p.n.	dàzhòng jiéyùn xìtǒng	34
Massachusetts	麻州	p.n.	Má Zhōu	89
masses	群众	n.	qúnzhòng	156
massive	海量	adj.	hǎiliàng	210
master, teacher	师傅	n.	shīfu	159
masterpiece	代表作	n.	dàibiǎozuò	103
match	配合	v.	pèihé	247
matter of opinion	见仁见智	phr.	jiànrén jiànzhì	69
May 4th Movement (1919) (an anti-imperialist, anti-feudal, political and cultural movement influenced by the October Revolution and led by intellectuals having the rudiments of Communist ideology)	五四运动	p.n.	Wǔ-Sì Yùndòng	96
McDonald's	麦当劳	p.n.	Màidāngláo	245
(measure word for ship)	艘	m.w.	sōu	10
(measure word) turn	番	m.w.	fān	69
media	媒体	n.	méitǐ	156
medical history	病史	n.	bìngshǐ	212
medical treatment	医疗	n.	yīliáo	212
medicinal materials, herbs	药材	n.	yàocái	10
Mediterranean Sea	地中海	p.n.	Dìzhōnghǎi	5
meet, welcome	迎接	v.	yíngjiē	153
Meiji Reformation	明治维新	p.n.	Míngzhì Wéixīn	94
Meili Snow Mountains (a mountain range in Yunnan Province, China)	梅里雪山	p.n.	Méilǐ Xuěshān	174
memory	回忆	n.	huíyì	90
merge	合并	v.	hébìng	40
metaphor	比喻	n.	bǐyù	211
Michelin-starred	米其林星级	phr.	Mǐqílín xīngjí	237
Microsoft	微软	p.n.	Wēiruǎn	190
Middle East	中东	p.n.	Zhōngdōng	15
migrant worker	农民工	n.	nóngmín gōng	119
millennials	千禧一代	phr.	qiānxǐ yí dài	62
Ming Dynasty (1368-1644)	明代	p.n.	Míngdài	9
mining and metallurgy	矿冶	n.	kuàngyě	90
miss	挂念	n.	guàniàn	147
miss one's hometown	思乡	v.	sīxiāng	148
mission school	教会学校	phr.	jiàohuì xuéxiào	89
mistake	差错	n.	chācuò	157
mobile	移动	adj.	yídòng	241
mobile payment	移动支付	phr.	yídòng zhīfù	205
mode, model	模式	n.	móshì	45
modern sense	现代感	n.	xiàndàigǎn	102
modernization	现代化	n.	xiàndàihuà	235
monarchy	君主制度	n.	jūnzhǔ zhìdù	95
mosque	清真寺	n.	qīngzhēnsì	5
Motorala	摩托罗拉	p.n.	Mótuōluólā	245
move in	迁入	v.	qiānrù	129
move out	迁出	v.	qiānchū	129
move to an earlier date	提前	v.	tíqián	128

English	Chinese	Part	Pinyin	Page
move, migrate	迁徙	v.	qiānxǐ	128
Mulan (a Hollywood movie)	花木兰	p.n.	Huā Mùlán	156
Museum of Islamic Art, Doha	多哈伊斯兰艺术博物馆	p.n.	Duōhā Yīsīlán Yìshù Bówùguǎn	103
Muslim	回民	n.	Huímín	5
myopia, short-sightedness	近视	n.	jìnshì	118

N

English	Chinese	Part	Pinyin	Page
narrow	窄	adj.	zhǎi	148
national defense	国防	n.	guófáng	235
National Geographic Magazine	国家地理杂志	p.n.	Guójiā Dìlǐ Zázhì	174
national hero	民族英雄	phr.	mínzú yīngxióng	156
national policy	国策	n.	guócè	63
natural and spontaneous	行云流水	phr.	xíngyún liúshuǐ	148
natural and unrestrained	潇洒自如	phr.	xiāosǎ zìrú	148
natural lighting (for an indoor space)	采光	v.	cǎiguāng	73
natural scenery	自然风光	phr.	zìrán fēngguāng	148
nature reserve	自然保护区	phr.	zìrán bǎohùqū	174
navigator	航海家	n.	hánghǎijiā	9
navy (a term used in ancient times)	水师	n.	shuǐshī	90
Nestle	雀巢	p.n.	Quècháo	245
network	网络	n.	wǎngluò	216
new and developing market	新兴市场	phr.	xīnxīng shìchǎng	159
New Culture Movement (around the time of the May 4th Movement in 1919)	新文化运动	p.n.	Xīn Wénhuà Yùndòng	96
new favorite	新宠	n.	xīnchǒng	235
new high	新高	n.	xīngāo	68
New York	纽约	p.n.	Niǔyuē	123
New York Times	纽约时报	p.n.	Niǔyuē Shíbào	123
Nobel Prize in Physics	诺贝尔物理奖	p.n.	Nuòbèi'ěr Wùlǐ Jiǎng	103
normal	正常	adj.	zhèngcháng	64
Northern Europe	北欧	p.n.	Běi Ōu	190
not in harmony	不协调	phr.	bù xiétiáo	237
nothing strange	不足为奇	phr.	bù zú wéi qí	69
novel	小说	n.	xiǎoshuō	68
numerous	众多	adj.	zhòngduō	35
numerous and close together	密密麻麻	adj.	mìmimámá	128
nurture	滋养	v.	zīyǎng	159

O

English	Chinese	Part	Pinyin	Page
obstacle, barrier	障碍	n.	zhàng'ài	90
obvious	明显	adj.	míngxiǎn	188
oil and gas pipelines	油气管道	phr.	yóuqì guǎndào	16
oil painting	油画	n.	yóuhuà	151
on behalf of	替	prep.	tì	217
on the verge of	濒临	v.	bīnlín	174
once	一旦	conj.	yídàn	217
once again	再度	adv.	zàidù	210
one after another, in succession	纷纷	adv.	fēnfēn	245
one-child policy	一胎化政策	phr.	yìtāihuà zhèngcè	62
online	在线	adj.	zàixiàn	247
online car charter	互联网包车	phr.	hùliánwǎng bāochē	130
Online Shopping Carnival	网购狂欢节	p.n.	Wǎnggòu Kuánghuānjié	241
only	唯一	adj.	wéiyī	184
only child	独生子女	phr.	dúshēng zǐnǔ	62
operate	运营, 操作, 运作	v.	yùnyíng, cāozuò, yùnzuò	34, 44, 123
Opium Wars (1840-1842; 1856-1860)	鸦片战争	p.n.	Yāpiàn Zhànzhēng	90
opposition	对立	n.	duìlì	237
optimize	优化	v.	yōuhuà	210
orange (color)	橘色	n.	júsè	44
order	秩序	n.	zhìxù	236
(purchase) order	订单	n.	dìngdān	212
ordinary people	老百姓	n.	lǎobǎixìng	68
organization	机构	n.	jīgòu	175
originate from	源自	v.	yuánzì	184
otherwise, else	否则	conj.	fǒuzé	39
outcome, result	结果	n.	jiéguǒ	237
outstanding	出色	adj.	chūsè	102
outstanding, excellent	优秀	adj.	yōuxiù	95
overcome	克服	v.	kèfú	90
overtaking at a turn	弯道超车	phr.	wāndào chāochē	236
overthrow	推翻	v.	tuīfān	95
overturn, subvert	颠覆	v.	diānfù	218

P

English	Chinese	Part	Pinyin	Page
Pablo Ruiz Picasso (1881-1973) (a famous Spanish painter)	毕加索	p.n.	Bìjiāsuǒ	152
pace	步伐	n.	bùfá	218
Pacific Ocean	太平洋	p.n.	Tàipíngyáng	183
pain point (a specific problem that prospective customers of a business are experiencing)	痛点	n.	tòngdiǎn	248
palace	宫殿	n.	gōngdiàn	158

English	Chinese	Part	Pinyin	Page
panda base	熊猫基地	phr.	xióngmāo jīdì	175
park (a vehicle)	停放	v.	tíngfàng	44
particular period	时期	n.	shíqī	10
pass down through the ages	流传千古	phr.	liúchuán qiāngǔ	147
passenger transportation during or around the Spring Festival	春运	n.	chūnyùn	128
pathway	通道	n.	tōngdào	5
pay	支付	v.	zhīfù	45
pay (a sum of money)	付款	v.o.	fùkuǎn	44
pay the bill	结帐	v.	jiézhàng	206
peak value	峰值	n.	fēngzhí	190
Pearl River Delta (a metropolitan region)	珠江三角洲	p.n.	Zhūjiāng Sānjiǎo Zhōu	124
pearls and jewels	珠宝	n.	zhūbǎo	10
penguin	企鹅	n.	qǐ'é	177
pepper	胡椒	n.	hújiāo	5
percent	百分	n.	bǎifēn	64
Père David's deer	麋鹿	n.	mílù	176
period	期间	n.	qījiān	128
period of time	一阵子	n.	yízhènzi	69
permit, license	许可	n.	xǔkě	39
person (referring to passenger traffic volume)	人次	m.w.	réncì	211
person traveling or residing in a place far away from home	游子	n.	yóuzǐ	148
pervade	渗透	v.	shèntòu	216
petroleum, oil	石油	n.	shíyóu	177
phenomenon	现象	n.	xiànxiàng	69
philosophy	哲理	n.	zhélǐ	158
photovoltaic system, solar power system	光伏发电装置	phr.	guāngfú fādiàn zhuāngzhì	189
physical store	实体店	n.	shítǐdiàn	241
physical strength	体力	n.	tǐlì	211
place an order	下单	v.	xiàdān	39
plan	计划	v.	jìhuà	129
planned economy	计划经济	phr.	jìhuà jīngjì	236
pledge, promise	誓约	n.	shìyuē	190
plot, story	情节	n.	qíngjié	102
Poet Immortal	诗仙	p.n.	Shīxiān	146
Poet-Sage	诗圣	p.n.	Shīshèng	146
polar bear	北极熊	n.	běijíxióng	176
policy	方针	n.	fāngzhēn	62
politics	政治	n.	zhèngzhì	16
poor	贫穷	adj.	pínqióng	236
popular	大众化	adj.	dàzhònghuà	34
popular sites	热门地段	phr.	rèmén dìduàn	72
popularize	普及	v.	pǔjí	96
population	人口	n.	rénkǒu	35
porcelain	瓷器	n.	cíqì	5
portray	塑造	v.	sùzào	157
post-90s generation (a Chinese term referring to people born between 1990 and 2000)	90后	phr.	jiǔlínghòu	45
postal	邮政	n.	yóuzhèng	16
potential	潜能	n.	qiánnéng	247
powerful	强大	adj.	qiángdà	210
pragmatism	实用主义	n.	shíyòng zhǔyì	236
premier	总理	n.	zǒnglǐ	90
prestige	威望	n.	wēiwàng	158
prevent	防止	v.	fángzhǐ	207
price of housing	房价	n.	fángjià	68
price-performance ratio	性价比	n.	xìngjiàbǐ	242
print	印	v.	yìn	207
privacy	隐私	n.	yǐnsī	207
produce	产生	v.	chǎnshēng	189
production	生产	n.	shēngchǎn	212
professor	教授	n.	jiàoshòu	4
project	项目, 工程	n.	xiàngmù, gōngchéng	4, 189
promise	承诺	v.	chéngnuò	190
promote	促进, 推销	v.	cùjìn, tuīxiāo	4, 241
promote, advocate	推行	v.	tuīxíng	207
promote, spread	推广	v.	tuīguǎng	45
promotional film	宣传片	phr.	xuānchuán piàn	242
promptly, without delay	及时	adv.	jíshí	212
propose, initiate	倡议	v.	chàngyì	15
prosperous	盛	adj.	shèng	10
prosperous and strong	富强	adj.	fùqiáng	94
protect	保护	v.	bǎohù	207
protege	徒弟	n.	túdì	159
provide food for thought	耐人寻味	phr.	nài rén xún wèi	158
province	省	n.	shěng	35
public	公立, 公共	adj.	gōnglì, gōnggòng	119, 123
public welfare	公益	n.	gōngyì	4
purchase	购买	v.	gòumǎi	45
purchase in advance	预购	v.	yùgòu	128
pure e-commerce	纯电商	p.n.	chún diànshāng	241
pursue	追逐	v.	zhuīzhú	124

Q

English	Chinese	Part	Pinyin	Page
Qatar	卡塔尔	p.n.	Kǎtǎ'ěr	103
Qing Dynasty (1644-1912)	清朝	p.n.	Qīng Cháo	89
QR code	二维码	n.	èrwéimǎ	44

English	Chinese	Part	Pinyin	Page
Qu, a form of poetry from the Yuan Dynasty	元曲	p.n.	Yuán Qǔ	148
quality	质量	n.	zhìliàng	119
queue, line up	排队	v.	páiduì	217

R

English	Chinese	Part	Pinyin	Page
race	种族	n.	zhǒngzú	218
railway	铁路	n.	tiělù	90
rainstorm	暴雨	n.	bàoyǔ	184
raise donations	募捐	v.	mùjuān	118
raise funds	融资	v.	róngzī	45
rapid	急剧	adj.	jíjù	211
rapid transit	捷运	n.	jiéyùn	34
rare	稀,罕见	adj.	xī, hǎnjiàn	62, 128
rare animal	稀有动物	phr.	xīyǒu dòngwù	174
rare, hard to come by	难得	adj.	nándé	188
rate, ratio	率	n.	lǜ	117
rather than	与其	conj.	yǔqí	146
ratio	比例	n.	bǐlì	64
reach (a consensus or agreement)	达成	v.	dáchéng	183
reach up to	高达	phr.	gāo dá	117
read	阅读	v.	yuèdú	216
real	真实	adj.	zhēnshí	157
realism	现实主义	n.	xiànshí zhǔyì	147
real-time	实时	n.	shíshí	129
reasonable	合理	adj.	hélǐ	219
receive (visitors, guests, etc.)	接待	v.	jiēdài	89
recitation	朗诵	n.	lǎngsòng	148
Red Sea	红海	p.n.	Hónghǎi	9
reflect	反思,反映	v.	fǎnsī, fǎnyìng	45, 68
reform	改革	v.	gǎigé	45
reform, transformation	变革	n.	biàngé	45
register	挂号	v.	guàhào	217
registered residence	户口	n.	hùkǒu	73
relaxed	舒心	adj.	shūxīn	69
rely on	凭	v.	píng	248
renewable	可再生	adj.	kězàishēng	189
renounce the world, keep aloof from worldly affairs	出世	n.	chūshì	148
rent	租	v.	zū	45
rental	租金	n.	zūjīn	74
replace	取代	v.	qǔdài	96
reproductive science	繁殖学	n.	fánzhíxué	175
Republic of China	中华民国	p.n.	Zhōnghuá Mínguó	90
researcher	研究员	n.	yánjiūyuán	174
reside	居住	v.	jūzhù	68
retail	零售	n.	língshòu	240
return	归来	v.	guīlái	157
reverse	逆向	v.	nìxiàng	129
Revolution of 1911 (the Chinese bourgeois democratic revolution led by Dr. Sun Yat-sen which overthrew the Qing Dynasty)	辛亥革命	p.n.	Xīnhài Gémìng	95
reward	奖励	n.	jiǎnglì	156
rich	富裕	adj.	fùyù	236
rise	涨	v.	zhǎng	72
rise	崛起	n.	juéqǐ	236
risk	风险	n.	fēngxiǎn	16
road, route	道路	n.	dàolù	4
roam about	出没	v.	chūmò	175
rob	抢劫	v.	qiǎngjié	207
robber	劫匪	n.	jiéfěi	207
roll out, launch	推出	v.	tuīchū	40
romanticism	浪漫主义	n.	làngmàn zhǔyì	148
roof of a building	楼顶	n.	lóudǐng	189
root word	词根	n.	cígēn	124
route	线路,路线	n.	xiànlù, lùxiàn	35, 129
route map	轨迹图	n.	guǐjì tú	128
Rural Education Action Program (REAP)	农村教育行动计划	phr.	Nóngcūn Jiàoyù Xíngdòng Jìhuà	117
Russia	俄罗斯	p.n.	Éluósī	184

S

English	Chinese	Part	Pinyin	Page
sacrifice	牺牲	v.	xīshēng	207
safe	安全	adj.	ānquán	35
sailing route	航路	n.	hánglù	9
salary	薪酬	n.	xīnchóu	45
San Francisco	三藩市	p.n.	Sānfānshì	40
Sanlitun (a popular destination for shopping, dining and entertainment in Beijing, China)	三里屯	p.n.	Sānlǐtún	235
satisfy	满足	v.	mǎnzú	248
save	拯救	adj.	zhěngjiù	159
save	挽救	v.	wǎnjiù	184
scale	规模	n.	guīmó	241
scan	扫	v.	sǎo	44
scene	幕	m.w.	mù	103
scene, atmosphere	气象	n.	qìxiàng	247
scene, sight	景象	n.	jǐngxiàng	147
scenery	风景线	n.	fēngjǐngxiàn	44
sea level	海平面	n.	hǎipíngmiàn	183
seal	海豹	n.	hǎibào	177
seas to the west of China	西洋	p.n.	Xīyáng	9
second child	二胎	n.	èr tāi	62
secret (of success)	秘诀	n.	mìjué	102
secret code	密码	n.	mìmǎ	103

English	Chinese	Type	Pinyin	Page
security guard	保安	n.	bǎo'ān	213
seeing is believing	百闻不如一见	phr.	bǎi wén bù rú yí jiàn	73
seek	寻求	v.	xúnqiú	183
Self-Strengthening Movement (1861-1895) (a drive to learn Western concepts of modernization)	洋务运动	p.n.	Yángwù Yùndòng	90
semester	学期	n.	xuéqī	4
senior fellow apprentices	师兄师姐	phr.	shīxiōng shījiě	158
sense	触觉	n.	chùjué	248
separate oneself from	脱离	v.	tuōlí	124
separation	分离	n.	fēnlí	148
Series D funding	D轮融资	phr.	D lún róngzī	247
serious, solemn	严肃	adj.	yánsù	102
settle a bill	结算	v.	jiésuàn	206
severe	严峻	adj.	yánjùn	64
sexual harassment	性骚扰	n.	xìngsāorǎo	219
Shaanxi (a province in Northwest China)	陕西	p.n.	Shǎnxī	236
shallow	浅	adj.	qiǎn	148
shame	耻辱	n.	chǐrǔ	157
Shangri-La (a county-level city in Yunnan Province, China)	香格里拉	p.n.	Xiāng Gé Lǐ Lā	174
sharp	敏锐	adj.	mǐnruì	248
Shenzhen (a city in Guangdong Province)	深圳	p.n.	Shēnzhèn	69
ship	船只	n.	chuánzhī	10
shop front	店面	n.	diànmiàn	190
short distance	短途	n.	duǎntú	44
show (a film)	放映	v.	fàngyìng	156
sign (an agreement)	签署	v.	qiānshǔ	183
Silicon Valley	硅谷	p.n.	Guīgǔ	74
Silk Road	丝绸之路	p.n.	Sīchóu zhī Lù	4
similar	相似	adj.	xiāngsì	74
simple	简单	adj.	jiǎndān	34
simple and easy	浅易	adj.	qiǎnyì	96
simple and honest	憨厚	adj.	hānhòu	158
simply, at all	简直	adv.	jiǎnzhí	69
simulate	模拟	v.	mónǐ	175
Singles' Day (November 11th)	双十一光棍节	p.n.	Shuāngshíyī Guānggùnjié	241
skyline	天际线	n.	tiānjìxiàn	123
skyscraping	摩天	v.	mótiān	123
slogan	口号	n.	kǒuhào	40
snub-nosed monkey	金丝猴	n.	jīnsīhóu	174
soar, surge	飙升	v.	biāoshēng	68
socialism	社会主义	n.	shèhuì zhǔyì	236
solar energy	太阳能	n.	tàiyángnéng	189
solar panel	太阳能板	phr.	tàiyángnéngbǎn	190
solution	方案	n.	fāng'àn	236
sooner than planned	提早	v.	tízǎo	190
South China tiger	华南虎	n.	Huánánhǔ	176
Southeast Asia	东南亚	p.n.	Dōngnányà	9
spacious	宽敞	adj.	kuānchang	73
speaker	音箱	n.	yīnxiāng	248
special	特殊	adj.	tèshū	151
species	物种	n.	wùzhǒng	177
spices	香料	n.	xiāngliào	5
spirited discussion	热议	n.	rèyì	156
splendid, brilliant	璀璨	adj.	cuǐcàn	151
spoil (a child)	溺爱	v.	nì'ài	64
spread, teach	传播	v.	chuánbō	10
Springfield (a city in Massachusetts)	春田市	p.n.	Chūntián Shì	89
spur on	带动	v.	dàidòng	124
square meter	平米	m.w.	píngmǐ	69
stabilize	稳定	v.	wěndìng	129
stable	安稳	adj.	ānwěn	69
stage	舞台	n.	wǔtái	68
Stanford University	斯坦福大学	p.n.	Sītǎnfú Dàxué	117
Starbucks	星巴克	p.n.	Xīngbākè	190
start a business	创业	v.	chuàngyè	45
start, create	开创	v.	kāichuàng	10
starting point	起点	n.	qǐdiǎn	4
start-up (company)	初创公司	phr.	chūchuàng gōngsī	246
state, realm	境界	n.	jìngjiè	158
statistics	统计	n.	tǒngjì	218
steal	偷窃	v.	tōuqiè	207
still	仍然	adv.	réngrán	39
straits	海峡	n.	hǎixiá	148
streets and lanes	大街小巷	phr.	dà jiē xiǎo xiàng	235
strive	奋斗	v.	fèndòu	74
strive for	争取	v.	zhēngqǔ	183
strong and vigorous	矫健	adj.	jiǎojiàn	175
strong, powerful	强劲	adj.	qiángjìn	241
structure, format	格局	n.	géjú	147
struggle	挣扎	v.	zhēngzhá	119
study abroad	留学	v.	liúxué	89
suburbs, outskirts	近郊	n.	jìnjiāo	35
succinct	精练	adj.	jīngliàn	148
suffer, encounter	遭到	v.	zāodào	183
sufferings of the people	民生疾苦	phr.	mínshēng jíkǔ	147
suite (measure word for houses)	套	m.w.	tào	68

English	Chinese	Part	Pinyin	Page
summer camp	夏令营	n.	xiàlìngyíng	4
Sun Yat-sen (1866-1925) (the first president and founding father of the Republic of China)	孙中山	p.n.	Sūn Zhōngshān	95
super	超级	adj.	chāojí	217
supply	供应	v.	gōngyìng	189
surprised	惊讶	adj.	jīngyà	35
survival rate	存活率	n.	cúnhuólǜ	175
survive	生存	v.	shēngcún	119
Suzhou Museum	苏州博物馆	p.n.	Sūzhōu Bówùguǎn	103
swift and strong	迅猛	adj.	xùnměng	245
sympathetic response	共鸣	n.	gòngmíng	68
system	系统	n.	xìtǒng	16

T

English	Chinese	Part	Pinyin	Page
tactics	策略	n.	cèlüè	176
tael (a unit of weight)	两	m.w.	liǎng	147
Tai chi (a type of Chinese martial art)	太极	p.n.	Tàijí	158
Taipei	台北	p.n.	Táiběi	34
Taiwan Taoyuan Airport	台湾桃园机场	p.n.	Táiwān Táoyuán Jīchǎng	34
take (a mode of transportation)	搭乘	v.	dāchéng	34
take one's father's place in the army	代父从军	phr.	dài fù cóng jūn	156
take photographs from a flying object (aerial photography)	航拍	v.	hángpāi	248
take place	发生	v.	fāshēng	35
take responsibility	负责任	v.o.	fù zérèn	207
take root, settle down in a place	扎根	v.	zhāgēn	73
talk show	脱口秀节目	phr.	tuōkǒuxiù jiémù	69
Tang Shaoyi (1862-1938) (the first premier of the Republic of China who took office in 1912)	唐绍仪	p.n.	Táng Shàoyí	90
tangled, torn between	纠结	v.	jiūjié	69
target audience	对象	n.	duìxiàng	247
taste	味道	n.	wèidào	5
teachers	师资	n.	shīzī	119
teaching	教学	n.	jiàoxué	119
team	团队	n.	tuánduì	175
technology	技术	n.	jìshù	10
telegram	电报	n.	diànbào	90
temperature	温度	n.	wēndù	182
temporarily	暂时	adv.	zànshí	39
Tencent (a Chinese multinational investment holding conglomerate specializing in Internet-related services and products, entertainment, AI, and technology)	腾讯	p.n.	Téngxùn	245
Tesla	特斯拉	p.n.	Tèsīlā	235
test	考验	n.	kǎoyàn	64
Texas	德州	p.n.	Dézhōu	68
that is settled then	一言为定	phr.	yì yán wéi dìng	124
thatched cottage	草堂	n.	cǎotáng	146
the greatest extent	尽量	adv.	jǐnliàng	190
The Big Boss (Hong Kong martial arts film starring Bruce Lee)	唐山大兄	p.n.	Tángshān Dàxiōng	101
The Wealth of Nations (Chinese translated work of Yan Fu, originally written by Adam Smith)	原富	p.n.	Yuán Fù	95
theme	主题	n.	zhǔtí	159
theory	理论	n.	lǐlùn	95
theory of evolution	进化论	n.	jìnhuàlùn	95
there is no lack of	不乏	v.	bùfá	190
think deeply, ponder	思索	v.	sīsuǒ	157
think deeply, ponder over	思考	v.	sīkǎo	237
thinking	思维	n.	sīwéi	248
Thomas Henry Huxley (1825-1895) (English biologist)	赫胥黎	p.n.	Hè Xūlí	95
threat	威胁	n.	wēixié	177
Three Gorges	三峡	p.n.	Sānxiá	146
throughout the year	终年	n.	zhōngnián	174
Tianjin (a municipality of China)	天津	p.n.	Tiānjīn	39
Tibetan antelope	藏羚羊	n.	Zànglíngyáng	176
Tibetan Ethnic Minority	藏族	p.n.	Zàngzú	174
tidal energy	潮汐能	n.	cháoxīnéng	189
tide, wave (figurative)	浪潮	n.	làngcháo	242
Time Magazine	时代周刊	p.n.	Shídài Zhōukān	40
time period	叶	n.	yè	184
times (multiplier)	倍	m.w.	bèi	184
Times Square	时代广场	p.n.	Shídài Guǎngchǎng	123
tire	轮子	n.	lúnzi	45
tolerance	包容性	n.	bāoróngxìng	218
tomb	坟墓	n.	fénmù	148
Tong Kwo On (1858-1913) (the founding president of Tsinghua University)	唐国安	p.n.	Táng Guó'ān	90
too ghastly to contemplate	不堪设想	phr.	bùkān shèxiǎng	184
topic	话题	n.	huàtí	210
total mileage	总里程	n.	zǒnglǐchéng	35
trace, mark	痕迹	n.	hénjì	207
traffic jam	堵塞	n.	dǔsè	39
transaction	交易	n.	jiāoyì	207
translate	翻译	v.	fānyì	34
transnational	跨国	adj.	kuàguó	190

English	Chinese	POS	Pinyin	Page
transport	运输	v.	yùnshū	128
trend	趋势	n.	qūshì	241
trends, developments	动态	n.	dòngtài	248
try	尝试	v.	chángshì	102
try to find out	摸索	v.	mōsuǒ	236
Tsinghua University	清华大学	p.n.	Qīnghuá Dàxué	90
Tsung-Dao Lee (an Asian American physicist)	李政道	p.n.	Lǐ Zhèngdào	103
Tung Meng Hui, Chinese Revolutionary League (founded in 1905)	同盟会	p.n.	Tóngménghuì	95
TV series	电视剧	n.	diànshìjù	68
twists and turns, setbacks	波折	n.	bōzhé	68

U

English	Chinese	POS	Pinyin	Page
U.S. dollar	美元	n.	měiyuán	69
Uber	优步	p.n.	Yōubù	40
unbearable	不堪	adj.	bùkān	45
undertake, shoulder	肩负	adj.	jiānfù	159
undo a lock, unlock	解锁	v.o.	jiěsuǒ	44
unexpected	意想不到	phr.	yìxiǎng búdào	245
unexpectedly	竟	adv.	jìng	123
unfamiliar	陌生	adj.	mòshēng	148
unfavorable situation, plight	处境	n.	chǔjìng	176
unicorn (a start-up that is valued at one billion dollars or more)	独角兽	n.	dújiǎoshòu	246
unimaginable, inconceivable	不可思议	adj.	bù kě sī yì	89
United Nations	联合国	p.n.	Liánhéguó	177
unprecedented	前所未有	adj.	qián suǒ wèi yǒu	129
urbanization	城镇化	n.	chéngzhènhuà	124
urban-rural gap	城乡差距	phr.	chéngxiāng chājù	119
urgent	迫切	adj.	pòqiè	218
use, employ	采用	v.	cǎiyòng	211
user	用户	n.	yònghù	128

V

English	Chinese	POS	Pinyin	Page
value of self	自我价值	phr.	zìwǒ jiàzhí	157
vast	辽阔	adj.	liáokuò	35
vehicle that runs on gasoline or diesel	燃油车	n.	rányóu chē	39
venture capital investment (an abbreviated form of 创业投资)	创投	phr.	chuàngtóu	247
verge, brink, edge	边缘	n.	biānyuán	74
Vernacular Language Movement	白话文运动	n.	Báihuàwén Yùndòng	96
veterinary science	兽医学	n.	shòuyīxué	175
vie	争夺	v.	zhēngduó	40
view, opinion	见解	n.	jiànjiě	152
village	农村	n.	nóngcūn	63
villages and towns	乡镇	n.	xiāngzhèn	118
Vincent Willem van Gogh (1853-1890) (a famous Dutch Post-Impressionist painter)	梵高	p.n.	Fángāo	152
vision, eyesight	视力	n.	shìlì	118
vision, horizon	视野	n.	shìyě	69
visit, look around	参观	v.	cānguān	123
visual	形象化	adj.	xíngxiànghuà	45
vivid	形象	adj.	xíngxiàng	148
voice (message)	语音	n.	yǔyīn	212
Volkswagen	大众汽车	p.n.	Dàzhòng Qìchē	241
volleyball	排球	n.	páiqiú	68
volume of passenger traffic	客流量	n.	kèliúliàng	211
volume of self-production	自产量	phr.	zìchǎnliàng	190
voucher	券	n.	quàn	118

W

English	Chinese	POS	Pinyin	Page
wait	等候	v.	děnghòu	218
wait expectantly	拭目以待	phr.	shì mù yǐ dài	242
Wall Street	华尔街	p.n.	Huá'ěrjiē	237
Walmart	沃尔玛	p.n.	Wò'ěrmǎ	190
walrus	海象	n.	hǎixiàng	177
Wangjing SOHO (a landmark in Beijing, China)	望京SOHO	p.n.	Wàngjīng SOHO	123
warehouse	仓库	n.	cāngkù	190
warm oneself	取暖	v.	qǔnuǎn	188
warning	警告	n.	jǐnggào	184
Washington, D.C. (the capital of the United States of America)	华盛顿	p.n.	Huáshèngdùn	176
wave	波	n.	bō	45
wealth	财富	n.	cáifù	237
wear	配戴	v.	pèi dài	118
web user, netizen	网民	n.	wǎngmín	219
WeChat Pay (a mobile payment platform)	微信支付	p.n.	Wēixìn Zhīfù	206
WeChat Wallet	微信钱包	p.n.	Wēixìn Qiánbāo	236
Weixi Lisu Autonomous County (an autonomous county in Diqing Prefecture, Yunnan Province, China)	维西傈僳族自治县	p.n.	Wéixī Lìsùzú Zìzhìxiàn	174
West Asia	西亚	p.n.	Xīyà	5
what is called	所谓	v.	suǒwèi	69
what on earth (used in a question for emphasis)	到底	adv.	dàodǐ	236
wheat	小麦	n.	xiǎomài	5
widely known	家喻户晓	phr.	jiā yù hù xiǎo	156
win	赢	v.	yíng	156

English	Chinese	Type	Pinyin	Page
wind power generation	风力发电	phr.	fēnglì fādiàn	189
within reach	触手可及	phr.	chù shǒu kě jí	242
withstand	抵御	v.	dǐyù	176
work as an intern	实习	v.	shíxí	69
work force	劳动人口	n.	láodòng rénkǒu	64
work hard in one's job	打拼	v.	dǎpīn	35
work overtime	加班	v.	jiābān	74
working class	打工族	n.	dǎgōngzú	35
workplace	职场	n.	zhíchǎng	248
World Bank (an international financial institution)	世界银行	p.n.	Shìjiè Yínháng	189
worldwide distribution	货通全球	phr.	huò tōng quánqiú	241
worried, vexed	烦恼	adj.	fánnǎo	72
worth a lot of money	寸金寸土	phr.	cùn jīn cùn tǔ	69
worthy of	值得	v.	zhídé	35
worthy of, deserve to be called	不愧	adv.	búkuì	152
write	编写	v.	biānxiě	74
writing	文字	n.	wénzì	217
Wudaokou (a neighborhood in Beijing)	五道口	p.n.	Wǔdàokǒu	206
Wu Guanzhong (1919-2010) (a renowned painter in contemporary China)	吴冠中	p.n.	Wǔ Guànzhōng	151

X

English	Chinese	Type	Pinyin	Page
Xiaomi (a Chinese electronics company)	小米	p.n.	Xiǎomǐ	245
Xinjiang (a province in Northwest China)	新疆	p.n.	Xīnjiāng	5

Y

English	Chinese	Type	Pinyin	Page
yak	牦牛	n.	máoniú	5
Yale University	耶鲁大学	p.n.	Yēlǔ Dàxué	89
Yale University Art Gallery	耶鲁大学美术馆	p.n.	Yēlǔ Dàxué Měishùguǎn	151
Yan Fu (1854-1921) (Chinese scholar and translator, President of Fudan University)	严复	p.n.	Yán Fù	95
Yangtze River Delta (a metropolitan region)	长江三角洲	p.n.	Chángjiāng Sānjiǎo Zhōu	124
Yangtze River Valley (a metropolitan region)	长江中游	p.n.	Chángjiāng Zhōngyóu	124
yearning	憧憬	n.	chōngjǐng	74
yearning for home	乡愁	n.	xiāngchóu	148
yin and yang (complementary forces in Chinese philosophy)	阴阳	n.	yīnyáng	158
Yitongxing (an app for payment)	易通行	p.n.	Yìtōngxíng	206
Yongshou County (a county in Shaanxi Province, China)	永寿县	p.n.	Yǒngshòu Xiàn	117
Youku (a video hosting service based in Beijing, China)	优酷	p.n.	Yōukù	217
young animal	幼仔	n.	yòuzǎi	175
young child	幼童	n.	yòutóng	90
Yu Kwang-Chung (1928-2017) (a famous Taiwanese writer, poet, educator, and critic)	余光中	p.n.	Yú Guāngzhōng	148
Yue (Chinese surname)	岳	n.	Yuè	205
Yung Wing (1828-1912) (the first Chinese to graduate from an American college)	容闳	p.n.	Róng Hóng	89
Yunnan (a province in Southern China)	云南	p.n.	Yúnnán	9
Yunnan and Tibet	滇藏	p.n.	Diān Zàng	175

Z

English	Chinese	Type	Pinyin	Page
Zhang Qian (an ancient diplomat)	张骞	p.n.	Zhāng Qiān	5
Zheng He (a famous navigator of China)	郑和	p.n.	Zhèng Hé	9
Zhengzhou (the capital city of Henan Province, China)	郑州	p.n.	Zhèngzhōu	130
Zhou Enlai (1898-1976) (the first premier of the People's Republic of China who took office in 1949)	周恩来	p.n.	Zhōu Ēnlái	96
Zhuangzi (369-286 BC) (an influential Chinese philosopher of the Warring States period)	庄子	p.n.	Zhuāngzǐ	158

ABBREVIATIONS FOR GRAMMATICAL TERMS

n.	noun	m.w.	measure word	num.	numeral
v.	verb	pron.	pronoun	aux.v.	auxiliary verb
adj.	adjective	prep.	preposition	phr.	phrase
adv.	adverb	conj.	conjunction	v.o.	verb-object construction

3. 语言点 LANGUAGE USE

UNIT 1 — page 1

1. Providing additional details: 不仅……也……
   西安<u>不仅</u>是10多个朝代的首都，<u>也</u>是"丝绸之路"的起点。

2. Describing the function of something: 以……为……
   那时中国输出到西方的商品<u>以</u>丝绸<u>为主</u>。

3. Indicating a means or method: 通过……
   中国的发明也<u>通过</u>丝绸之路传入欧洲。

4. Introducing an outcome: 从……可以看出……
   <u>从</u>一碗牛肉面<u>可以看出</u>文化的交流和融合。

5. Promoting something on a large scale: 向……传播……
   郑和的船队<u>向</u>各国<u>传播</u>中国的技术。

6. Describing one's role: 扮演……角色
   郑和的船队一直都在<u>扮演</u>友善大使的<u>角色</u>。

7. Expressing a sense of pride for something or someone: 为/以……（而）感到自豪
   中国人都<u>为</u>郑和七下西洋与各国人民和平共处的历史事迹<u>而感到自豪</u>。

8. Highlighting one's contributions: 为……作出了很大贡献
   郑和开创了海上丝绸之路的极盛时期，<u>为</u>世界航海业<u>作出了很大贡献</u>。

9. Clarifying a term: ……是指……
   "一带一路"<u>是指</u>丝绸之路经济带和21世纪海上丝绸之路。

10. Useful verb: 带来……
    这个经济带能为中国和世界<u>带来</u>什么好处？

11. Indicating a perspective taken: 从……角度来看
    我们可以<u>从</u>文化、经济和政治三个不同的<u>角度来看</u>。

12. Facing a certain situation: 面临……
    很多国家担心这个计划太大，会<u>面临</u>很大的风险和挑战。

UNIT 2 — page 30

1. Emphasizing a state that holds true in all circumstances: 无论……都/也……
   中国的地铁<u>无论</u>从外观、票价、便捷、安全这几个角度来看，<u>都</u>是一流的。

2. Expressing something that is worthy of a certain response: 值得……骄傲/庆祝/纪念/学习
   除了地铁以外，高铁更<u>值得</u>我们<u>骄傲</u>。

3. Making a conjecture: 恐怕……
   堵塞<u>恐怕</u>是大城市都要面对的问题。

4. Introducing a method: 通过/用……来……
   <u>用</u>打车软件<u>来</u>打车非常容易。

5. Highlighting two characteristics: 既……又……
   拼车<u>既</u>省钱<u>又</u>节能。

6. Describing a condition to be fulfilled for a certain result: 只要……就……
   <u>只要</u>扫车上的二维码，<u>就</u>能把车解锁。

7. Expressing successive or repeated occurrences: 一……又一……
   这是时代带来的<u>一</u>波<u>又一</u>波的变革。

UNIT 3　　　　　　　page 59

1. Indicating a time or event in relation to a continuing situation: 自从……
   自从2015年开放二胎，我有些朋友已经开始考虑生二胎了。

2. Emphasizing the reason for an outcome: 毕竟……
   我有些朋友已经开始考虑生二胎了，毕竟有个兄弟姐妹比较好。

3. Giving further explanation: 也就是说……
   也就是说，一般千禧一代、90后都是独生子女。

4. Describing the treatment of someone or something: 加以……
   人口政策是按照社会情况，随时加以调整的！

5. Expressing amazement: 简直……
   100多平米的公寓就要200万美元一套，我简直不能相信。

6. Summarizing an explanation: 这就是所谓的……
   这就是所谓的"寸金寸土"。

7. Disregarding earlier considerations: 反正……
   这些选择让年轻人觉得很纠结，反正是不同的人有不同选择，可谓"见仁见智"。

8. Describing cause and effect or purpose and action: 为……而……
   毕业生为选择工作的城市而烦恼。

9. Describing the layout of a house: ……室……厅……卫
   这是一套三室一厅一卫的房子。

UNIT 4　　　　　　　page 85

1. Expressing coincidence: ……正好……
   他们到耶鲁参观的时候，接待的同学正好是中国人。

2. Giving examples: 比如……
   也有在外交和在教育界发展的，比如：中华民国的第一任总理唐绍仪和担任清华大学第一任校长的唐国安。

3. Deepening one's understanding of something: 加深……对……的认识/了解
   他们的后人有很多珍贵的照片和回忆，能加深我们对早期留美学生的认识。

4. Emphasizing someone or something: 尤其……
   他促进了中国人尤其是年轻知识分子对外国先进科技思想的认识。

5. Introducing someone or something in a group: 其中……
   那是因为庚子赔款选拔了很多优秀的学生来美国学习，其中就有胡适。

6. Giving credit to someone or something: 没有……就没有……
   可以说没有留学生，就没有今天的现代化的中国。

7. Describing someone or something in a group: 是……之一
   他也是《时代周刊》选出的20世纪最具影响力的百位名人之一。

8. Pointing out another issue relating to the previous topic: 至于……
   至于贝聿铭，我好像在哪里听过他的名字。

9. Describing the result of combining two elements: 结合……，形成……的风格/特色/习惯
   贝聿铭18岁以前在中国受教育，后来在美国上大学，所以他能结合东西方艺术，形成他个人的独特风格。

10. Expressing a proportion: ……占……的……分之……/百分之……/大多数
    差不多有400多万华裔，大约占美国人口的百分之一。

UNIT 5　　　　　　　　page 114

1. Emphasizing a situation: 连……也/都……
   打工子弟学校就连农村的学校也不如。

2. Emphasizing the equal importance of two aspects: 固然……（但是）……也……
   我们的主任常跟我们说在乡下的"留守儿童"固然不容易，跟父母进城的打工子弟也遇上不少挑战。

3. Describing a dismal situation: 在……边缘
   很多打工者和他们的孩子都在社会的边缘挣扎生存。

4. Useful verb: 提供……
   听说SOHO还经常邀请一些成功企业家提供讲座和论坛。

5. Useful verb: 打造……
   中国现在正在打造五大城市群。

6. Making connections: ……跟……有关系
   你看世界的文明发展跟城市有多密切的关系！

7. Stating two aspects of an action: ……一方面……（另）一方面……
   当然一方面发展城市，一方面也得保留传统的文化。

8. Welcoming something: 迎来……挑战/高峰/机遇
   每年都迎来一个前所未有的新高峰！

9. Emphasizing one part to reflect the whole situation: ……仅……就（有）……
   中国有那么多人，仅北京地区就有800万外地人。

10. Refuting an argument: 并非……
    春运并非只有文化的原因，还有经济发展不平衡的原因。

UNIT 6　　　　　　　　page 143

1. Expressing preference: 与其……（倒）不如……
   与其在饭馆门前排长队、在商场的人群里挤，倒不如跟朋友一起出行，到成都和三峡旅游。

2. Expressing concession: 即使……也……
   即使对我这样的外国学生来说，这个名字也绝对不陌生。

3. Emphasizing the process of an experience: 经过……
   经过数十年的努力后，他画出了很多影响深远的作品。

4. Describing someone's accomplishments: 不愧是……
   吴冠中真不愧是中西融合的大师！

5. Expressing relevance or connection: 关系到……
   因为你的一举一动都关系到你家族的光荣和耻辱。

6. Stating a way of doing something: 以……的形式
   影片以喜闻乐见的艺术形式给全世界的电影观众带来了惊喜。

UNIT 7　　　　　　　　page 171

1. Referring to different groups: 有的……，有的……，还有的……
   那时候金丝猴离我们很近，有的在攀爬树枝，有的在互相追逐，还有的在吃野果和树叶。

2. Stating the effect before the cause: 之所以……，是因为……
   熊猫数量之所以稀少，是因为它们不容易受孕。

3. Expressing a purpose: 为了……
   为了对外国表示友好，中国把国宝赠送给美国。

4. Pressing for an exact answer: 究竟……
   究竟什么是"全球变暖"？

5. Useful verb: 达成……
   这是世界各国为了解决气候变化问题而达成的第一个国际协议。

6. Expressing a consequence: 不然/要不然……
   人类必须把气温的变化控制在摄氏两度之内，不然"末日的时钟就要敲响了"。

7. Expressing an actual situation: 其实……
   其实北京的雾霾并没有想象中的那么严重。

8. Useful verb: 不乏……
   其中不乏知名的公司，比如苹果、谷歌、微软、沃尔玛、星巴克等。

UNIT 8   page 202

1. Catering to certain needs: 迎合……需求/需要/口味
   出租车为了迎合中国游客的需要，都可以使用支付宝了。

2. Establishing a connection between two items: 在……和……/他们之间搭建起桥梁/联系/平台
   移动支付最大的好处就是能在顾客和商家之间搭建起桥梁。

3. Expressing an amount: ……高达/长达/多达……
   每年春运铁路、公路、航空等客流量高达30亿人次。

4. Emphasizing that something will still be true even if another thing happens: 就算……也……
   机器人就算24小时不间断地工作，也不会觉得累。

5. Expressing agreement: 可不是吗
   可不是吗？我不敢想象没有网络的生活。

6. Expressing a consequence when something happens: 一旦……就……
   以前一旦外国有了新事物，中国就出现模仿它们的东西。

UNIT 9   page 231

1. Emphasizing a result that remains unchanged: 不管……都……
   不管黑猫白猫，能捉老鼠的都是好猫。

2. Emphasizing puzzlement or doubt: 到底……
   那到底中国是先进的还是落后的？是富裕的还是贫穷的？

3. Expressing supposition: 如果……就……
   如果这些差距现象得不到缓解，就会造成分化和对立。

4. Expressing the discontinuation of a situation: 不再……了
   现在消费人群不再局限于年轻人了，连中老年人也加入其中。

5. Expressing the meaning of "basically": 基本上……
   这基本上是一个O2O（online to offline）的商业模式，实现了线上线下的完美结合。

6. Expressing double negation: 不可不……
   除了我们熟悉的谷歌、脸书以外，还有不可不知的中国三巨头——百度、阿里巴巴和腾讯，简称为BAT。

7. Parallelism
   她们凭着敏锐的触觉，活跃的思维，充沛的精力，成为了初创企业的领军人物。

4. 中国地图 MAP OF CHINA

Photo Credits

Every effort has been made to trace all sources and copyright holders of images in this book before publication, but if any have been inadvertently overlooked, the publisher will ensure that full credit is given at the earliest opportunity.

Cover: Izf/iStock/Thinkstock, auleit/iStock/Thinkstock, Jess_Yu/iStock/Thinkstock.

Pages: vii (l to r, t to b) iStock.com/hakule, iStock.com/Nikada, iStock.com/bluejayphoto, iStock.com/PeopleImages, dibrova/iStock/Thinkstock, Hemera/Thinkstock, iStock.com/nicholashan, artJazz/iStock/Thinkstock, PhonlamaiPhoto/iStock/Thinkstock, iStock.com/XiXinXing; **1** iStock.com/hakule; **3** Peter Dennis/Thinkstock; **4** LindaWang/iStock/Thinkstock; **8** (l to r, t to b) bingdian/iStock/Thinkstock, axz66/iStock/Thinkstock, bingdian/iStock/Thinkstock, TkKurikawa/iStock Editorial/Thinkstock; **9** Cengage Learning Asia; **10** John Vanderlyn/Wikipedia; **14** (l to r, t to b) gianliguori/iStock/Thinkstock, SeanPavonePhoto/iStock/Thinkstock, LuoJun/iStock/Thinkstock, bingdian/iStock Editorial/Thinkstock; **15** hakule/DigitalVision Vectors/Thinkstock; **21** (l to r) http://tupian.baike.com, http://www.hwjyw.com, pressdigital/iStock/Thinkstock, www.bswj.net, http://mingrenw.cn, OceanFishing/iStock/Thinkstock, Maynagashev/iStock/Thinkstock; **22** View Stock/Thinkstock; **24** (t to b) axz66/iStock/Thinkstock, kuriko917/iStock/Thinkstock; **26** Rat0007/iStock/Thinkstock; **28** iStock.com/MATTHIASRABBIONE; **30** iStock.com/Nikada; **32** (t to b) zhudifeng/iStock/Thinkstock, mppriv/iStock/Thinkstock, Wimage72/iStock/Thinkstock, Peter Dennis/Thinkstock; **33** (t to b, l to r) vanbeets/iStock/Thinkstock, ssuaphoto/iStock/Thinkstock, TonyYao/iStock/Thinkstock, Izf/iStock/Thinkstock, metamorworks/iStock/Thinkstock, Andrey Suslov/iStock/Thinkstock, Sylphe_7/iStock/Thinkstock; **34** Jui-Chi Chan/iStock/Thinkstock; **36** (t to b, l to r) iStock.com/alessandro0770, iStock.com/Winnytony, KittisakJirasittichai/iStock/Thinkstock, VIPDesignUSA/iStock/Thinkstock, iStock.com/YiorgosGR; **37** (t to b, l to r) aurielaki/iStock/Thinkstock, LuckyBusiness/iStock/Thinkstock, Wavebreakmedia Ltd/Wavebreak Media/Thinkstock, Purestock/Thinkstock, XiXinXing/iStock/Thinkstock; **38** Beijing Subway; **40** iStock.com/alla_snesar, iStock.com/visualspace; **43** (l to r, t to b) tarasov_vl/iStock/Thinkstock, Rost-9D/iStock/Thinkstock, OnstOn/iStock/Thinkstock, iStock.com/sankai, VladislavStarozhilov/iStock/Thinkstock; **44** iStock.com/kool99; **47** (l to r) KhaoYaiBoy/iStock/Thinkstock, chuyu/iStock/Thinkstock; **48** Zhuwq/https://en.wikipedia.org/wiki/File:%E6%B8%85%E6%98%8E%E4%B8%8A%E6%B2%B3%E5%9B%BE.jpg; **49** livechina/iStock/Thinkstock; **51** iStock.com/FatCamera; **53** Tzido/iStock/Thinkstock; **56** Cengage Learning Asia; **59** iStock.com/bluejayphoto; **61** (l to r, t to b) Dian_S_Cahya/iStock/Thinkstock, Jetta Productions/DigitalVision/Thinkstock, iStock.com/DragonImages, icholakov/iStock/Thinkstock, iStock.com/Stas_V, Volodymyr Kotoshchuk/iStock/Thinkstock; **62** Tomwang112/iStock/Thinkstock; **63** View Stock/Thinkstock; **64** imtmphoto/iStock/Thinkstock; **67** (l to r) lena_volo/iStock/Thinkstock, yangchao/iStock/Thinkstock; **68** qingwa/iStock/Thinkstock; **72** imtmphoto/iStock/Thinkstock; **73** Tomwang112/iStock/Thinkstock; **74** LewisTsePuiLung/iStock/Thinkstock; **76** (l to r) kpalimski/iStock/Thinkstock, BardoczPeter/iStock/Thinkstock, BardoczPeter/iStock/Thinkstock; **77** (t to b, l to r) chineseposters.net, chineseposters.net, chineseposters.net; **78** (l to r) leremy/iStock/Thinkstock, Cengage Learning Asia, Cengage Learning Asia; **79** (l to r) eternalcreative/iStock/Thinkstock, Wavebreakmedia Ltd/Wavebreak Media/Thinkstock; **81** (t to b) iStock.com/fstop123, iStock.com/Liderina; **82** XiXinXing/iStock/Thinkstock; **83** iStock.com/monkeybusinessimages; **85** iStock.com/PeopleImages; **87** (t to b) southtownboy/iStock/Thinkstock, Photosensia/iStock/Thinkstock; **88** (t to b) RuslanKaln/iStock/Thinkstock, RudyBalasko/iStock/Thinkstock, dabldy/iStock/Thinkstock; **89** Richard Rummell/Collection of Arader Galleries/https://en.wikipedia.org/wiki/File:Rummell,_Richard_Yale_University_cropped.jpg; **90** https://en.wikipedia.org/wiki/File:Zhangtianyoux.jpg; **93** (l to r) Rusheng Yao/iStock/Thinkstock, zhudifeng/iStock/Thinkstock, Top Photo Group/Thinkstock, Top Photo Group/Thinkstock, kiankhoon/iStock/Thinkstock; **94** https://en.wikipedia.org/wiki/File:Sun_Yat-sen_1924_Guangzhou.jpg; **95** https://en.wikipedia.org/wiki/File:Sun_Yat_Sen_together_with_the_members_of_the_Singapore_Branch_of_Tongmen_Hui.png; **97** (t to b) John Thomson/Beinecke Rare Book & Manuscript Library/https://en.wikipedia.org/wiki/File:NANKING_ARSENAL.jpg, https://en.wikipedia.org/wiki/File:1912Jimingxiaoling2.jpg, https://en.wikipedia.org/wiki/File:La_Jeunesse.jpg; **101** https://www.flickr.com/photos/edrost88/5986775507; **102** National General Pictures/https://en.wikipedia.org/wiki/File:Bruce_Lee_1973.jpg; **103** PaulCowan/iStock/Thinkstock; **107** Gilbert H. Grosvenor Collection, Prints and Photographs Division, Library of Congress/https://en.wikipedia.org/wiki/File:Alexander_Graham_Telephone_in_Newyork.jpg; **111** Robert Foothorap/https://en.wikipedia.org/wiki/File:Amy_Tan.jpg; **112** iStock.com/vchal; **114** (l to r) dibrova/iStock/Thinkstock, Hemera/Thinkstock; **116** (l to r, t to b) cozyta/iStock/Thinkstock, SeanPavonePhoto/iStock/Thinkstock, shansekala/iStock/Thinkstock, dk1234/iStock/Thinkstock, yaner1105/iStock/Thinkstock, 冷咖啡/Own work/https://en.wikipedia.org/wiki/File:Baoding3.jpg, shansekala/iStock/Thinkstock, dk1234/iStock/Thinkstock, shansekala/iStock/Thinkstock, greir/iStock/Thinkstock; **117** zhaojiankang/iStock/Thinkstock; **118** Jupiterimages/PHOTOS.com>>/Thinkstock; **119** kertu_ee/iStock/Thinkstock; **122** bingdian/iStock Editorial/Thinkstock; **127** (l to r) iStock.com/jacus, hanhanpeng/iStock/Thinkstock, tupiku/iStock/Thinkstock; **128** iStock.com/Nikada; **130** Tero Vesalainen/iStock/Thinkstock; **133** Cengage Learning Asia; **135** (l to r) Hey Darlin/DigitalVision Vectors/Thinkstock, zrfphoto/iStock/Thinkstock; **136** (l to r, t to b) zhanghaitao/iStock/Thinkstock, voyata/iStock/Thinkstock, choness/iStock/Thinkstock, John Foxx/Stockbyte/Thinkstock; **137** Booblgum/iStock/Thinkstock; **138** (l to r, t to b) Sean3810/iStock/Thinkstock, stocksnapper/iStock/Thinkstock, f11photo/iStock/Thinkstock, Mathew Brady/https://en.wikipedia.org/wiki/File:Mark_Twain,_Brady-Handy_photo_portrait,_Feb_7,_1871,_cropped.jpg, vwalakte/iStock/Thinkstock, GeorgiosArt/iStock/Thinkstock, SeanPavonePhoto/iStock/Thinkstock, Ch.Andrew/https://en.wikipedia.org/wiki/File:Yu_Guangzhong_20110527_YLSH_4.jpg; **139** (t to b) iStock.com/real444, iStock.com/urf; **143** iStock.com/nicholashan; **145** (l to r, t to b) 张择端/FOTOE, https://commons.wikimedia.org/w/index.php?curid=936207, Cengage Learning Asia; **146** iStock.com/loonger; **147** iStock.com/jejim; **148** Ch.Andrew/https://en.wikipedia.org/wiki/File:Yu_Guangzhong_20110527_YLSH_4.jpg; **151** https://www.vcg.com/editorial/408540516; **152** Zheng Jingkang/Scanned from China Photography issue 1978.6 by 維基小霸王/https://commons.wikimedia.org/w/index.php?curid=37898454; **153** (l to r, t to b) vanbeets/iStock/Thinkstock, SeanXu/iStock/Thinkstock, silkwayrain/iStock/Thinkstock, bpperry/iStock/Thinkstock, KingWu/iStock/Thinkstock, mamahoohooba/iStock/Thinkstock, Jess_Yu/iStock/Thinkstock; **154** (t to b, l to r) iStock.com/KreangchaiRungfamai, Foundations World Economic Forum/Enabling eCommerce: Small Enterprises, Global Players/https://commons.wikimedia.org/w/index.php?curid=68575690, iStock.com/AdrianHancu, iStock.com/SeanXu; **156** Cengage Learning Asia; **157** http://www.movieposterdb.com/poster/35b70595; **158** (t to b) iStock.com/all_is_magic, iStock.com/Eloku; **159** (l to r) iStock.com/grki, Warner Bros. Pictures/https://en.wikipedia.org/w/index.php?curid=57212947; **162** (t to b) https://commons.wikimedia.org/wiki/File:LuXun1930.jpg, https://commons.wikimedia.org/w/index.php?curid=4827061; **163** https://commons.wikimedia.org/w/index.php?curid=63461181; **167** Tencent Video; **168** iQiyi; **169** iStock.com/Meinzahn; **171** artJazz/iStock/Thinkstock; **173** (l to r, t to b) iStock.com/Eloku, iStock.com/lightkitegirl, iStock.com/Lesia_G, iStock.com/ElenaMedvedeva, iStock.com/rudall30, iStock.com/Panacea_Doll; **174** Eva Hejda/http://fotos.naturspot.de/Wikipedia; **175** iStock.com/leungchopan; **176** (t to b) iStock.com/setimino, iStock.com/mb-fotos; **177** iStock.com/Mario_Hoppmann; **178** Cengage Learning Asia; **179** (t to b) Cengage Learning Asia, Cengage Learning Asia, Cengage Learning Asia; **181** (l to r) zjzpp163/iStock/Thinkstock, zjzpp163/iStock/Thinkstock, Hemera/Thinkstock; **182** iStock.com/mycola; **183** iStock.com/martin_33; **184** (l to r) iStock.com/WhitcombeRD, iStock.com/WildandFree, iStock.com/DurkTalsma; **186** (l to r) ego450/iStock/Thinkstock, Top Photo Group/Thinkstock; **187** (l to r, t to b) iStock.com/simonmasters, iStock.com/luoman, iStock.com/Thaisign, iStock.com/donvictorio, iStock.com/LuCaAr, iStock.com/myronhensel; **188** iStock.com/WangAnQi; **189** (l ro r) iStock.com/typhoonski, iStock.com/menabrea; **192** (l to r, t to b) iStock.com/vivalapenler, Maurizio Pesce/https://commons.wikimedia.org/wiki/File:Elon_Musk,_Tesla_Factory,_Fremont_(CA,_USA)_(8765031426).jpg, iStock.com/Yongyuan Dai, iStock.com/stockcam; **193** (t to b) iStock.com/articular, iStock.com/heyengel, iStock.com/SAKhanPhotography; **194** iStock.com/DimaBerkut; **197** iStock.com/piyaset; **199** iStock.com/Biletskiy_Evgeniy; **200** (l to r, t to b) iStock.com/Olga Zelenina, iStock.com/Galyna_P, iStock.com/Nikiteev_Konstantin, iStock.com/flowerstock; **202** PhonlamaiPhoto/iStock/Thinkstock; **204** (l to r, t to b) iStock.com/JGalione, iStock.com/AndreyPopov, iStock.com/Visivasnc, iStock.com/andresr; **205** Cengage Learning Asia; **206** (l to r) Cengage Learning Asia, Cengage Learning Asia; **208** (l to r) iStock.com/BigGabig, xurui/iStock/Thinkstock, Jess_Yu/iStock/Thinkstock; **209** (l to r) xudonghu/iStock/Thinkstock, cl2004lhy/iStock/Thinkstock; **210** iStock.com/PhonlamaiPhoto; **212** iStock.com/JIRAROJ PRADITCHAROENKUL; **213** iStock.com/metamorworks; **216** (t to b) iStock.com/wutwhanfoto, iStock.com/Sitthiphong; **217** iStock.com/imtmphoto; **218** iStock.com/metamorworks; **219** iStock.com/Graficaprint; **221** (l to r) chuyu/iStock/Thinkstock, Top Photo Group/Thinkstock; **222** (t to b) Cengage Learning Asia, Cengage Learning Asia; **223** (l to r) Cengage Learning Asia, Cengage Learning Asia; **224** (t to b) iStock.com/aleksvrn51, iStock.com/metamorworks, iStock.com/leremy; **226** iStock.com/metamorworks; **229** (l to r) iStock.com/Chesky_W, iStock.com/PhonlamaiPhoto; **231** iStock.com/XiXinXing; **233** (t to b) Haier, iStock.com/tbradford, iStock.com/wonry, iStock.com/RomanBabakin; **234** (t to b) iStock.com/zorazhuang, BuildYourDreams, http://www.li-ning.com/; **235** iStock.com/ispyfriend; **237** iStock.com/FernandoChee; **240** iStock.com/zhudifeng; **241** iStock.com/wonry; **242** Cengage Learning Asia; **244** (l to r) nobiggie/iStock/Thinkstock, mamahoohooba/iStock/Thinkstock, long8614/iStock/Thinkstock; **246** (t to b) iStock.com/wonry, iStock.com/wonry; **247** Cengage Learning Asia; **251** (t to b) Cengage Learning Asia, Cengage Learning Asia; **256** iStock.com/Philiphotographer; **258** iStock.com/baona.